FOLKLORE OF THE
HOLY LAND

Moslem, Christian and Jewish

J. E. Hanauer

DOVER PUBLICATIONS, INC.
Mineola, New York

Published in the United Kingdom by David & Charles, Brunel House, Forde Close, Newton Abbot, Devon TQ12 4PU.

Bibliographical Note

This Dover edition, first published in 2002, is an unabridged republication of the new and enlarged 1935 edition of the work first published by The Sheldon Press, London, in 1907.

International Standard Book Number: 0-486-42493-6

Manufactured in the United States of America
Dover Publications, Inc., 31 East 2nd Street, Mineola, N.Y. 11501

TO

THE MEMORY OF

MY DEAR WIFE

WITHOUT WHOSE ENCOURAGEMENT THIS
BOOK WOULD NEVER HAVE BEEN
WRITTEN AND WITHOUT WHOSE HELP
ITS MATERIALS COULD NEVER HAVE
BEEN COLLECTED ; IT IS NOW MOST
AFFECTIONATELY DEDICATED

J. E. H.

FOREWORD

BEHIND the passage of invading armies, behind the turmoil of political struggles, behind the procession of the pilgrims and their deep devotion at the Holy Places, Palestine has had through the ages her own life of the soil and the harvest, with its rhythm of toil and rest, of rain, fruitfulness and drought.

The peasant in the Egyptian Delta toils all the year round in the intensive cultivation of any plot to which Nile water can be caused to flow. But in Palestine the very marked rhythm of the climate brings to the peasant his happy pauses, when the dry fields lie at rest till the breaking of the rains, or when on some winter day the heaven opens and every path runs with the torrents that fall from heaven. Therefore in the villages of Palestine, as compared with those mud villages of the Egyptian Delta, we find a richer harvest of the fruits of leisure. Women's dresses flower out into embroideries, dancers know how to improvise a song to the rhythmical clapping of the neighbours' hands, and above all, the story comes into its own.

As one who has spent holiday weeks in collecting fairy tales from the villages of both countries, I can testify to a freer, wilder, more romantic and less muddy imagination in the tales of Palestine. But the longer story that beguiles a winter evening is set in a whole world of lesser imaginings and *jeux d'esprit*—word-plays on local place names, explanations of the shape of some hill or rock, tales of the saint or prophet whose tomb lies beside the village, stories of the mysterious power of certain waters or the virtues of certain plants, and legends woven round the names that everyone knows and loves, Abraham, El Khidr, Solomon the great King, or Mary and her Son. All this is interwoven in the happiest way with jest or pious saw or rhyming proverb. These things are the bright inflorescence of talk unspoilt by hurry, in houses where books were unused and evening lights were dim. Too precious to forget, these tales and saws were stored in the memory and brought out again and again for the regalement of some circle " smelling the air " in their September vineyard, or huddling together for warmth in a January downpour. And so, with no formal handing down, such tales and word-plays have lived on from generation to generation, until our own day, when that village life is threatened by new forces and new ways that may prove either its ruin or its salvation.

There is no need nowadays to expound the value of this quaint and happy flowering of the human mind, the unconscious expression of a people's nature. Too late in some lands of the West, and with labour of professors and folk-lore societies, these flowers of the countryside—now seen to be the rightful heritage of the children of the land—are garnered and labelled as specimens, or planted awkwardly—poor little field flowers that they are—in formal gardens where cultivated flowers hold the eye.

But if there is matter for regret in the loss of the folk-lore of any land, the loss of that of Palestine would be a calamity, not only for the children of her villages, but for the studious world. The folk-lore of *this* land has news to tell, for those trained to read it, not only of the past of places, tribes, peoples and language, but of the daily life and interactions at this their meeting-place, of the three great religions that have sprung up on Semitic soil; and, again, of primitive and less noble religious material—animistic and magical— officially rejected and ignored by the great faiths, but surviving with the survival power so often possessed by lower forms of life. And yet again, in this mass of floating material have we not the very matrix (or at least a fair picture of it) from which were taken the stories of much Jewish or Syriac or Arabic literature? Here, then, is material for scholarship.

Canon Hanauer's book did not come into the world as a labelled and indexed work of scholarship, but as the fruit of the playtime of an unselfish life. The Canon, known throughout Jerusalem as the depositary of all manner of lore about the city's past, has made Palestine his home for longer years than are granted to most men. Even the games of his boyhood were played among the ancient places. As a youth he induced a Jerusalem carpenter to make something approaching a cricket bat, the first ever seen in the land; and when he taught the Arab boys of the Bishop Gobat School to use this instrument in their narrow playground at the south-west corner of the ancient city battlements, too strong a hit would send the ball into the deeps where the Valley of Hinnom joins the Lower Pool of Gihon.

Palestine is Canon Hanauer's land by length of days and love, his place of work and his playground, and these stories are the fruit of his understanding friendship and unfailing joy in the little twists of thought and humour shown him without shyness by his friends who knew that, like themselves, he was bound to that land in love and long custom.

Here, then, is a book to reveal new vistas, even to the passing pilgrim who would understand and love the Holy Land. But for those who are able to learn the Arabic tongue Canon Hanauer has opened a door of entrance to his own kingdom of intimacy. He leaves this fruit of his friendship to those who would follow him as friends.

CONSTANCE E. PADWICK.

Cairo.

INTRODUCTION TO THE EDITION
OF 1907

By MARMADUKE PICKTHALL

MY aim in this preface being to afford the untravelled reader of the following stories such a glimpse of the country and people which produced them as may render them intelligible, if not coherent, I shall begin with a glance at the past history of the Holy Land as illustrated in its present folk-lore.

Of Old Testament times the fellahìn have countless stories, more or less reminiscent of their religious instruction at the mouth of Greek priest or Moslem Khatìb,* vivified by the incorporation in the text of naïve conjectures, points of private humour, and realistic touches from the present-day life of the country, which shock the pompous listener as absurd anachronisms. Thus the disguise of a Russian pilgrim †—a figure now commonly to be met with on the road from Jerusalem to the Jordan—is given to Satan when he beguiles the Patriarch Lot (Sect. I. chap. vi.); and our father Adam has been described to me as sitting under the Tree of Knowledge, " smoking his narghileh." Nebuchad-nezzar and Titus become one person (Bukhtunussur) and the personality of Alexander the Great (Iskender Dhu el Karneyn) is stretched so as to include more ancient conquerors. Moreover, the desire inherent in Orientals to know how everything came to be, content with any hypothesis provided it be witty, has produced any number of delicious little fictions which, to all ends but the scientific, are much better than fact. Such *jeux d'esprit* abound in the

---

* Village preacher and schoolmaster.

† The Russian Church and the Coptic still include a pilgrimage to the Holy Places among the duties of the devout Christian.

following pages, as, for instance, the story of Noah's daughter (Sect. I. chap. iii.) ; and of how the mosquito came to buzz (Sect. III. chap. x.) ; and they are useful to be known by all who must converse with Orientals, since for the latter they are a part of learning. Mr. Kipling's *Just So Stories* are examples of this vein of Eastern humour.

Of Our Lord and the Apostles and the Blessed Virgin there are sheaves of legends extant, many of them current among Moslems as well as Christians; for it must not be forgotten that the followers of Muhammad have great reverence for Jesus Christ, whom their Prophet named Ruh' Allah, the Spirit of God. They believe in His Immaculate Conception and all His miracles, but deny His Divinity. Only St. Paul is anathema to them, because they say he took the pure faith of El Islàm, the faith of Adam and Noah and Abraham, as restored by Jesus, and made of it a new religion. With the very doubtful exception of the quaint story of Francesco and the Angel of Death (Sect. III. chap. v.), no legend concerning the New Testament period has been included in this work; for the reason that such legends ceased long ago to be local, and are most, if not all, of them elsewhere accessible, in the Apocryphal Gospels or one or other of the multiplied Lives of the Saints.

To most legends of the centuries between Christ and Muhammad, called by the Moslems " the Interval," a like objection seemed to apply. The stories of the Seven Sleepers and of the Martyrs of the Pit, of St. Helen's Dream and the consequent finding of the cross, no longer belong to Palestine, though they are still told there. But the legend of the Tree of the Cross (Sect. I. chap. vi.) and that of St. George in the chapter on " El Khudr " (Sect. I. chap. ix.), with a tradition, given in Sect. II. chap. vi., concerning some caves in Wady Isma 'in, called " the Upper Chambers of the Maidens," undoubtedly belong to this period. The romantic deeds of 'Antar and Abu Zeyd, with all the wealth of the stories ascribed to the Arabs of the Ignorance,* though known to natives of Palestine, have not been localised. They belong

---

* The Time of the Ignorance is the name given to the days before Muhammad, when a majority of the Arabians were idolaters.

to the Arabic language and literature, and must be set down
as acquired.

With the conquest of Jerusalem by the armies of the Calif
Omar ibn el Khattab begins the historical memory in this
folk-lore as distinct from the Scriptural and fabulous; and
I have heard Christians as well as Moslems extol the
character of Omar and depict it not amiss. They relate
that when the homely old man arrived, unattended, upon
the camel which had borne him all the way from El Medìneh,
to receive in person the submission of a place as holy as
Jerusalem, the splendid slaves of the Byzantine government,
cringing, led him to the Church of the Holy Sepulchre;
fully expecting him to say his prayers there, and turn the
church into a mosque. But he declined to pass the threshold,
praying from without on the name of Jesus. He was led
thence to other churches, but would enter none of them,
preferring for the scene of his devotions the summit of Mount
Moriah, site of Herod's Temple and of Solomon's, which was
at that time a waste of ruins. This was the Beyt el Makdas,
the House of the Sanctuary, to which angels came in pilgrimage long before the creation of Adam—that "further
temple" to which Muhammad was carried in his sleep from
Mecca, and whence he started on his marvellous "night
journey" through the Seven Heavens. Here the conqueror
caused to be built a noble shrine, the Dome of the Rock,
which we to this day call the Mosque of Omar.

Omar's severity towards the Christians was so much below
their anticipations that he figures in the popular memory
almost as a benefactor of their religion. They were deprived
of their church bells, but kept their churches; and if large
numbers of them embraced El Islàm, it was through self-
interest (or conviction) and not at the point of the sword as
has been represented. Indeed, the toleration displayed by
the Moslems towards the vanquished, though less than we
should practise nowadays, is without a parallel in Europe
till many centuries later. It was not emulated by the
Crusaders,* who, rushing to wrest the Holy Sepulchre from

* Many of the Crusaders were so ignorant as to believe that the
Moslems were idolaters.

the clutch of the " foul Paynim," were astonished to find it in the hands of Christians, whom, to cloak their disconcertion, they denounced as heretics.

From the Moslem conquest downward—with the exception of the mad destructive inroads called Crusades, and the short-lived Frankish kingdom (often referred to by the Mohammedan fellahìn as the Time of the Infidels)—one tradition has prevailed in the land till quite recent years. In that conquest the East reclaimed her own, the young civilisation of the Arabs overpowered the luxury of the moribund Roman Empire: a judgment from God, it is said. It was a return to the time of David at least, if not of Abraham; and this tremendous relapse must be borne in mind of those who would deduce from existing conditions in Palestine the life that was led there in the time of Christ. From Omar's time, with the reservation already made, the fellahìn, whether ruled in chief from Baghdad, Cairo or Constantinople, have been subject to an Oriental form of government, rough in the hand but genial in the head, which, allowing great liberty to the individual, has furnished rich material for song and story. A vast majority of the stories here collected have the keen Oriental flavour of this period.

In the fourth decade of the last century the Pasha of Egypt, Muhammed Ali, rebelled against his sovereign lord the Sultan, when an Egyptian force under Ibrahìm Pasha invaded Syria and occupied it for some time. Owing to French influence, European ideas had already made some way among the governing class in Egypt, and the radicalism of Ibrahìm made his rule offensive to the conservative notables of Syria. Still, he was the kind of tyrant to appeal most strongly to Orientals—heavy-handed but humorous, knowing how to impart to his decisions that quaint proverbial savour which dwells in the mind of the people and makes good stories; and his fame among the fellahìn is that of a second Solomon (see " Detective Stories," Sect. II. chap v.). With him begins the age of progress in the Holy Land. Since the withdrawal of the Egyptian troops in 1840, things have moved fast in a European direction; till there is now

such an inflow of civilisation and education as to threaten
the very source of folk-lore, making some such Noah's Ark
as this seem necessary if aught is to survive the banal deluge.

The region from which Mr. Hanauer has drawn these
stories is the hill-country between Bethel in the north and
Hebron in the south. It is holy land for the Mohammedan
and the Jew hardly less than for the Christian, and its
population comprises all three branches of that monotheistic
faith whose root is in the God of Abraham. The Moslems,
who are the dominant class, are the offspring of the Arab
conquerors and of such of the conquered as espoused El
Islàm; the Christians, the descendants of those old inhabitants of Syria, subjects of the Byzantine Empire, who at the
conquest preferred their religion to worldly advancement.
Their stories against one another, though abounding in sly
hits, breathe as a rule the utmost good-nature. Only in the
Jewish legends one detects a bitterness which, in view of the
history of their race, is pardonable.

In the Middle Ages there existed in Jerusalem and
Hebron, as in the cities of Europe, small despised com-
munities of Jews, strictly confined to one quarter, the gates
of which were locked at night. To these were added some
three hundred years ago a company of Spanish Jews
(Sephardim), fleeing hither from the Inquisition with their
wives and families; who still at this day form a separate
group and use among themselves an antiquated kind of
Spanish which they pronounce oddly.

Another company of old-time immigrants, whose descendants have preserved individuality, were the Mughàribeh
(sing. Mughrabi) or Moorish Jews. Pure Orientals in dress,
speech and character, they have earned a bad name in the
land as charlatans, many of them being professed wizards
and conjurers. But a vast majority of the large and growing Jewish population are immigrants of the last fifty years,
borne to Palestine on the waves of the Zionist movement,
and looking about them surlily, with foreign eyes. Coming
from the towns of East and Central Europe, the agricultural
life expected of them is as strange as the country, and at first
hostile. The Jew is a foreigner in the Holy Land; and the

standpoint and posture of his ancestors of the time of Christ to-day is found with the Moslem, who also claims descent from Abraham.

About one-third of the matter here presented has been published in America * in another version, and the chapters on the Animal and Plant lore were originally contributed to the Palestine Exploration Fund Quarterly Statement, from which they are reprinted by permission of the committee. Stories spread fast and far in the East, and are soon localised (I have found a considerable number of these current among the people of Lower Egypt), and it may well be that some of the following have found their way into print; but the author would have it clearly understood that he has derived them all from the legitimate source of folk-lore, the lips of the people themselves. Where he has observed a coincidence or similarity he has endeavoured to point it out, but neither he nor his editor is a skilled folk-lorist. There are sure to be many such kinships which have escaped our vigilance.

Although this compilation is but a pailful from the sea, as compared with the floating mass of folk-lore which exists in Palestine, I know of no other attempt at collection on anything like so large a scale; and it has been our object so to present the stories as to entertain the casual reader without impairing their value for the student of such matters. With much that is puerile, they contain both wit and humour, and withal not a little of that Heavenly Wisdom, the Wisdom of Solomon and of the Son of Sirach, to which, in the East, churches were once dedicated.

N.B.—Notes in square brackets with the initials " M. P." were contributed to the edition of 1907 by Mr. Pickthall.

* *Tales told in Palestine*, by J. E. Hanauer. Edited by H. G. Mitchell. Cincinnati: Jennings and Graham; New York: Eaton and Main. (Copyright (1904) by H. G. Mitchell.)

A MOHAMMEDAN LEGEND

Introductory and Apologetic

" Tainting the air, on a scirocco day, the carcase of a hound,
all loathsome, lay in Nazareth's narrow street. Wayfarers
hurried past covering mouth and nostrils, and at last, when
purer air they reached, in Eastern style they cursed the dog,
and the dog's owner's ancestors, and theirs who, bound to
care for public cleanliness, yet left the nuisance there to
poison all around. Then, that same way, there came 'Isa,
the son of Mary, of great fame for mighty deeds performed in
Allah's Name. He said, ' How lovely are its teeth, so sharp,
and white as pearls: ' then went his way."

Be the lot, Reader, thine, 'midst many faults to note some
beauty shine: some lesson new in Eastern legends old: and,
'mid much dross, to find some grains of gold.

J. E. H.

CONTENTS

CONTENTS

SECTION II

CONTAINING LEGENDS AND ANECDOTES POSSIBLY
FOUNDED ON FACT

CONTENTS

SECTION III

CONTAINING STORIES AND ANECDOTES ILLUSTRATING
SOCIAL IDEAS, SUPERSTITIONS, ANIMAL AND
PLANT LORE, ETC.

SECTION I

CONCERNING THE CREATION AND DIVERS
SAINTS, SINNERS AND MIRACLES

SECTION I

I

KNOW that the very first thing which Allah created was the marvellous Tablet of Destiny upon which is written not only all that happened in the Past, or that will happen in the Present or the Future, but also every human being's lot for ever: whether he will be happy or wretched, rich or poor in this life; and whether he will be a true Believer and inherit Paradise hereafter, or a Kafir and go to Jehennum. The Tablet of Destiny was made out of an immense white pearl, and it has two leaves like those of a door. There are learned men who assert that these leaves are formed out of two red rubies of incomparable size and beauty, but Allah alone knows if they speak truth.

Allah next created a great pen formed out of a single gem. The pen is so long that it would take one five hundred years to travel from end to end of it. It is split at one end like an ordinary pen, and pointed, and from the point light flowed forth in the same way that ink flows from common pens, or water gushes from a fountain. Then the voice of Allah thundered forth the one word " WRITE," and the sound caused the pen, which was full of life and intelligence, to tremble, and immediately the point began to race across the tablet from right to left, and to inscribe the things that had been, and that then were, and that would happen until the Day of Resurrection. When the tablet was filled with writing the pen dried up, and it and the tablet were removed, and are preserved in the Treasury of Allah, who alone knows all that is written.

The next thing which Allah created was water, and then a

[1] See p. 237.

great white pearl of the size of the heavens and the earth. As soon as the pearl was formed Allah spoke to it, and, trembling at His Voice of Thunder, it melted and became water which, meeting that first created, formed great billows, deep smiting against deep, and surge upon surge. Then Allah's command again went forth, and all was still— a great expanse of pure undisturbed water, without wave or ripple or foam.

Then Allah created His Throne, the seat of which was formed of two great jewels, and He placed it floating upon the face of the waters.

There are those, however, who maintain that the Throne was created before the water and the heavens and the earth ; saying that human builders lay the foundation of a structure before they put on the roof, but that Allah, in order to display His Almighty Power, put up first the roof, which is His Throne.

The wind, which He furnished with wings, was the next thing God created.   None but Allah knows how much wind there is, nor how far the atmosphere extends.   Allah commanded the wind to bear up the water, in the same way in which the water was supporting the Throne.

After this Allah made a great serpent which lies in a circle surrounding the Throne.[2]   The head of this serpent is a great white pearl, its body is of gold, and its eyes are two sapphires.   None but Allah Himself knows the size of the serpent.

Now the Throne is the Throne of Might and Greatness, and the Seat that of Glory and Majesty, and they were not created because Allah was in need of them, but only to display His Greatness and His Glory Who existed from all Eternity.

Then Allah told the wind to smite the sea, thereby causing great foaming waves to rise with vapour and showers of spray.   By Allah's command the foam became solid earth which was caused to float upon the surface of the water, whilst the vapour and spray became the clouds.   It took

[2] See p. 237.

Allah two days' time to do all this. The waves were then in their turn congealed, so as to form mountains which serve to keep the earth steady and prevent it from floating about. The mountain-bases are all connected with the roots of the great Kàf[3] range, which surrounds the world like a high rim of a circular baking-tray and keeps its contents from falling into space.

Allah next arranged that the water remaining on the surface of the earth should be formed into seven concentric seas, separated from each other by as many continents, but nevertheless connected by divers gulfs and straits, and containing an infinite number and diversity of living creatures, as well as of the nourishment that sustains them. The seven continents likewise vary in their climates and conditions, as in the plants and animals that abound therein. It took Allah two further days to set these things in order.

Now the earth used to rock and roll like a ship at sea, so that all living creatures were very sick. Therefore Allah commanded a strong angel to go beneath the earth and support it. The angel did so, and stretching one arm towards the east, and the other towards the west, he upheld the world. Then, in order that the angel might have something to stand on, Allah created a great rock of green emerald, which He commanded to roll in beneath his feet and support them. Then, as there was nothing for the rock to rest upon, a great bull[4] was created, and ordered to go under the rock and bear it up; some say on his horns, and others on his back. Those who make the former statement explain earthquakes as caused by the movement of the bull's head when he shifts the rock from one horn to the other. He has eyes so fiery red that no one can look in them without blindness. He is named Behemoth, and stands on the back of a great whale, which swims about in an ocean which Allah created for the purpose. Beneath the ocean, and surrounding it and the world, is air, which rests upon darkness, through which in their appointed seasons move the sun, moon and stars, created for no other service than to give light to the earth.

[3] Caucasus. See p. 237.   [4] See p. 239.

It sometimes happens that the sun or the moon is eclipsed, and the explanation of the phenomenon is in each case simple. When the moon is at the full, and her light falls upon that part of the great sea in which the whale is swimming, the monster will sometimes open his mouth and seize her. He would doubtless swallow her up whole if Allah permitted it, but he is compelled to relinquish his prey—most speedily if the worshippers of the Unity make great and loud lamentations, and offer prayers. The cause of eclipses of the sun is different. They are signs vouchsafed from Allah, and solemn warnings against sin. The first that ever happened was to bid men heed the preaching of Ibrahìm the friend of Allah, on whom be peace; and in our own days the wonder is of frequent occurrence to the end that all mankind may take heart to the teaching of the Apostle of Allah, on whom be prayer and peace.[5]

Thus, as I have explained, the world rests upon the shoulders of an angel, and the angel upon a great emerald rock, and the rock upon the horns or shoulders of a bull, and the bull upon the back of a great whale, and the whale or dragon swims in a great sea which is upborne by air, which is surrounded by darkness. The heavenly bodies whine at certain seasons through the darkness; but what there is beyond the darkness Allah knows!

Do you ask me how all these wonders came to be known and understood of man? Know then, that, having thus created the world, Allah next called Intellect or Mind into being. And Allah said to the Mind, " Imbibe knowledge," and it imbibed knowledge. Then Allah said to it, " Receive the ability to manage matters," and it did so. Therefore also Allah has declared by the mouth of His Prophet, on whom be prayer and praise: " The wise man is he who is truthful and patient in his temper; and it is Mind that delivers mankind from Evil." For this cause Allah allows Mind an entrance into Paradise to discover all mysteries,

---

[5] It is also said that the sun and moon are a married couple, who come together once every month, at which time the moon is invisible. See p. 239.

and He will not punish the wise in the day of Resurrection
in the same manner in which He will punish the ignorant,
who flatter with their lips, and lie with their tongues, and
meddle in matters that concern them not by asking questions
about things which they are unable to comprehend, even
though they may possibly know how to read and write.

Two stories told by a Mohammedan notable of Damascus
to the present writer illustrate a modern educated Moslem's
views about the value of Prayer.

I. An old and corpulent but very pious Kadi was incessantly fingering his rosary and invoking the Name, except
when obliged to speak about other things in the way of duty
or business.

One rainy day, just before putting his left foot into the
stirrup in order to mount his donkey, he ejaculated, " O
Allah! help me." A strong effort enabled him to get into
the saddle, from which his over-great exertion in mounting
caused him to tumble off into the muddy street on the other
side of the ass. Having been helped to arise, and whilst
his defiled garments were being wiped by compassionate
by-standers, he exclaimed, " O Allah! as Thou bestowest
so much more, and that the opposite of what I asked for, I
shall be careful in future what petitions I present. However,
as I have escaped with my life, I say ' El Hamdu lillah.' "

II. In the camp of the Beni-Israel in the wilderness there
was a poor but righteous fisherman who possessed a very
handsome wife and an only son. The man was so poor that
he did not own even " a house of hair," that is, a rough goats'-
hair-cloth tent, and the only shelter he and his family had
was a pit dug out in the ground and scantily roofed with
bushes and desert plants. He maintained a precarious
existence by fishing with a hand-net from the shore of the
Red Sea. One day, however, seeing Musa, the Prophet, to
whom be salaams, starting on one of his periodical visits to
the top of Mount Sinai, the poor man, falling at the feet of
the Great " Kallim ullah," the speaker to Allah, besought
him to intercede with the most High on his behalf. The
Prophet promised to do this; and on his return from the

Mount, told the suppliant that he was allowed to present three petitions which would be granted.

Full of joy, the fisherman returned to his dug-out and informed his wife of his great good fortune and added, " We must consider well what we ask for, and must not be hasty in framing our requests; let us therefore think the matter over during the night."

Wearied with the day's toil, the man soon fell asleep; but the woman lay awake thinking. " If my husband ask for wealth he will be sure to become tired of me when I grow old, and he will marry another woman; let me therefore benefit by at least one petition."

Next morning as soon as her man awoke, she told him to pray that she might always remain as beautiful as she was when a bride. The husband obeyed willingly, and then went to throw his net from the shore, which was only a couple of hundred paces distant.

While he was thus engaged, a fierce Amalekite, riding past the dug-out, saw the handsome female, and leaping from his horse, seized her, and in spite of her shrieks, lifted her on to his horse, mounted behind her, and galloped off. The noise she and her boy made called the attention of her husband to what had happened; and he, being unable to follow the robber and recover his wife, called out, " O Allah, I beseech Thee, turn her into a pig." The request was granted instantly, to the horror of the Amalekite, who found himself carrying a great struggling and noisy sow. Now it is well known that the desert is the abode of jinns, ghouls and other evil spirits, and the robber, concluding that the sow was one of them, at once dropped her and fled.

When the fisherman reached the place and realised what had happened, he at once besought Allah to restore her to her normal condition. The prayer was answered; but we learn from this instructive story that no prayers can alter " what is written on the Tablet of Destiny."

II

ALLAH formed Adam out of a handful of dust. Some say that this handful was taken from the Sakhrah, or Holy Rock in Beyt el Makdas; but they are more probably right who assert that the dust of which the first man was made had been collected from different parts of the world and consists of various kinds of soil, which accounts for the divers colours of men and women. Others say from mud taken from the root of a palm. When Allah had formed Adam He left the figure lying lifeless forty days, some say forty years, while notice was given to the Angels, the Jinn, and the Jân to be ready to worship and do him honour as soon as Allah had put breath into his nostrils. Though most of them obeyed, yet Iblìs, moved with pride and envy, refused to do so, and was therefore cast out of the Celestial Garden, and became the Satan doomed to stoning, cause of all man's tribulation.

At the first Adam was male and female in one body, man on one side, woman on the other. In due time the female part separated from the male, and became a perfect woman; Adam remaining a perfect man; and the couple mated. But they were not happy, as the female refused to submit to the male, saying they were made of the same dust, and he had no right to order her about. So she was turned out of Paradise, and consorting with Iblìs, became the mother of devils.[1] She is called " El-Karìneh " by the Arabs, both Christian and Moslem, and " Lilith " by the Jews generally; " La-Brûsha " by the Sephardim, or Spanish Jews. She is the deadly enemy of all women, especially such as have recently become mothers. These must be carefully nursed and watched, and, together with their new-born babes,

[1] See p. 240.

fenced round with charms and holy amulets, and heads of
garlic, lumps of alum, blue beads, and so forth, lest the
Karìneh strangle them in her jealous fury or frighten the
mother into madness. European doctors, who pretend to
know everything, do not know the dreadful dangers to which
they expose women in childbed when they forbid other
women to visit and amuse them.

When " El-Karìneh " had been driven from Paradise,
Allah created our mother Hawa, that is, Eve, out of one of
Adam's ribs, which he had extracted from the latter whilst
he slept. Adam and Hawa were very happy together till
Iblìs succeeded in getting back into Paradise concealed in the
hollow of the serpent's fangs. The Evil One had bribed the
serpent with the promise that it should have the richest and
most luscious of food, which, as Iblìs said, was human flesh.
How the serpent was outwitted by the swallow we shall,
Inshallah, tell later on in this book. Having entered the
garden, Satan succeeded in persuading Hawa to eat of the
forbidden fruit, which, according to some of the learned,*
was wheat. Adam, having been persuaded by his wife to
share her offence, was, as a punishment, cast out of Paradise,
together with Hawa, Iblìs and the serpent. He had, however, the sense to snatch up, and bring down to earth with
him, an anvil, a pair of tongs or pincers, two hammers, and
a needle. He was cast out of Paradise at the gate named the
Gate of Penitence; Hawa from the Gate of Mercy; Iblìs at
the Gate of Malediction; and the serpent at the Gate of
Calamity. So all four of them fell to the earth, each coming
down in a different place: Adam at Serendib or Ceylon;
Hawa at Jiddah; Iblìs at 'Ailah or 'Akabah; and the
serpent at Isfahan in Persia. Two hundred years elapsed
before Adam and Hawa met once more at Jebel 'Arafat, the
mountain of Recognition, near Mecca; and, in the meantime, fresh horrors had been enacted, for, being under the
curse, Hawa had borne offspring of the seed of devils, and
Adam had got many children by female jinns.[2] The
descendants of those unclean monsters under the name of

* Moslem belief.
[2] See p. 240.

afrìts, rassad, ghouls, marids, and so on, still people the earth
and try to harm mankind.

What happened at the end of two centuries, how Adam
repented and was taken by Gabriel to find Hawa at 'Arafat,
and how the forgiven couple went and lived in Ceylon we
need not tell, nor the story of their sons Habil, Kabil,[3] and
Seth, seeing that this is known to all the People of the Book,
whether Moslems, Christians, or Jews. What, however, is
not generally known, is that Allah showed Adam all his
posterity, even all men that should ever live, between his
own days and the Day of the Resurrection. It came to pass
in this manner: Allah stroked Adam's back, and forthwith
there issued from the latter's loins multitudes of men,
thousands upon tens of thousands, each man no bigger than
an ant; and when these had all borne witness that there is
no God but Allah, and that Mûsa should be the one to whom
Allah would speak, and Ibrahìm El Khalìl should be the
Friend of Allah, and 'Isa ibn Maryam the one who should
be born of Allah's Spirit, and that Mohammed should be the
Apostle of Allah, and when each individual had confessed
his belief in the World to come and the Day of the Resurrection, they all returned into Adam's loins.

Adam was a tall man, taller than any palm tree. The
hair of his head was also very long. The angel Gabriel
visited him twelve times. When he died, his progeny had
grown to the number of forty thousand persons.

Some say, there being others who contradict the statement,
that it was he who first built the Beyt el Makdas. There are
also different opinions as to the place where he is buried;
some stating that his tomb is near Hebron, and others that
he was buried with his head at Jerusalem and his feet
stretching all the way to Hebron. Others say the case is
just the reverse, and that Adam's head rests at Hebron, but
his feet at El-Kûds. Allah knows![4]

THE CAUSE OF HUMAN DEPRAVITY

A story told by Herr Liebler, a German missionary, who
stated that he heard it related by an Arab at Nineveh.
Retailed to the present writer about Easter-tide 1934.

[3] Kimchi on Genesis v. 1-3. See p. 240.   [4] See p. 24.

ADAM was at work in the field, and Eve attending to her home duties when she heard the wail of an infant. She at once rushed out and was surprised to find a beautiful little boy lying exposed. It was, though she knew it not, a devil's brat which Iblìs, anxious to do the fallen parents of the human race some further harm, had left close to their habitation. Eve picked up the baby and did all she could to quiet it.

When Adam returned home and saw the child, he at once snatched it from Eve's arms and tossed it into the river, where he saw it sink.

Next day, after Adam had gone to work, Iblìs came and called out, " Imp, where are you? " " Here I am," answered the little demon, emerging from the river. " Just remain here till my return," said the parent-devil. When Adam returned and found the foul though handsome creature, he promptly tossed it into the fire and burnt it to ashes.

Next morning Iblìs came along again and called his offspring, who at once came to life out of the cold ashes.

When the father of the human race returned from his labours in the evening and found the little devil that he had believed drowned and burnt to ashes, alive again, he said to Eve, " The only way to rid ourselves of this most dangerous enemy is to kill, cook and eat him."

This was done, but when next morning the Arch-demon turned up and called out, " Imp, where are you? " a double voice issuing from the bodies of Adam and Eve respectively replied, " Here I am, and very comfortable." " That is just what I all along intended," said the Evil One. Thus it has come to pass that since then every human being has a good deal of what is devilish in him.

III

NOAH, on whom be peace, was one of the six greatest prophets that ever lived, though he left no writings behind him, as did his grandfather Idrìs,* who was the first human being to use a pen, wherewith he wrote thirty books of divine revelation—besides works on astronomy and other sciences, which are now lost—before Allah removed him to Heaven. Another name of Noah was 'Abd el Ghâfar, which means Servant of the Forgiving One. He was born one hundred and fifty years after the translation of Idrìs. He lived at Damascus till Allah sent him to warn mankind of the Flood and build the ark. By Allah's command and direction he made the first *nâkûs* or gong, such as those which are used to this day in Oriental churches and convents.[1]

With the exception of the hammers and pincers which, as already related, Adam had brought out of Paradise and later on bequeathed to his descendants, the only tool Noah possessed was a great knife. As this was an inadequate supply of instruments for so great an undertaking as the building of the ark, the Patriarch received the mysterious promise that his most formidable enemy should become his best assistant. Noah, confiding in this promise, bravely started to cut down the branch of a great tree. The knife, however, became so firmly wedged in the cleft it had made that, try as he would, the holy man could not get it out again. He pulled and tugged at it for several hours, but in vain, and finally went home. Iblìs then happened to pass by. Seeing the knife, he extracted it easily, and delighted with the thought that he would, by spoiling it, make it useless for Noah, he carefully notched the blade along its edge. When the

* Enoch.
[1] See p. 242.

Patriarch returned to work next morning, he found an excellent saw ready for him.

Noah's efforts to convert mankind were in vain. He was beaten and mocked even by his own wife Wa'ileh, an unbeliever, as well as by his wicked son Canaan, and the latter's son Uj bin 'Anak (Og the son of Anak). Anak was the daughter of Adam, a vile woman,* and the first of witches. These four persons did their best to persuade everyone that Noah was mad.

The Flood burst forth from underground out of a *tannúr* or oven, the site of which is uncertain, some placing it at Gezer and others at Damascus. The ark was upborne by the rising waters, which were swollen by torrential rains. Noah and his family (his wife, Anak and Og excepted), together with a company of other believers, the number of whom some say was six, others twelve, and even seventy-eight or eighty, half of them men and half women, including Jorham the elder, the preserver of the Arabic language, were saved, as well as animals which Allah had caused to enter the ark. Among the latter was the ass, under whose tail Iblìs had hidden, disguised as a fly. This donkey, reluctant to enter the ark bearing the Evil One with him, was driven in by Noah with hard blows. To compensate the donkey for this injustice, it had been predestined that one of his descendants should enter Paradise. This happened when the ass of 'Ozair † was raised to life again and admitted into the Heavenly Garden.

The waters of the Deluge destroyed all mankind except those inside the ark, and Og.‡ The latter was so tall that when the Flood came its waters only reached up to his ankles. He repeatedly tried to destroy Noah and his crew by submerging the ark, but in vain. The pitch with which it had been coated had made it so difficult to grasp that it always slipped from his hands and came safely up to the surface. When hungry, Og would squat down on his haunches and take up a handful of water. Straining it through his

---

* Awwal sharmûteh kânet fi'd-dunyah.

† *i.e.* Jeremiah, Esdras, or Lazarus of Bethany: three saints who have got confused in Syrian Hagiology.

‡ Tale told the compiler by a Druze muleteer in 1869.

fingers, he always found a good many fish left in his grasp. These he could roast by holding them up to the sun. When thirsty, all he had to do was to put out his hands close together and catch the rain which was tumbling in bucketfuls from the skies. He lived several centuries after the Flood till the time of Mûsa. One day, as he was standing on Jebel esh Sheykh,* he wanted to stride across El-Beka'a,† but, misjudging the distance, he stepped, not on to the Lebanon range, as he had intended, but far beyond it, into the great sea. At another time when, suffering from fever, he lay down to rest, he stretched from Banias, where the Jordan gushes forth, as far as the Lake Merom. As he lay thus, some muleteers passed Banias on their way southward. When they approached his face, he said to them, " I am too ill to move. For the love of Allah, when you reach my feet, drive away the mosquitoes that are tickling them and cover them up with my 'abâyeh.[2] The men promised to do as he said; but, when they reached his feet, they found no mosquitoes, but a crowd of jackals.

Og died at last by the hand of Mûsa, in the following manner.‡ In order to destroy the Israelites on their way through the wilderness, the giant pulled up a great rock out of the earth. It was so large that it would have crushed the whole camp of Israel, which covered a square league of country. Og was carrying it upon his head, meaning to drop it on the camp, when Allah sent a bird that pecked through the stone a hole so large that the mass slipped down over Og's head and on to his shoulders, in such a way that he could not get rid of it nor see where he was going. Hereupon Mûsa, whose stature was ten *dra'as*,§ and whose miracle-working rod was the same length, leapt up to the height of ten *dra'as* and just managed to hit Og on his ankle, so that he fell down and was killed. Stones were heaped upon his body as high as a mountain.

To return to Noah: ¶ the ark floated to and fro on the surface of the Flood till it came to the place where Mecca is

* Mount Hermon.   † The wide plain of Cœle-Syria.
‡ Tale told by a Sephardi Jew.
§ The modern *dra'a* or " peak " = 27 inches.   ¶ Moslem tale.
[2] See p. 242.

situated, and there it lay motionless for seven days. Then it moved northward till it reached the site of Jerusalem, where, being endowed with speech by Allah, it informed Noah that here the " Beyt el Makdas " or House of the Sanctuary, would be rebuilt and inhabited by many prophets, his descendants.[3] After the Flood, when the men and women who had been saved in the ark had gone forth to re-people the earth, the Patriarch was left alone with his daughter, who kept house for him, his wicked wife (Wa'ileh) having perished.[4] One day a suitor for the girl appeared, and Noah promised her to him on condition of his preparing a suitable home for her.* The man took his leave, promising to return within a certain time. The term having passed without his reappearance, Noah promised his daughter to another man, upon the same condition. He also departed and failed to appear at the time stated, so when a third suitor came, with a home quite ready, Noah consented to the marriage taking place at once. Hardly, however, had the wedded pair departed when the second suitor came to claim his bride. Unwilling to disappoint him, the Patriarch, by invoking the name of Allah, turned a she-ass into a girl resembling his daughter, and gave her to the expectant bridegroom. Soon after the pair left, the first suitor appeared demanding his bride. Noah then turned his bitch into a girl and married her to the laggard. Since then there have been three sorts of women in the world. First, the God-fearing, who are true helpmeets to their husbands; secondly, stupid and indolent slatterns, who want driving with a stick; and thirdly, shrews, who, scorning both admonition and discipline, continually snarl and snap at their owners.

Noah lived for three hundred years after the Deluge.† Being healthy and industrious, he planted a vineyard. Unknown to him, however, the Evil One slew apes, lions and swine, mingled their blood and by night manured the young vines with the horrid mixture. This is the reason why people who drink wine too freely, at first become as ridiculous

---

* Tale told in 1885 by a fellâh from Abu Shusheh (Gezer).
† Tale told by an Ashkenazi or Polish Jew in 1883.
[3] See p. 242.   [4] See p. 243.

as apes, then as fierce and dangerous as lions, and finally as besotted, degraded and unclean as pigs. Noah, when the vintage was come, made wine and, not knowing this, indulged much in its use. Consequently, and to the consternation of his sons, he babbled of his intention to marry again and breed a new race. When they protested, he became furious and violent, and afterwards fell asleep on the ground. Hereupon his two elder sons left him, but Canaan, in order to prevent his father from marrying again, did him a horrible bodily injury. That, say the Jews, was why Noah, on awaking from his drunken sleep, cursed Canaan and all his descendants (see Genesis ix.).

IV

JOB AND HIS FAMILY

AYÛB, on whom be Peace, was a very rich man with a large family.[1] In order to prove the sincerity of his professed piety, Allah deprived him, not only of all his worldly possessions and his children, but of his health as well. He was afflicted with a skin disease so loathsome that, on account of the smell from his ulcers, nobody but his wife would come within fifty yards of him. In spite of these misfortunes the Patriarch continued to serve Allah and to give Him thanks as in the day of prosperity. His patience, though great, did not equal that of his wife, who was a daughter of Ephraim the son of Joseph, or else of Manasseh. She not only nursed her husband with great devotion, but supported him by her earnings, and, when she could get no work, used to carry him about on her back in an *abáyeh*, while she begged from door to door.* This she did for seven years without a murmur. One day, when she had been forced to leave her husband for a short time, Iblìs appeared to her, and promised that if she would worship him he would cure her husband and restore his lost possessions. The woman, sorely tempted, went to ask leave of Ayûb, who was so angry with her for daring to parley with the devil that he swore, if Allah would restore him to health, to give her a hundred lashes. He then uttered this prayer: "O my Lord, verily evil hath afflicted me; but Thou art the most merciful of those who show mercy." Hereupon Allah sent Gabriel, who took Ayûb by the hand and raised him. At the same instant the fountain which supplies Bìr Ayûb in the valley below Jerusalem sprang up at the Patriarch's feet. The latter, by the

---

* Tale told by an Orthodox Greek priest to a member of his flock; and also by fellahìn of Siloam to me.

[1] See p. 243.

Angel's direction, immediately drank thereof, and the worms in his wounds at once fell from his body; and when he had bathed in the fountain, his former health and beauty were restored. Allah then restored his children to life, and made his wife so young and handsome that she bore him twenty-six sons. To enable the Patriarch to support so large a family, and also to compensate him for the loss of his wealth, the threshing-floors close to Bìr Ayûb, which belonged to him, were filled with gold and silver coinage rained down by two clouds sent for the purpose. Softened by these evidences of the Almighty's mercy, Ayûb began to regret his rash oath; but could not see how to evade its performance. In this difficulty Gabriel came again to his relief. At the Angel's suggestion, the Patriarch took a palm branch which had a hundred fronds, and giving his wife one tap with it, considered that she had received the promised beating.

Besides his devoted wife, Ayûb had a relative who, from all accounts, was one of the most remarkable men that ever lived. He is generally called " El Hakìm Lokman," [2] though I have also heard the name " El Hakìm Risto " applied to him.*

This personage was the son of Baura, who was the son or grandson either of Ayûb's sister or of his aunt. He lived for several hundreds of years, till the time of David, with whom he was acquainted. He was extremely ugly, of a black complexion, with thick lips and splay feet; but, to make up for these deformities, Allah gave him wisdom and eloquence. Offered the choice between the gifts of prophecy and wisdom, he chose the latter. The prophet David wished him to be King of Israel, but he declined so onerous a position,† content to remain a simple Hakìm.

Having been taken and sold into slavery by the Bedû who raided the Hauran and carried off Ayûb's cattle, he obtained

* The latter name, which is only, and that seldom, heard amongst Christians, suggests that of Aristotle, but he is more easily identified with the Greek Æsop; all the fables attributed to the latter being current in Palestine and ascribed to Lokman.

† I received this information from a learned Moslem, a Sudanese.

[2] See p. 243.

his liberty in a remarkable manner. His master, having one day given him a bitter melon to eat, was greatly surprised at his obedience in consuming the whole of it, and asked him how he could eat so unpleasant a fruit. Lokman answered that it was no wonder that he should, for once in a while, accept an evil thing from one who had conferred so many benefits on him. This answer so pleased his owner that he set him free.

The well-known fables excepted, the following story is that most related of this sage.

* A certain rich man was very ill, and the doctors said he must die, because there was some animal inside him, clutching at his heart. It was thought it might be a serpent, for it is well known that if people sleep in the fields where yellow melons are growing they run the risk of young serpents slipping through their open mouths into their stomachs, and thriving there on the food that ought to nourish their victims.³ El Hakìm Lokman was called in as a last resource. He said there was one operation which might save the patient, but to perform it would be very dangerous. The sick man clutched at this last chance of life. He sent for the Kadi, the Mufti, and the whole Council of notables, and in their presence signed and sealed a document which exonerated Lokman from all blame in case he died under the operation. He then took leave of his friends and relatives.

Lokman invited all the other doctors in the city to assist at the operation: first making them swear that they would not interfere through jealousy.

One physician, however, he did not invite, and that was his sister's son, of whom he was very jealous, but who, nevertheless, attained ultimately even greater skill than Lokman himself. (That enmity should exist between such relatives is natural, for his sister's son is commonly a man's worst rival: † a circumstance which has given rise to the

* Tale told me in 1865 by an Orthodox Greek peasant from Bethlehem, whom I met in the Kaiserswerther Deaconesses hospital at Jerusalem.

† Opinion expressed by a native Christian from Es Salt, in Transjordania.

³ See p. 244.

common saying: "If thou hast no sister's son, but art so foolish as to desire one, take a lump of clay and mould one for thyself, and to thine own liking, and then, when he is perfect, behead him lest he perchance come to life and do thee an injury.") This nephew, though uninvited, determined to witness the operation, so he climbed on to the house-top, where he knew of a small window through which he could look into the sick-room, and see all that was going on. In the meantime Lokman administered *benj* [4] to the sufferer and, as soon as the anæsthetic had taken effect, proceeded to lay him open. So doing, he revealed a huge crab clinging to the heart.

At the sight even Lokman himself lost courage, and said, "There, sure enough, is the cause of sickness, but how to remove the beast I know not. If anyone here knows a way, for Allah's sake let him name it." The physicians replied, "We cannot tell how to remove the creature, for, if we use force, it will only cling more tightly to the heart, and the man will die." Hardly had these words been spoken when, to Lokman's surprise and shame, the unseen watcher on the house-top shouted into the room, "Ilhak bi 'n-nâr ya homâr!" "Follow up with fire, thou ass!" On hearing this most opportune advice, Lokman sent one of his colleagues running to the Butchers' Street, to ask the keeper of the first Kobab-broiling-shop to lend him an iron skewer. Others were told to prepare a brazier; others to fetch cotton wool. When all was ready, the great Hakìm wrapped a wet cloth round one end of the iron skewer for a handle, and thrust the other in the fire till it was red-hot, while one of the attendant physicians, by his orders, manufactured two small pads of cotton wool. When the skewer was red-hot the operator touched one of the claws with it. The sudden pain caused the crab to lift that claw, when one of the pads was put beneath it. In this way all the claws were loosened, and the crab could be removed without danger to the patient.

Lokman was then going to clean the wounds with a silver spoon; but his nephew on the roof cried: "Beware of

[4] See p. 244.

touching a human heart with metal." He therefore took a piece of wood that lay handy, and fashioned it into a spoon for his purpose. Having anointed the wounds in the heart, he sewed up the chest of the patient, who thereafter recovered and enjoyed long life.

V

ABRAHAM, "THE FRIEND OF GOD" *

IBRAHÌM, whose surname is Khalìl Allah, or the Friend of God, was the son of Azar or Terah, a sculptor, and also wazìr to Nimrûd, King of Kûtha. The impiety of Nimrûd was so great that he compelled his subjects to worship him as a god.

A dream which greatly disturbed him was interpreted by soothsayers to portend the speedy birth of a great prophet who should overthrow idolatry and cause Nimrûd's ruin. To prevent this the tyrant collected all men into a large military camp, had every male infant in his dominions massacred, and ordered that all women likely to become mothers should be closely watched and their offspring, if male, destroyed at birth.

In spite of these precautions, Azar's wife was delivered of Ibrahìm without the knowledge of any mortal but herself. When the hour of her trouble approached, she was led secretly by angels to a concealed and well-furnished cavern.† Her trial was rendered painless by Allah's grace, and, leaving her new-born babe in the care of celestial ministrants, she returned to her home in perfect health and vigour.

Azar, who, like all other men, was away from home in constant attendance upon Nimrûd, was for a long time ignorant of what had happened during his absence. His wife was allowed to visit her child every few days, and was every time surprised at his growth and extraordinary beauty. In one day he grew as much as any ordinary child would in a month, and in one month as much as another would in a year. He was also fed in a marvellous

* These are tales told both by Jews and Moslems.
† Moslem tradition shows this cave at the village of Barzeh, near Damascus. See also Josephus, *Antiq.*, Bk. I, ch. vii, 2.

manner. Entering the cave one day, his mother found the infant sitting up and sucking his fingers with great gusto. Wondering why he did this, she examined his fingers, and found that from one there gushed forth milk, from the next honey, whilst butter and water respectively exuded from the others. It was most convenient, and she ceased to be surprised that the child throve so remarkably. At the age of fifteen months he could already speak fluently, and, being very inquisitive, put the following shrewd questions to his parent: "Mother, who is my Lord?" She answered, "I am." "And who is thy Lord?" "Thy father." "And who is my father's Lord?" "Nimrûd." "And who is Nimrûd's Lord?" "Hush!" said the mother, striking the child on its mouth. She was, however, so delighted that she could no longer keep the child's existence hid from Azar. The wazìr came and was conducted to the cavern. He asked Ibrahìm whether he really was his son. The infant Patriarch answered in the affirmative, and then propounded to his father the same series of questions that he put to his mother, and with the same result.

One evening Ibrahìm begged his mother to allow him to go out of the cave. His request being granted, he marvelled greatly at the wonders of creation, and made the following remarkable declaration. "He that created me, gave me all things needful, fed me, and gave me drink, shall be my Lord, and none but He." Then, looking skywards, he perceived a bright star, for it was evening, and he said, "Surely this is my Lord!" But the star, as he watched it closely, sank to westward and disappeared, and Ibrahìm said, "I love not things that change. This could not have been my Lord." In the meantime the full moon had risen and was shedding her mild beams on all around, and the child said, "Surely this is my Lord!" and he watched her all through the night. Then the moon also set, and, in great distress, Ibrahìm exclaimed, "Verily I was in error, the moon could not have been my Lord; for I love not things that change." Soon after this the sky was tinged with all the glorious colours of the sunrise, and the sun arose in all his brightness, waking men and birds and insects to life and energy, bathing all things in a golden glory. At his splendour, the boy cried, " Surely this is my Lord ! " But, as the hours wore on, the sun also began to sink westwards, and the shadows to lengthen, till at last the shades of night again covered the earth, and in bitter disappointment the child said, " Verily I was again in error, neither star nor moon nor sun can be my Lord. I love not the things that change." And in the anguish of his soul he prayed: " O Allah, Thou Great, Unsearchable, Unchangeable One, reveal Thyself to Thy servant, guide me, and keep me from error."

The petition was heard and Gabriel was sent to instruct the earnest seeker after truth. As a child of ten years of age, Ibrahìm already began to exhort the people to worship Allah only. One day he entered the idol temple, and, finding nobody present, he broke all the images except the largest with an axe, which he then laid on the lap of that which he had spared. When the priests entered the temple they were very angry, and, seeing Ibrahìm, accused him of sacrilege. He told them there had been a quarrel amongst the gods, and that the greater one had destroyed those who had provoked him. When they answered that this could not be, he showed them from their own mouths the folly of their idolatrous belief. Hereupon they accused him to Nimrûd, who had a great furnace built, filled with fuel and set on fire. He then ordered Ibrahìm to be thrown into the fire. The heat, however, was so great that nobody dared to venture near enough to carry out the command. Then Iblìs showed Nimrûd how to construct a machine by means of which the young martyr, bound hand and foot, was hurled into the flames. But Allah preserved him, and the furnace was to him as cool and pleasant as a rosegarden watered by fountains. He came out of the fire unhurt. Nimrûd then declared that he must either see this God of Ibrahìm's or kill Him. He therefore had a lofty tower built, from the top of which he hoped to get into heaven. When the tower had reached the height of seventy stories, each storey being seventy *dra'as* high, Allah confounded the speech of the workmen. Seventy-three languages were thus suddenly spoken all at one and the same time and in the same place, causing great babbling, wherefore the tower was called Babel. Pilgrims from Mosu and Baghdad declare that its ruins exist in their country to this day. Foiled in this attempt, Nimrûd constructed a flying-machine, as simple as it was ingenious. It was a box with one lid at the top and another at the bottom. Four eagles which had been specially trained, and had attained their full size and strength, were tied one to each of the four corners of the box; then an upright pole was fixed on to the chest, and to this pole a large piece of raw meat was fastened. The birds flew upwards in order to get at the meat, and in so doing carried the box, into which Nimrûd and an attendant archer had entered, with them. The harnessed eagles could not get at the meat, and so the flying-machine rose higher and higher. When it had ascended so high that the earth could hardly be seen, the giant ordered his companion to shoot an arrow heavenwards. Before ascending, Nimrûd had taken the precaution to dip the tips of the arrows in blood. Arrow after arrow was shot heavenwards, and, when the quiver was emptied, the pole with the meat on it was taken down and thrust through the opening in the bottom of the box. On finding themselves thus balked of their food, the wearied eagles of course began to descend, and on reaching the earth, Nimrûd pointed to the arrows which had fallen back to the earth as a proof that he had wounded Allah; while the latter as he boasted, had been unable to do him the least harm. This blasphemy completely deceived the people, whose confidence in Nimrûd had been rudely shaken by Ibrahìm's deliverance from the fiery furnace, and they began to worship the cunning giant. Allah, however, did not let his wickedness go unpunished. The more clearly to show the greatness of His power, the Almighty employed the smallest of His creatures in order to humble the most arrogant. A sand-fly was sent to enter the giant's nostrils and make its way to his brain, where for two hundred years it tormented Nimrûd day and night until he died. Towards the end his agony was so intense that he could only get relief by employing a man to strike him constantly on the head with an iron hammer.

In the meantime, however, when Nimrûd found that he could do no harm to Ibrahìm, and that many people were being converted to his faith, he banished the prophet from his dominions.* But hardly had he taken this step ere he regretted it, and sent a troop of soldiers, mounted on mules which had been used to carry fuel to the furnace, in order to recapture him. When the Patriarch, who was riding a donkey, saw the soldiers at a distance, he realised that, unless he abandoned his beast and found some hiding-place, there was no hope for him. So he got off and took to his heels.

After running for some time he came across a flock of goats, and asked them to protect him. They refused and he was obliged to run on. At last he saw a flock of sheep, which, at the same request, at once agreed to hide him. They made him lie flat on the ground, and huddled together so closely that his enemies passed him by. As a reward for the sheep, Ibrahìm asked Allah to give them the broad and fat tails for which Eastern sheep are remarkable; and, to punish the goats, he procured for them little upright tails, too short for decency; while the mules, which till then had been capable of bearing young, were now made barren, because they willingly carried fuel to the furnace and bore the soldiers of Nimrûd swiftly in pursuit of El-Khalìl.

After this, Ibrahìm had various adventures both in Egypt and at Bir-es-Seba,† following which came events which I cannot do better than tell in the words of one of the sheykhs of the great Mosque at Hebron, who gave me the following account.

"Having escaped from Nimrûd, El-Khalìl was commanded to go to Mecca and build the *Maram* or sanctuary there. On reaching his destination, he received instructions first to offer up his dear son Ismaìn (Ishmael) as a sacrifice upon Jebel 'Arafat, the mountain where Adam had recognised Hawa. Iblìs, hoping to make trouble between the Patriarch and his friend, went to our Lady Hagar, on whom

* This tale was told by a fellâh of Siloam.   † Beersheba.

be peace, and implored her to dissuade her husband from the cruel deed. She snatched up a stone and hurled it at the tempter. The missile did him no harm, but the pillar against which the stone dashed is still shown to pilgrims. From this incident he has the name ' Ash Sheytan er Rajìm,' meaning ' Satan, the stoned One,' or ' who is to be stoned.' "

Having finished the Ka'aba, Ibrahìm was directed to build another *Haram* at El-Kûds. This he did, and was then ordered to build a third at Hebron. The site of this last sanctuary would, he was informed, be shown to him by a supernatural light which would shine over it at night. This is one account. Another account says that three angels in human form having appeared to the Patriarch, he, supposing them to be men, invited them to his tent, and then went to slay a fatling as a meal for them. In some way or other the calf eluded Ibrahìm, who followed it till it entered a certain cave. Going in after it, he heard a voice from the inner chamber informing him that he stood in the sepulchre of our Father Adam, over which he must build the sanctuary. A third story runs that a strange camel was to come and guide El-Khalìl to the appointed place. This time Iblìs succeeded in deceiving the Father of the Faithful, who began to build at Ramet el Khalìl, an hour from Hebron, but, after he had laid the few courses which are still to be seen there, Allah showed him his mistake, and he moved on to Hebron.

* Hebron was then inhabited by Jews and Christians, the name of whose patriarch was Habrûn. Ibrahìm went to visit him, and said he wished to buy as much land as the *furweh* or sheepskin jacket which he was wearing would enclose if cut into pieces. Habrûn, laughing, said, " I will sell you that much land for four hundred golden dinàrs, and each hundred dinàrs must have the die of a different sultan." It was then the '*asr*,† and Ibrahìm asked leave to say his prayers. He took off his *furweh* and spread it on the ground for a prayer-carpet. Then, taking up the

---

* Some of the details in the ensuing narrative remind one of the story of the founding of Carthage.

† [Hour for afternoon prayer, half-way from noon to sunset.—M. P.]

proper position, he performed his devotions, adding a petition for the sum demanded. When he rose from his knees and took up his jacket, there lay beneath it four bags, each containing a hundred gold dinàrs, and each hundred with the die of a different sultan.

He then, in the presence of forty witnesses, told the money into Habrûn's hand and proceeded to cut his *furweh* into strips with which to enclose the land thus bought. Habrûn protested, saying that was not the agreement; but Ibrahìm appealed to the witnesses, who decided that the size or number of the pieces into which the *furweh* was to be cut had not been specified.

This made Habrûn so angry that he took the forty witnesses to the top of the hill south-west of the city, where the ruins of Deyr el Arba'in * now stand, and there cut their heads off. But even that did not silence them, for each head, as it rolled down the hill, cried: " The agreement was that the jacket should be cut." El-Khalìl took their corpses and buried them, each in the place where the head stopped rolling.

Next to his implicit faith in Allah's Providence, Ibrahìm was chiefly noted for his hospitality. He used often to say, " I was a poor penniless outcast and fugitive, but Allah cared for and enriched me. Why, therefore, should I, in my turn, not show kindness to my fellow-men? " He had a hall built in which there was a table set ready for the refreshment of any hungry wayfarer, as well as new garments for such as were in rags. Before taking his own meals he was wont to go forth out of his camp to the distance of one or two miles in hopes of meeting guests to keep him company. In spite of his liberality he was not impoverished, but actually grew richer, by Allah's blessing. One year there was a sore famine in the land, and the Patriarch sent his servants to a friend he had in Egypt, asking the latter to send him a supply of corn. The false friend, thinking that he had now an opportunity for ruining the Friend of Allah, answered that, had the grain been wanted for the use of Ibrahìm and his own household

* *i.e.* Convent of the Forty.

and no others, he would have gladly furnished it; but that, as he knew that the food, which was so scarce all the world over that year, would only be wasted on vagabonds and beggars, he felt that he would be doing wrong to send any.

Ibrahìm's servants, very loyal to their master, were ashamed of being seen returning to his camp with empty sacks, so they filled them with fine white sand, and, reaching home, related what had happened. The Patriarch was much grieved at his friend's treachery, and whilst thinking on the matter he fell asleep. Sarah, who knew nothing of what had occurred, opened one of the sacks and found it full of the most beautiful flour, of which she made bread. Thus when earthly friends failed, Allah succoured El-Khalìl.

Being so hospitable himself, Ibrahìm could not understand how others could be the contrary. One day he was obliged to leave his tents and visit a distant part of the country, where some of his flocks were pasturing in the charge of shepherds. On reaching the place where he expected to find them, he was told by a certain Bedawi that they had gone to other pastures a good way off. He therefore accepted the Arab's invitation to enter his tent and rest awhile. A kid was killed to furnish a repast. Some weeks later, El-Khalìl had again occasion to go the same way, and met the same Bedawi, who, in answer to his inquiry as to the whereabouts of his shepherds, answered, " So many hours north of the place where I killed a kid for thee." Ibrahìm said nothing, but passed on his way. Not long after this he had occasion to make a third journey, and on meeting the Bedawi the latter told him that the flocks he was seeking were at such a distance south of " the place where I killed a kid for thee." The next time El-Khalìl met the man, he told him that the sheep were so and so far east of the place where that precious kid had been killed. " Ya Rabbi, O my Lord," exclaimed Ibrahìm, past patience, " Thou knowest how ungrudgingly I exercise hospitality without respect of persons. I beseech Thee, therefore, that as this man is constantly throwing his wretched kid in my teeth, I may be enabled to vomit it out, even though it be so long a time since I partook thereof." The prayer received an instant answer, and the slaughtered kid was restored alive and whole to its churlish owner.

Amongst other things which, according to Moslem tradition, began with Ibrahìm, we may mention three. The first of these was the rite of circumcision,[1] which was instituted in order that the corpses of Moslems slain in battle might be distinguished from those of unbelievers and receive decent burial. The second was the wearing of the wide Oriental trousers called *Sirwâl*. Till the time of Ibrahìm the only clothing worn was that which pilgrims to Mecca have to wear on approaching that city. It is called the *Ihrâm*, and consists of a woollen loin-cloth, and another woollen cloth thrown over the shoulders. Finding these garments insufficient for the demands of modesty, the Patriarch asked Allah that they might be supplemented, and accordingly Gabriel was sent from Paradise with a roll of cloth. Out of this he cut the first pair of *sirwâls*, and instructed Sarah (who was the first person since the time of Idrìs to use a needle) how to make them up. Iblìs, however, being jealous of the angel's tailoring, told the infidels that he knew a better and more economical way of cutting cloth, and, in proof, produced the Frank trousers, which, in these depraved and degenerate days, are being adopted by some Easterns. The third thing which began with El-Khalìl was grey hair. Before his time it was impossible to distinguish young men from old, but the Patriarch, having asked Allah for some sign by which the difference might be known, his own beard became snow-white. He was also the inventor of sandals; for people went altogether bare foot before his time.

Ibrahìm had obtained from Allah the promise that he should not die until he expressly wished to do so, and thus when the predestined day arrived, the Almighty was obliged, since his "Friend" had not expressed the wish, to inveigle it from him.

[1] See p. 244.

As before said, Ibrahìm was very hospitable. One day, seeing a very old man tottering along the road to his encampment, he sent a servant with a donkey to his assistance. When the stranger arrived, Ibrahìm made him welcome and set food before him. But when the guest began to eat, his feebleness seemed to increase. It was with difficulty he carried the food to his mouth.

At last El-Khalìl, who had been watching him with surprise and pity, inquired, " What ails thee, O Sheykh? " " It is the weakness of old age," was the reply. " How old are you? " asked Ibrahìm, and, on hearing the answer, " What! " he exclaimed, " shall I, when I am two years older, be as you are now? " " Undoubtedly," replied the stranger. At that El-Khalìl cried out: " O Lord God, take away my soul before I reach so pitiful a condition! " Hereupon the sheykh, who was Azrael in disguise, sprang up and received the soul of the Friend of Allah.

Ibrahìm was laid to rest in the cave of Machpelah at Hebron, by the side of Sarah his wife. His son Isaac and his grandson Jacob were also, as time rolled on, buried in the same place. However, it is a mistake to say that they are in tombs and dead, for as a matter of fact they are not dead, but living.[2] These prophets, like David and Elijah, still appear sometimes in order to save God's servants in times of danger or distress, as in the following story, which I relate as it was told me * by the chief rabbi of the Jews at Hebron.

Some two centuries ago, a Pasha, deputed to collect the taxes in Palestine, came to Hebron, and informed the Jewish community that, unless within three days they paid a large sum of money, their quarter would be looted and wrecked.

The Jews of Hebron were very poor, and had no hope of procuring so much money. They could only fast and pray for succour in their dire extremity. The night before the day on which the money must be paid was spent by them in ceaseless prayer in the synagogue. About mid-

* About 1876.
2 See p. 244.

night they heard loud knocking at one of the gates of their quarter. Some of them went and tremblingly asked who it was who thus disturbed them. " A Friend," was the reply. Still they dared not open. But the man without thrust his hand through the solid door and placed a large bag in a hole of the wall within. The arm was withdrawn again, and all was still. The bag was found to contain the exact sum of gold demanded by the Pasha. The Jews next morning presented themselves before their oppressor and laid the money at his feet. At sight of the bag he blenched and asked how they came by it. They told their story, and he confessed that the bag and its contents had been his until the middle of last night, when, though his tent was strictly guarded, a sheykh in bright raiment had come and taken it, threatening him with instant death if he moved or said a word. He knew that it was El-Khalîl, come to rescue the Jews, and begged their pardon for his harsh exactions. The Jews of Hebron still show the hole in the wall in which the bag of money was placed by Ibrahìm.

VI

LOT AND THE TREE OF THE CROSS *

Our father Adam, on his death-bed, was so terrified at the thought of dissolution, that he sent his son, the Patriarch Seth, to the gate of Paradise to beg the cherub on guard there to give him a single fruit from the Tree of Life. The Angel, unable to grant the request, yet, touched with pity for the fallen race, by Allah's leave plucked a branch that had three twigs, and gave it to the messenger. Seth returned to find his father dead. He planted the branch at the head of Adam's grave, where it took root and grew through the centuries. Though it survived the Flood, it was forgotten by mankind.

Now the Patriarch Lot, whose wife had been changed into the huge column of rock-salt which is still a sight of wonder near Jebel Usdum on the southern shores of the sea which bears his name, fell into sin so grievous that, when his conscience awoke, he despaired of salvation. He might have killed himself had not an angel from Allah appeared and told him to take a jar full of water from the Jordan, and go into the hill-country to water a small tree that he would find growing at the head of Adam's grave. The angel also told him that the plant, if it throve, would be the means of grace for all mankind. Lot sped with joy on his errand. It was a terribly hot day, and a fierce sirocco-wind was blowing when Lot set out to do the angel's bidding. As he toiled up the steep ascent to the spot where the khan, called the "Inn of the Good Samaritan," now stands, he saw a pilgrim (some say a Russian pilgrim) lying beside the road, apparently at the last gasp. Lot, being kind of heart, knelt down and offered him a draught of water. Great was his astonishment when the pilgrim, who was no other than the Evil One in human form, at one draught emptied the jar.

* Orthodox Greek legends.

Without a word Lot trudged back to the Jordan and refilled the vessel; but again, when he had brought it a good part of the way, Satan, in the guise of a worn-out pilgrim, abused his kindness and drank all the water. A third attempt was frustrated in the same way. At last the penitent, overwhelmed by this third failure, threw himself on the ground, moaning: " If I fail to relieve the suffering I shall add another to the sins which weigh me down. Yet, if I give drink to every thirsty man I meet, how shall I water the tree of my salvation? " Overcome by fatigue and sorrow he fell asleep where he lay, and in a dream the angel once more appeared to him and told him who the pretended pilgrims really were, adding that his unselfishness had proved acceptable to Allah, and that his sins were forgiven; while, as for the tree, it had been watered by angels.

Lot died in peace, and the tree grew and flourished, but the devil ceased not to scheme for its destruction till at length he succeeded in persuading Hiram to cut it down for the building of Solomon's temple. Thus the trunk was carried to Jerusalem, but the architect, finding no use for it, had it thrown into the valley eastward of Jerusalem, where it served as a foot-bridge across the torrent of the Kedron, and was thus used till Belkis, Queen of Sheba, came to visit Solomon. As she drew near to the city she was inspired with consciousness of the precious nature of the bridge she had to cross, and on reaching it she refused to set foot on it, but knelt and worshipped. The wise King of Israel, who had come forth to meet his guest, was greatly surprised at her behaviour; but when she told him whence the trunk came, and the purpose it was destined to serve, he had it taken up, carefully cleaned, and preserved in one of the treasure-chambers of the Temple. There it remained until it was required to make the cross on which Christ died. Anyone who cares to examine the present stone bridge over the Kedron, close to Absalom's Pillar, can see some of the large stones where the trunk once lay.[1]

[1] See p. 245.

VII

THE DEATHS OF AARON AND MOSES

ON reaching the confines of Palestine the Beni-Israel encamped in the country near the Wady Mûsa.* One evening, soon after they had reached it, Harûn pointed out to
Mûsa a place on a distant hillside which looked very green
and beautiful in the light of the evening sun, and expressed
his wish to visit it. Mûsa promised that they should do so
next day. Accordingly, on the following morning, the two
brothers, accompanied by their sons, set off on an expedition to the spot. By the time they reached it they were
glad to shelter from the sun in an artificial cave they found
there. On entering they were much surprised to see a
handsome couch to which was attached an inscription
stating that it was intended for the use of the person whose
stature it would fit. The bedstead was tried in succession
by all the party, and when Harûn came to lie there, it
exactly suited him. While he was yet on the bed a stranger
entered the cavern, and, respectfully saluting those present,
introduced himself as Azrael, the Angel of Death, and
stated that he had been specially sent by Allah to receive
the soul of Harûn. The venerable high-priest, though submissive to the Almighty Will, wept much as he took leave
of his brother, sons and nephews, commended his family
to the care of Mûsa, and bade him give his blessing to the
people. Azrael then begged the others to leave the cave a
minute. When he allowed them to return, the high-priest
lay dead upon the couch. They then carried out the body,
washed and prepared it for burial, and, having offered
up prayers over it, took it back and laid it on the bed.
Then, having carefully closed up the mouth of the sepulchre,
they returned sorrowfully to the camp and told the people

* Petra.

that Harûn was dead. The children of Israel, who were fond of Harûn, on hearing these words accused Mûsa of having murdered his brother.   To clear His servant of this accusation, Allah caused angels to carry the couch with Harûn's dead body through the air, and hover with it over the camp in the sight of all Israel; and, at the same time, to proclaim that Allah had taken the soul of Harûn and that Mûsa was innocent of his death.

Of the death of the great Lawgiver himself there are two different accounts.   The first briefly relates, how Allah having informed Mûsa that the time of his decease was at hand, the latter spent the few days of life left him in exhorting Israel to abide in the fear of Allah and keep His commandments.   Then, having solemnly appointed Joshua his successor, and laid down the government, Mûsa died while studying the Law.

The other legend, which is more common, runs as follows:—

Mûsa, on whom be peace, had, like Ibrahîm el Khalîl, received a promise that he was not to die until he, of his own free-will, laid himself down in the grave.

Feeling himself to be secure in that promise, the prophet simply refused to die when the Angel of Death informed him that his hour had come.   He was so angry with Azrael that the latter, affrighted, returned to his Maker and complained of the prophet's conduct.   The angel was sent back again to expostulate and make certain alluring promises: for instance, that Mûsa's grave should be annually visited in pilgrimage by believers,[1] and that the very stones of the place should be fit for fuel.[2]   Azrael also reminded Mûsa of all the favour which, during his life, he had received from Allah, and told of yet greater honours in store for him in Paradise.   All in vain.   The prophet turned a deaf ear to every argument, and at length, disgusted with the dread angel's persistency, he told him to be off, and himself left the encampment and wandered forth over the hillsides to the west of the Dead Sea.   Here he came across the shepherd to whom the charge of Sho'aib's*

* Jethro's.
[1] See p. 246.   [2] See p. 246.

and Mûsa's own flock had been entrusted when the latter was sent on his mission to deliver Israel out of Egypt, and he entered into conversation. The man was surprised to see the Lawgiver, and inquired what reason he had for leaving the haunts of men. When Mûsa told him, the shepherd, to his great displeasure, took the part of Azrael, and suggested that, seeing the Prophet was simply going to exchange the burdens, toils and sorrows of this life for unending joys at Allah's right hand, he ought to greet the announcement of his approaching change with joy. " I myself," continued the shepherd, " greatly fear death, but that is only natural, seeing that I am only a poor sinful being; but you, who are so high in Allah's favour, ought to rejoice at the prospect."

On being thus admonished, Mûsa lost his temper, saying: " Well, then, as you say you are afraid of death, may you never die! " " Amen," replied the man to this wish, little guessing it was a curse.

When the shepherd had lived out his days he swooned away, and his friends, supposing him dead, buried him in the place where his grave is still shown, not far from the shrine of Neby Mûsa.* But he is not dead, for in consequence of Mûsa's words, " May you never die," he cannot find rest in death, but is still alive and wanders about pasturing the ibex. He is sometimes seen by wandering Bedû and hunters of the wild goats in the district around the Dead Sea, and in the wadys on the west of the Jordan valley, as far north as the Sea of Tiberias. He is sometimes mistaken for El Khudr. He has been seen in the act of casting himself from a precipitous cliff, attempting suicide in his despair; but in vain. He is described as a very tall old man, covered with white hair, his beard and nails exceeding long. He always takes to flight if one tries to approach him.

To return to Mûsa. On leaving the shepherd, the Prophet wandered further along the chalky hillsides till he unexpectedly came upon a group of stone-cutters who were excavating a chamber in a wall of rock. Having greeted them Mûsa inquired what they were about, and was told that the king of the country had a very precious treasure which he wished to hide carefully from human sight, and

* Tale told by a Moslem from the village of Abn-dis, near Bethany.

that therefore he had commanded them to hollow out a rock-chamber in this lonely spot in the wilderness. It was now midday, and very hot. Feeling tired, and as there seemed to be no shade anywhere else, the Lawgiver asked permission to enter the cave and rest there. Permission was courteously granted. The weary Prophet was not in the least aware that he had asked leave to rest in his own predestined sepulchre. Hardly had he assumed a recumbent posture when the leader of the gang of workmen, who was the Angel of Death in disguise, offered him an apple. Mûsa, having accepted and smelt at it, expired immediately. His funeral rites were then performed by the supposed workmen, who were, in fact, angels expressly sent for the purpose.

VIII

DAVID AND SOLOMON

(Some of the Best Traditions.*)

DAÜD (on whom be peace) was singularly pious and anxious to do his duty to Allah as well as to his neighbour. He therefore used to divide his time into three parts, devoting one day to the worship of Allah and the study of Scripture, the second to matters of State, and the third to domestic duties and the earning of a livelihood. He was led to work with his own hands for the support of his family by the following circumstances.

When he first came to the throne he was anxious to know whether his people were satisfied with his rule, and, knowing how worthless is the praise of courtiers, he resolved to find out for himself. He therefore went about disguised among the common people and heard what was thought of his administration. On one such occasion he was informed by an angel in human form that the great fault of his government was that the king lived at the expense of the public treasury, instead of working with his hands for daily bread. On hearing this, Daûd was greatly troubled, and besought Allah to show him some kind of trade by the proceeds of which both he and his family might be able to live without burdening the nation. Hereupon Gabriel was sent to teach the king the art of making coats of mail. Thenceforth, during his leisure hours, the king was always to be found at work in his armoury, and there was a great demand for his handiwork, as the armour he made was proof against all weapons. The usual price of a full suit of mail was six thousand dinârs. The king made them at the rate of one a day. One-third of the proceeds went towards the support

* Moslem–Jewish legends.

of his family, one-third in alms, and the remainder to purchase materials for the building of the Temple. Suleyma also had a trade. He knew the art of kneading stone, and moulding it into various shapes, in the same way that a pastry-cook or a baker moulds dough. Some *colonnettes* with curiously twisted, rope-like marble shafts in the Dome of the Rock of Jerusalem are shown as his work.

Daûd made a pilgrimage to the graves of the patriarchs at Hebron, and, on his return to Jerusalem, expressed in prayer a longing to be as favoured of Allah as they were. He even went so far as to say that he was sure that, if exposed to their temptations, he would overcome them; with a prospect of a like reward. In answer to this prayer Allah told Daûd that his petition would be granted, but that, seeing how the race of Adam had degenerated, the All Merciful, in granting his request, had added a favour with which the patriarchs had not been indulged: that he should be informed of the exact time of his trial. The date and hour were thus announced to the pious king.

When the day arrived, Daûd, full of confidence, shut himself up in the tower which still bears his name,[1] and gave orders that he was on no account to be disturbed. He passed the time in reading and meditation. Then, as now, many wild rock-doves flew around the tower, and the king was presently roused from his devotions by a flutter of wings. Looking up, he saw, just outside the window, a most wonderful pigeon, its plumage gleaming with prismatic colours, and looking as if it had feathers of gold and silver studded with precious jewels. The king threw some crumbs on to the floor, and the bird came in and picked them up at his feet, but eluded every attempt at capture. At last it flew to the window and settled on one of the bars. Daûd tried again to catch it, but the creature flew away, and it was then, as he was looking after it, that he saw that which led to his great crimes in the matter of Uriah.

Two angels were some time afterwards sent, in human form, to reprove the fallen monarch. On their arrival at the gate of Daûd's tower they were refused entrance

[1] See p. 246.

by the guards; but, to the latter's great astonishment, they easily scaled the fortress wall and entered the royal chamber. Surprised at their coming in unannounced and without leave, Daûd demanded to know their business with him. He was thunderstruck when, having related the parable of the one ewe lamb,* they denounced his iniquity. When they had fulfilled their mission they departed, leaving the king so full of remorse at his failure to resist the temptation sent in answer to his prayer, that he wept day and night. Mountains and hills, trees and stones, beasts and flying things, which had been wont to echo his songs of praise to Allah, now joined in his lamentations. There was universal weeping, and the tears of Daûd himself flowed so copiously that they filled both the Birket es Sultan † and the Birket Hammâm el Batrak.‡ At last a prophet was sent to tell the contrite sinner that, in consideration of his penitence, Allah pardoned the sin against Himself, but that, for the crime against his fellow-man, he must obtain forgiveness from the person injured. The king then made a pilgrimage to the tomb of Uriah, and there confessed his sins, when a voice came from the tomb saying: " My Lord the King, since your crime has secured me Paradise, I forgive you with all my heart." " But, Uriah," said Daûd, " I did it to get possession of your wife." To this there was no answer, until Daûd, in despair, prayed Allah to make Uriah forgive him. Then the voice came again from the tomb: " I forgive thee, O King, because for one wife torn from me on earth, Allah has given me a thousand in heaven."

In the southern wall of the Dome of the Rock, often erroneously called the Mosque of 'Omar, on the right-hand side, just outside the door, there are two small slabs of marble which, having been sliced from the same block, show the same veining, and have been fastened side by side

* 2 Sam. xii. 1–6.
† Traditionally known as the Lower Pool of Gihon.
‡ Traditionally known as the Pool of Hezekiah.

in such a way that the vein-lines form a figure which re-
sembles two birds perched on opposite sides of a vase.
The picture is framed in marble of a darker colour. Connected with the picture is the following story.

The great Suleymân el Hakîm was sitting one day near a
window of his palace, listening to the love-talk of two
pigeons upon the house-top. Said the male bird loftily:
" Who is Suleymân the King? And what are all his buildings to be so proud of? Why, I, if I put my mind to do it,
could kick them down in a minute! "

Hearing this, Suleymân leant out of the window and called
the boaster, asking how he could tell such a lie. " Your
Majesty," was the cringing reply, " will forgive me when I
explain that I was talking to a female. You know one cannot help boasting in such circumstances." The monarch
laughed and bade the rogue begone, warning him never
to speak in that tone again. The pigeon, after a profound
reverence, flew to rejoin his mate.

The female at once asked why the king had called him.
" Oh," came the answer, " he overheard what I was
saying to you, and asked me not to do it." So enraged
was Suleymân at the irrepressible vanity of the speaker
that he turned both birds into stone, as a warning to men
not to boast, and to women not to encourage them.*

Suleymân was well acquainted with the language of
plants. Whenever he came across a new plant he asked
its name, uses, the soil and cultivation by which it flourished,
and also its properties; and the plant answered. He laid
out the first botanical garden.

One day, in the Temple courts, he noticed a young plant
of a kind unknown to him. He promptly asked its name.
" El Kharrûb," ² was the answer. Now El Kharrûb
means the destroyer. " Of what use art thou? " continued
the king. " To destroy thy works," replied the plant.
On hearing this Suleymân exclaimed in sorrow, " What!

* Cf. " King Solomon and the Butterflies " in Mr. Rudyard Kipling's
Just So Stories.
² See p. 246.

has Allah prepared the cause of the destruction of my works during my lifetime? "

Then he prayed that his decease, whenever it should occur, might be hidden from the Jân till all mankind should be aware of it. His reason for making this petition was his fear that if the Jân should know of his death before mankind knew of it, they would seize the opportunity to do mischief and teach men iniquity. Having prayed thus, the king dug up the Kharrûbeh and planted it close to a wall in his garden, where, to prevent, as far as might be, any harm coming from it, he watched it daily till it had grown into a strong, stout sapling. He then cut it down and made of it a walking-stick on which he would lean when he sat superintending the labours of the evil spirits he kept slaving for him, to prevent them from exercising their power and ingenuity against mankind.

Now, many years before, Belkis, Queen of Sheba, had come to prove Suleymân with hard questions, one of which was how to pass a silk thread through a bead, the perforation in which was not straight through, but winding like the body of a moving serpent. It had been a hard task, but it was performed, at the king's request, by a small white worm or maggot which, taking the end of the thread between its teeth, crawled in at one end and out at the other. To reward this insignificant creature for its work, the king granted its request that it might lodge inside the seed-vessels and other parts of plants and feed thereon. Unknown to Suleymân it had found a home under the bark of the young Kharrûb tree, his staff, and had penetrated to the very centre of the trunk. The time arrived for the king to die, and he happened to be sitting as usual, leaning on his staff, when Azrael came and took away his soul, unknown to the Jân, who worked on steadily for full forty years not knowing that the king was dead, because the staff upheld his corpse just as if it had been alive. At last, however, the worm hollowed out the staff, which suddenly broke in two, so that the body of Suleymân rolled to the ground and the evil spirits knew that their tyrant was dead. To this day the traveller in the East is shown a huge unfinished stone [3] in the quarries at Ba'albec, and others in different parts of the country, and is informed that they are some of the tasks left unfinished by the Jân, when at last they were sure that Suleymân el Hakìm was dead.

[3] See p. 246.

EL KHUDR *

ONE of the saints oftenest invoked in Palestine is the
mysterious El Khudr or Evergreen One. He is said to have
been successful in discovering the Fountain of Youth,
which is situated somewhere near the confluence of the two
seas.† This fountain had been vainly sought for by other
adventurers, including the famous Dhu'lkarneyn,[1] the
two-horned Alexander, who with his companions came to
the banks of the stream that flowed from it, and actually
washed the salt fish which they had brought with them as
provision in its waters, and yet, though the said fish came
to life again and escaped them, failed to realise the happiness
within their reach. They went on their way till they came
to the place where the sun sets in a pool of black mud, and
their leader built eighteen cities, each of which he called
Alexandria, after himself; but neither he nor his companions
became immortal, because they had failed to see and use
the one opportunity of a lifetime.

El Khudr, more fortunate or more observant, not only
found the fountain, but drank of its waters, so he never dies,
but reappears from time to time as a sort of avatar, to set
right the more monstrous forms of wrong and protect the
upright. He is identified with Phinehas, the son of Eleazar,
with Elijah the prophet, and with St. George. Jewish
mothers, when danger threatens their children, invoke him
as " Eliyahu ha Navi," Christian as " Mar Jiryis " and
Moslem as " El Khudr "; and his numerous shrines in
different parts of the land are visited in pilgrimage by
adherents of all three religions.

Though it is believed that prayers addressed to him at all

* Jewish, Moslem and native Christian legends.
† The Mediterranean and the Red Sea.
[1] See p. 247.

46

these places are efficacious, yet on Fridays he himself worships Allah at different sanctuaries in succession: one Friday at Mecca, the next at Medina, and then in turn at Jerusalem, El Kûba and Et Tûr. He takes only two meals a week, and quenches his thirst alternately at the well Zemzem in Mecca and that of Solomon in Jerusalem. He bathes in the fountain at Silwan (Siloam).

One of the shrines dedicated to El Khudr is situated about a mile to the north of Solomon's Pools near Bethlehem, and is a sort of madhouse. Deranged persons of all the three faiths were taken thither * and chained in the court of the chapel, where they were kept for forty days on bread and water, the Greek priest at the head of the establishment now and then reading the Gospel over them, or administering a whipping, as the case demanded.

The following legend concerning this convent was related by a native of the neighbouring village of Beyt Jala:—

A very long time ago, in the days of the ancestors of our great-grandfathers, the Greek priest was administering the Holy Communion in the church of El Khudr. Now, as you know, the Greeks crumble the consecrated bread into the cup of wine, and administer both the elements at the same time, by means of a spoon. Whether the celebrant was drunk or not I cannot tell, but this much is certain, that whilst about to put the spoon into the mouth of a communicant kneeling in front of him, somehow or other he spilled its sacred contents. They fell on to his foot, made a hole right through it, and a mark on the flagstones beneath. The wound which the body and blood of the Saviour made in the foot of the priest never healed, but was the cause of his death. Some time afterwards, however, a man afflicted with a grievous disease visited this same church of Mar Jiryis, and, without being aware of the fact, knelt down on the flagstone which had received a mark from the falling upon it of the consecrated bread and wine, and prayed for his recovery. To his great joy, and to the surprise of all present, he was healed on the spot. The fame of his cure brought many others who were stricken with incurable maladies to El Khudr, and, as soon as they knelt on the sacred stone, they were cured, to the glory of God and of

* Before the British occupation of Palestine.

Mar Jiryis; so that the reputation of the church became widely spread, and even reached the ears of the Sultan of the Muscovites, who, jealous that so holy a stone should be kept in such an out-of-the-way village, coveted it for the benefit of himself and his people. He sent a man-of-war to Jaffa, bearing a letter to the Patriarch of Jerusalem, saying that the slab should be taken up at once and transported to Jaffa. As the Sultan of the Muscovites was a good friend, benefactor, and protector of the Church, the Patriarch did not hesitate to obey his order, and had the stone conveyed to Jaffa. It was placed in a boat belonging to the warship in order to be taken on board, but all the efforts of the rowers to reach the vessel were in vain, for Mar Jiryis himself appeared, and repeatedly pushed the boat back to the shore with his lance. This happened so often that the Muscovites were obliged to desist from their purpose; and when it was reported to the Patriarch, he realised his error, and had the stone brought back and reverently deposited in the church at El Khudr, where it is shown to this day.

As already stated, there are many churches and convent chapels dedicated to St. George. Within the walls of Jerusalem there are at least two Greek and one Coptic convent of that name; whilst just outside the Jaffa Gate, and on the western side of the traditional Valley of Gihon or Upper Hinnom, nearly opposite the Citadel, is another. The Moslems believe that, at the Last Day, Christ will slay Antichrist, and some of them maintain that this convent marks the spot where that will happen. They found their opinion on the statement that what is now known as the Jaffa Gate was formerly called the Gate of Lydda.

On the northern slope of Mount Carmel there is another celebrated centre of El Khudr worship.[2] It is frequently visited by Jewish, Christian, Moslem and Druze pilgrims who are in search of bodily or mental healing. Some very remarkable cures are said to have been performed at this place. The following example was told me by the late Dr. Chaplin, who was for many years head of the L.J.S. Medical Mission at Jerusalem. One day there was brought

[2] See p. 247.

to him a young Jewess, suffering from a nervous complaint which he considered curable, but only by long treatment. The girl's relations at first agreed to leave her at the hospital, but afterwards took her away in spite of his remonstrances. They said that they were sure that she was not really ill, but only under the influence of a *dibbuk* or parasitical demon, and they intended to treat her accordingly.

Some months later the doctor happened to meet the girl in the street, and found, to his surprise, that she was well again. Asking how the cure, which seemed to him astounding, had been effected, he was told that her friends had sent her to Mount Carmel and locked her up one night in Elijah's cave. Shut up alone, she said, she fell asleep, but was roused at midnight by a light that shone on her. Then she saw an old man all in white, who came slowly towards her, saying, "Fear not, my daughter." He laid his hand gently on her head and disappeared. When she awoke next morning she was perfectly well.

Among the Jews Eliyahu is considered not only as the special guardian of Israel, but also as the invisible attendant at every circumcision, and, as such, a special seat is prepared for him. In like manner a chair and a cup of wine are placed ready for him at the time of the Paschal anniversary. Amongst the Armenian Christians at Jerusalem there is a belief that if, at a meal, a loaf, or even a slice of bread, happen accidentally to fall or otherwise get into such a position that it stands on edge on the table, it is a sign that Mar Jiryis is invisibly present as a guest, and has condescended to bless the repast.

The story of St. George and the Dragon is, of course, well known in Palestine. The saint's tomb is shown in the crypt of the old Crusaders' church * at Lydda; and at Beyrût the very well into which he cast the slain monster, and the place where he washed his hands when his dirty work was done. The following is, briefly, the tale told by the Christians:—

* [If I remember rightly the tomb is half in the present Christian church and half in the adjoining mosque, the old Crusaders' church having been thus divided.—M. P.]

There was once a great city that depended for its water-supply upon a fountain without the walls. A great dragon, possessed and moved by Satan himself, took possession of the fountain and refused to allow water to be taken unless, whenever people came to the spring, a youth or maiden was given to him to devour. The people tried again and again to destroy the monster; but though the flower of the city cheerfully went forth against it, its breath was so pestilential that they used to drop down dead before they came within bowshot.

The terrorised inhabitants were thus obliged to sacrifice their offspring, or die of thirst; till at last all the youth of the place had perished except the king's daughter. So great was the distress of their subjects for want of water that her heart-broken parents could no longer withhold her, and amid the tears of the populace she went out towards the spring, where the dragon lay awaiting her. But just as the noisome monster was going to leap on her, Mar Jiryis appeared, in golden panoply, upon a fine white steed, and spear in hand. Riding full tilt at the dragon, he struck it fair between the eyes and laid it dead. The king, out of gratitude for this unlooked-for succour, gave Mar Jiryis his daughter and half of his kingdom.

As already remarked, Elijah frequently appears in Jewish legends as the Protector of Israel, always ready to instruct, to comfort, or to heal—sometimes condescending to cure so slight a complaint as a toothache, at others going so far as to bear false witness in order to deliver Rabbis from danger and difficulty.*

The modern Jewish inhabitants of Palestine devoutly believe in his intervention in times of difficulty. Thus, among the Spanish Jewish synagogues at Jerusalem, there is shown a little subterranean chamber, called the "Synagogue of Elijah the prophet," from the following story:—

One Sabbath, some four centuries ago, when there were only a very few Jews in the city, there were not men enough to form a *minyan* or legal congregational quorum. It was found impossible to get together more than nine, ten being the minimum number needed. It was therefore announced that the customary service could not be held, and those

* See Edersheim's *Life and Times of Jesus the Messiah*, App. VIII.

present were about to depart, when suddenly a reverend-looking old man appeared, donned his *talith* or prayer-shawl, and took his place among them. When the service was over, " the First in Zion," as the chief Rabbi of the Jewish community at Jerusalem is entitled, on leaving the place of worship, looked for the stranger, intending to ask him to the Sabbath meal, but he could nowhere be found. It was thought this mysterious stranger could have been no other than the famous Tishbite.

The following story, a version of one told in the Koran,* is related by the Moslems of El Khudr :—

The great Lawgiver was much perplexed and troubled when he thought about the apparently confused and strange dealings of Divine Providence, and besought Allah to enlighten him. He was told, in answer to his prayer, to go on a certain day to a certain place where he would meet a servant of the Merciful, who would instruct him. Mûsa did as he was told, and found at the rendezvous a venerable derwìsh, who, to start with, made him promise not to make remarks or ask questions concerning anything he might see him do while they journeyed together. Mûsa promised, and the pair set out on their travels.

At sunset they reached a village, and went to the house of the sheykh, a man rich and kindly, who bade them welcome and ordered a sheep to be killed in their honour. When bed-time came they were conducted to a large, well-furnished room. The *tusht* and *ibrìk*,† which in most houses are of tinned copper, were here of silver-plate set with jewels.

Mûsa, being tired out, soon fell asleep; but long ere daylight his companion woke him, saying they must start at once. Mûsa objected, finding the bed comfortable. He declared it ungrateful to leave so early while their host was still abed and they could not thank him. " Remember the terms of our compact," said the derwìsh sternly, while to Mûsa's amazement he coolly slipped the silver *tusht* or wash-hand-basin into the bosom of his robe. Mûsa then rose in silence and they left the house.

That evening, quite worn out, they reached another village, and were once more guests of the sheykh, who proved the very opposite of their host of the previous night. He

---

* Sûra xviii. 50 ff. † Vessels for ceremonial ablution.

grumbled at the necessity he was under of harbouring vagrants, and bade a servant take them to a cave behind the stable where they could sleep on a heap of *tibn*.* For supper he sent them scraps of mouldy bread and a few bad olives. Mûsa could not touch the stuff, though he was starving, but his companion made a good meal.

Next morning, Mûsa awoke very early, feeling hungry and miserable. He roused his guide and suggested that it was time to rise and start. But the derwìsh said, "No, we must not sneak away like thieves," and went to sleep again.

Some two hours later the ascetic rose, bade Mûsa put the fragments of the night's meal into his bosom, and said, "Now we must bid our host farewell." In the presence of the sheykh, the derwìsh made a low reverence, thanking him for his hospitality towards them, and begging him to accept a slight token of their esteem. To the amazement of the sheykh, as well as Mûsa, he produced the stolen basin, and laid it at the sheykh's feet. Mûsa, mindful of his promise, said no word.

The third day's journey was through a barren region, where Mûsa was glad of the scraps which, but for the derwìsh, he would have thrown away. Towards evening they came to a river, which the derwìsh decided not to attempt to cross till next morning, preferring to spend the night in a miserable reed-built hut, where the widow of a ferryman dwelt with her orphan nephew, a boy of thirteen. The poor woman did all in her power to make them comfortable, and in the morning made them breakfast before starting. She sent her nephew with them to show the way to a ruinous bridge further down the river. She shouted instructions to the boy to guide their honours safely over it ere he returned. The guide led the way, the derwìsh followed him, and Mûsa brought up the rear. When they got to the middle of the bridge, the derwìsh seized the boy by the neck and flung him into the water, and so drowned him. "Monster! murderer!" cried Mûsa, beside himself. The derwìsh turned upon his disciple, and the Prophet knew him for El Khudr. "You once more forget the terms of our agreement," he said sternly, "and this time we must part. All that I have done was predestined by Divine mercy. Our first host, though a man of the best intentions, was too confiding and ostentatious. The loss of his silver

* Chopped straw.

basin will be a lesson to him. Our second host was a skin-
flint. He will now begin to be hospitable in the hope of
gain; but the habit will grow upon him, and gradually
change his nature. As for the boy whose death so angers
you, he is gone to Paradise, whereas, had he lived but two
years longer, he would have killed his benefactress, and
in the year following he would have killed you."

The " former " rains having failed during the months of
November and December 1906, prayers for rain were
offered up in all places of worship, Moslem, Jewish and
Christian. About that time the following tales were circulated at Jerusalem. A woman who had just filled her
pitcher, drop by drop, from a scanty spring near Ain
Kârim was suddenly accosted by a horseman bearing a long
lance, who ordered her to empty her vessel into a stone
trough and water his horse. She objected, but yielded to
his threats. To her horror it was not water but blood that
ran from her pitcher. The horseman bade her inform her
fellow-villagers that had Allah not sent the drought, pestilence and other calamities would have befallen them.
Having given her this charge, he vanished. It was El
Khudr.

A Moslem woman at Hebron, giving drink to an aged
stranger at his request, was told to give to the Hebronites
a message similar to the above, and to add that Allah would
send rain after the Greek New Year. We certainly did
have some very wet weather after that date.

X

In the upper part of the Kedron Valley, not far from the point north of Jerusalem where it is crossed by the road to Nablus, is an old rock-hewn sepulchre. Inside the walled-up vestibule, the entrance to which is closed by a modern door, is an ancient but purposely mutilated and little noticeable Latin inscription, which proves that at one time this rock-tomb, which during the course of ages has been much altered and now serves the purpose of a synagogue, was the last resting-place of a noble Roman lady named Julia Sabina.

In spite of this fact, however, the Jews of Jerusalem assert that this is the tomb of Simon the Just, and make pilgrimages to it on the thirty-third day of 'Omer, and also on the Feast of Weeks, seventeen days later.

Simon II, son of Onias, lived during that period of Jewish history which intervenes between the time of Zerubbabel and that of the Maccabees. His surname, "the Just," shows the respect in which he was held by his contemporaries. He towered both in body and mind above other high-priests of the period, and worthily closed the long line of ancient Israelitish worthies preceding the heroes of the house of Asmon.

Jesus the son of Sirach (Ecclesiasticus l.) describes his work in the repairs and fortifications of the city and Temple, and dwells with enthusiastic reverence on his majestic appearance when he came from behind the veil hiding the Holy of Holies, into the midst of the people as they thronged the Temple courts on the great annual Day of Atonement. It was like the morning star bursting from a cloud, or the moon at the full (vers. 5, 6), like the sun's rays reflected from the golden pinnacles of God's house, or the rainbow when it shines out clear from the black background of the storm. It was like roses, like to lilies by a stream, like the fruit-laden olive tree, like the stately fir tree, like the fragrance of the frankincense, like the beauty of a golden vessel set with jewels. Every movement of the Pontiff is described with glowing admiration. The high-priestly garments of glory and beauty seemed all the more gorgeous from the manner in which he wore them. His form towered above those of his fellow-priests, as does a cedar in a palm grove; and all his ceremonial acts, the pouring out of the libations, to a blast of silver trumpets, the shouting of the multitude, the harmony evoked by the band of Levitical musicians and singers, above all Simon's delivery of the final benediction, were things never to be forgotten of the witness.

Nor was it his physical beauty alone which drew out the love of those who knew him. Various are the stories told of his influence with men, and the prevailing power of his prayers with God. According to one tradition, he was the last survivor of the " Great Synagogue " which fixed the Old Testament Canon. Another says that it was he who met Alexander the Great when that conqueror (known in Arab folk-lore as the second Iskander Dhu'lkarnein, the first of that name having been a prophet contemporary with El Khalil, and to whom we alluded when speaking of El Khudr and the Fountain of Youth) came to Jerusalem about 330 B.C.; while a third asserts that it was Simon the Just who tried to dissuade Ptolemy Philopator from intruding into the Temple at Jerusalem. The whole city was panic-stricken when the monarch announced his resolution. The dense crowds sent heavenward a shriek so piercing that it seemed as if the very walls and foundations shared in it. In the midst of the tumult was heard the prayer of Simon, invoking the All-seeing God. And then, like a reed broken by the wind, the Egyptian king fell on the pavement and was carried out by his guards.

It is also related that, till the days of Simon the Just, it was always the right hand of the high-priest that drew the lot for the scapegoat; but that afterwards the right and left

wavered and varied. Till his time the scarlet wool bound
round the horns of the animal turned white in token of the
atonement being accepted and all sin forgiven; but after his
days its changing colour was never certain. In his days
the golden candlestick in the holy place burned without
failing; afterwards it frequently went out. Two faggots
daily were sufficient to keep the flame on the great altar of
burnt-offering in front of the Temple porch alive in his
time; but later, piles of wood were not enough. In the
last year of his life he is said to have foretold his own death
from the omen that, whereas on all former occasions he was
accompanied to the entrance to the Holy of Holies on the
solemn yearly fast-day by an angel in the form of an aged
man clad in white from head to foot, this year his mysterious
companion was clothed in black, and followed him as he
went in and came out. His teaching may be judged of by the
saying ascribed to him: " There are three foundations of the
universe—the Law, Worship and Almsgiving."

He greatly disliked receiving the ascetic dedication of the
Nazarites. On one occasion, however, he made an exception. A tall, handsome youth of splendid bearing, with
beautiful eyes and long locks of hair falling in magnificent
clusters on his shoulder, arrived one day from a place in the
south of Palestine and presented himself before the high-
priest as anxious to take the vows. " Why? " inquired
Simon. " Would you shave off that glorious growth of
hair? " The young man replied: " I was keeping my
father's flocks when, one day, whilst drawing water from a
well, I beheld, with vainglorious feelings, the reflection of
my own image in the water, and was, in consequence,
tempted to give way to a sinful inclination and be lost. I
said to myself, ' Thou wicked one! wilt thou be proud of
that which does not belong to thee, who art but worms and
dust? O God, I will cut off these locks for the glory of
heaven.' " On that, Simon embraced the youth, exclaiming, " Would there were many such Nazarites in
Israel! "

With such a record of his life, it is no wonder that in
modern times the Jews of Jerusalem ascribe miraculous

power to the intercessions of this saint, and offer vows and prayers at his shrine, as in the following story:—

About two hundred years ago, when Rabbi Galanti was " The First in Zion," there came a year of great distress for lack of rain. The whole population of the city fasted and prayed, the Christians holding services and reciting litanies in their churches, the Moslems in their mosques, and the Jews at their Place of Wailing; but in vain. Infants, Christian, Jewish and Moslem, were also kept for hours without food and water, in order that their sufferings and cries might bring down the desired blessing, since Allah loves the prayers of little children; and the pupils in the Mohammedan schools marched in procession all through and round the city, chanting prayers and passages from the Koran; but still the heaven was as brass, and the All-Merciful seemed to have forgotten His chosen Land and City.

In consequence of this fearful drought, popular prejudice was roused against the Jews, and a Moslem sheykh told the Pasha that Allah was keeping back the rain because they were allowed to live in Jerusalem. Hearing this, the Pasha sent word to Galanti that, unless rain fell within three days, the Jews should be driven out.

The consternation caused by this message may be imagined. The Jews spent the next two days in constant prayer. Before sunrise of the third day, Galanti bade his people clothe themselves for wet weather, and accompany him to the tomb of Simon the Just, to give thanks for the heavy rain that would fall before evening.

The Jews believed their Rabbi had gone mad, yet dared not to disobey " The Crown of the Head of Israel." As the procession passed out at the Damascus Gate, the Moslem sentries mocked them for wearing winter clothing on that intolerably hot day, under that burning sky. But the Jews trudged on their way regardless of ridicule.

On reaching the shrine of Simon the Just their Rabbi's faith infected them, and they joined him with fervour in thanksgiving; when suddenly the sky was overcast and rain came down in torrents. Indeed so heavy was the downpour that, in spite of their winter clothing, they were drenched to the skin.

As they returned, the soldiers at the gate, who had mocked them going out, fell at Galanti's feet and asked forgiveness. The Pasha, likewise, was much impressed, and for a long while afterwards they were held in honour by the populace.

SECTION II

CONTAINING LEGENDS AND ANECDOTES POSSIBLY
FOUNDED ON FACT

SECTION II

I

BÂB EL KHALÌL, THE JAFFA GATE AT JERUSALEM [1]

IN Mohammedan eschatology Bâb el Khalìl figures as the
Gate of Lydda where 'Isa ibn Maryam [2] will destroy Antichrist, though some amongst the learned, for instance
Abulfeda and Kemâl-ed-din, assert that the event will take
place near the entrance to the town of Lydda, and, as a
matter of fact, a well inside a small domed building situated
about half-way between Lydda and Ramleh, and called
" Bir es Zeybak " or the Quicksilver Well, is pointed out as
the exact spot where the *Dejjâl* (lit. impostor) or Antichrist
will be slain.

Just inside the gateway, and on the left-hand side after
passing the portal, there are two cenotaphs in an enclosure
behind an iron railing. Old jars and tins, saddles, etc.,
placed beside the cenotaphs, or piled up in the corners of
the open space around them, show that two *Welis* or saints
are buried here. As the once existing inscriptions are now
quite effaced, no one knows exactly who they were. Some
think the tombs are those of the two architect brothers under
whose supervision the present city wall was built in the early
part of the sixteenth century. Others have informed the
writer that the monuments mark the graves of *Mujahedìn*, or
warriors of Islam, in the days either of Bûkhtûnnussur
(Nebuchadnezzar) * or of Salah-ed-din (Saladin), while
still another story relates that the *wely* buried here was a

---

* [Nebuchadnezzar and Titus are often confused by Moslem Arabs.
Thus St. John the Baptist's blood is said to have continued welling up
like a fountain under the great altar till the Temple was destroyed by
Bûkhtûnnussur, and even then not to have stopped till Bûkhtûnnussur
had slain a thousand Jews.—M. P.]

[1] See p. 248.   [2] See p. 248.

namesake and contemporary of Salah-ed-din who was in charge of the gate when the Christians besieged the city,* and when he fell in the battle, his severed head seized hold of his scimitar with its teeth and kept the Christians off seven days and nights.

Concerning Nebuchadnezzar, it is related that long before the destruction of the pre-exilic Jerusalem, Jeremiah or 'Ozair (Esdras), the prophet, knew him as a starving lad, afflicted with a scabby head and covered with vermin. Having foretold his future greatness, the prophet obtained from the youth a letter of *Amân* or safety for himself and particular friends to be available when the disasters predicted by the prophet should come upon the unhappy Beyt-el-Makdas. When, many years later, Jeremiah heard that the Babylonian hosts were actually on their way, he went down to Ramleh, presented the document to Bûkhtûnnussur, and claimed the protection promised. This was granted; but when the prophet begged that the city and Temple might also be spared, the invader said that he had received command from Allah to destroy them.

In proof of his statement, he bade Jeremiah watch the flight of three arrows which he shot at random. The first was aimed westwards, but turned in an opposite direction and struck the roof of the Temple at Jerusalem. The second arrow, which was pointed northwards, acted in the same manner, and so did the third, which was shot southwards. The city and Temple were utterly destroyed, and the golden furniture of the latter conveyed by Nebuchadnezzar's orders to Rome (*sic*).

'Ozair,† however, received a promise from Allah that he should be privileged to behold the restoration of Jerusalem. Passing the ruins one day, with a donkey and a basket of figs, he could not help expressing a doubt if this were possible, when Allah caused him to fall asleep for a whole century, at the end of which he was restored to life and found

* Which, by the way, did not happen in the time of Salah-ed-din; it was the other way about.

† Compare the classic story of Epimenides of Crete, Talmudic of Jechonia Ha Ma'agal and Washington Irving's *Rip van Winkle*.

the city rebuilt, populous and prosperous. The skeleton of his ass, being restored to life and covered with flesh and skin, began to bray, and was admitted into Paradise, as a reward to that one of its ancestors which had been wrongfully beaten for refusing to convey Iblìs into the ark. On beholding the resurrection of his donkey, 'Ozair was convinced that his experiences were real and that he had actually been asleep for a hundred years. He then, in obedience to the Divine command, entered Jerusalem and instructed its inhabitants in Allah's Law. The very spot where the prophet slept is shown at El Edhemìeh, north of the Holy City, in the large cave called Jeremiah's Grotto; [3] and a story like that of 'Ozair is read in the Greek churches during the service appointed for November 4th, when the fall of Jerusalem is commemorated.

Jewish traditions state that the celebrated Hebrew poet, Rabbi Judah ha Levi, of Toledo,* met his death at this Bab el Khalil. From his earliest youth he had yearned to visit the Holy Land and city, but had been prevented. At last, in his old age, the obstacles in his path were removed. But he never entered Jerusalem. On coming up to the gate he was seized with such emotion that he prostrated himself in the dust and lay there weeping, heedless of danger. A band of armed horsemen came galloping towards the town. The old man neither saw nor heard them; and so rapid was their approach, that before anyone had time either to warn or rescue the aged Jew, he had been trampled to death.

Many of the orthodox Jews of Jerusalem believe that, concealed within the gate-posts, there exists a *Mezûzah,* or case like those to be seen at the doorways of Jewish dwellings, placed here by the Almighty and containing a parchment upon which are written, by the finger of God Himself, the texts Deut. vi. 4–9 and xi. 13–21. In consequence of this belief many pious Jews, at passing in or out, touch the gate-post slightly and reverently, and then kiss their fingers.

* The author of many hymns, and particularly of the elegies for the 9th day of Ab, anniversary of the death of Moses, as also of the destruction of Jerusalem, first by Nebuchadnezzar and then by Titus many centuries later.

[3] See p. 249.

II

TURBET BIRKET MAMILLA * : JOHHA

THE most conspicuous object in this cemetery [1] is a small
domed building marking the grave of the Amìr Ala ed din
'Aidi Ghadi ibn 'Abdallah el Kebkebi, who died A.H. 688
(A.D. 1289), according to the inscription over the doorway. Inside the edifice is a remarkable cenotaph, the
ornamentation of which leads one to suspect that it probably
at one time stood over the tomb of some distinguished
Crusader, a conjecture which seems to be strengthened by
two traditions which contradict the statements of the above-
mentioned inscription.

One affirms that the Amìr here buried was a black man
of gigantic strength, who, on one occasion, when fighting
the Christians, cleft his opponent in twain, with a single
blow, from the crest of his helmet downwards.† The other
declares the mausoleum to be that of the person in whose
charge Saladin left Jerusalem after wresting it from the
Crusaders in A.D. 1187. The date of the inscription suggests
the time of Beybars.

A third story is that the edifice covers the grave of Johha,
a famous jester, who is by the peasantry generally confounded with the equally celebrated Abu Nowâs, and
occupies in Eastern folk-lore a position analogous to that of
Eulenspiegel or Dr. Howleglas in European. Here are a
few of the stories told of Johha. The majority are unfit for
reproduction.

When he was quite young, his mother one day sent him
to the market to fetch some salt and also some *semneh* or
clarified butter. She provided him with a dish for the

* Cemetery of the Pool of Mamilla.
† A feat said to have been performed by Godfrey de Bouillon,
leader of the first Crusade.
[1] See p. 249.

latter, and took it for granted that the grocer would put the salt in a piece of paper. On reaching the shop, the boy handed the vessel he had brought to the shopkeeper, in order that the latter might place the butter in it. He then turned it upside down, and directed the grocer to place the salt on the bottom of the dish. Going home, he said, " Here is the salt, mother." " But, my son," said she, " where is the *semneh*? " " Here," replied Johha, turning the dish right side up. Of course the salt was lost in the same way that the butter had been.

When Johha grew old enough to work for his living he became a donkey-driver. One day, being in charge of twelve donkeys employed to carry earth to the city, it occurred to him, before starting with the laden animals, to count them. Finding the tale complete, he took them to their destination and unloaded them. He then mounted one of them, and was going to return when he found one donkey missing. At once dismounting, he put them all in a row, and was astonished and greatly relieved to find the twelve there. He thereupon remounted and set off again, wondering as he rode along how it was that he had missed one donkey. Suddenly the suspicion flashed upon him that possibly the second count had been faulty, so he counted again, to find once more that only eleven were racing along in front of him. Terribly disconcerted, he again got down off the creature he was riding and, stopping the others, once more counted them. He was puzzled to find that there were again twelve. So absorbed was he by this mystery, that he went on counting and recounting the donkeys till his master, surprised at his long absence, came and solved his difficulty by obliging him to follow his asses on foot.

On his father's death, Johha inherited the family property, a small house. Being in need of money, he managed to raise it by selling the building all but one *kirât*,*[2] which he refused to part with; and, in order to mark that portion of the property which he was resolved to retain, he drove a tent-peg into the wall, having stipulated with the purchasers

* The twenty-fourth part of anything.
[2] See p. 251.

that that part of the edifice was to be set apart for his own unquestioned use. The new owners of the house were for a time allowed to live there undisturbed. One day, however, Johha appeared bearing a sack of lentils, which he hung upon the peg, no one making any objection. Some days later he removed this, and hung up a basket containing something else equally objectionable. He continued this procedure for some time without meeting with any remonstrance, seeing that he was only exercising his undoubted rights. At last, however, he one day appeared with a dead cat, which he left there till the occupants of the house, finding that neither remonstrances, entreaties, nor threats could induce him to remove the nuisance, and knowing that an appeal to law would be useless, seeing that Johha had the Kadi's ear, were glad to resell the house to him for a nominal sum. Ever since that time, the phrase " a peg of Johha's " has been used proverbially by Orientals in much the same sense in which Englishmen speak of " a white elephant."

One day Johha borrowed a large *tanjera*, or copper saucepan, from a neighbour for domestic use. Next day he returned it together with a very small but quite new one. " What is this? " asked the surprised owner. " Your tanjera gave birth to a young one during the night," replied the jester, and, in spite of the incredulity of the other man, maintained his assertion, refusing to take back the smaller tanjera, on the ground that the young belonged to the parent and the parent's owner. Besides, it was cruel to separate so young a child from its mother. After a deal of protestation, the neighbour, believing him mad, resolved to humour him, and took the small tanjera, greatly wondering at the jester's whim. Its point was revealed to his chagrin, some days later, when Johha came and borrowed a large and valuable copper *dist*, or cauldron. This he did not return, but carried it off to another town, where he sold it. When its owner sent to Johha to reclaim it, the knave said that he regretted his inability to send it back, but the utensil had unfortunately died and been devoured by hyænas. " What! " exclaimed the owner angrily, " do you think me fool enough to believe that? " " Well, my friend," was the reply,

" wonderful things sometimes happen. You allowed yourself to be persuaded that your tanjera, for instance, gave birth to a young one; why, then, should you not believe that your dist, which is simply a grown-up tanjera, should die?" In the circumstances, the argument seemed unanswerable, especially when, after searching through Johha's house, the cauldron could not be found.

Johha's neighbours, incensed by such practical jokes, put their heads together. They succeeded in persuading the joker to accompany them on an expedition to a lonely part of the coast. Having got him there, they told him they were going to drown him unless he swore a solemn oath to leave off his pranks, and " eat salt " with them. " I dare not eat salt with you," replied the rascal, " because I have a covenant and have eaten salt with the Jân. I shall not break my compact with them just to please you." " Very well," said his neighbours, " you have your choice. We shall bind you to this tree, and leave you here till midnight, when, unless you change your mind, and eat salt with us, we shall drown you." " Do your worst," said Johha. Whereupon they bound him fast to the tree and went away.

Johha cudgelled his brains to devise some means of escape. Great was his joy when, late that afternoon, he saw, at a distance, a shepherd with a large flock of sheep. He called the shepherd and persuaded him to set him free. When asked by his deliverer why he had been so bound, he told him: " For refusing to taste sugar." The shepherd seemed astonished at that, observing that he himself was fond of sugar. Johha then proposed that he should take his place. The simpleton, in the hope of sugar, consented, and after they had exchanged clothes, and the shepherd had taught the buffoon his special sheep-call, the former let himself be bound to a tree, whilst Johha promised to take charge of the flock, lead it to a certain cave and there await the shepherd's return. He felt sure that the man would be allowed to go his way when it was discovered that he himself had escaped. This was, however, not the case, for in their haste, and owing to the darkness of the night, the whistling of the wind, the sound of the waves, and the fact that the shepherd

mimicked Johha's voice to a tone, the enemies of the latter
never suspected the trick; and when the poor shepherd told
them that he would eat sugar, they pitched him into the sea.

Great was the surprise and terror of Johha's enemies
when, three days later, he marched cheerfully into the village
followed by a fine flock of sheep.* They ventured to
approach and ask him how he had escaped the sea, and
whence he had brought the animals. " I told you," was
his answer, " that I am in league with the Jân. Had I eaten
salt with you they would have treated me as a traitor, and
done me some grievous ill; as it is, however, they not only
spared my life but gave me this flock as a reward for my
loyalty."

Johha's neighbours were greatly impressed by this statement, and asked his forgiveness for their past ill-will. They
then also inquired in what way they also might obtain the
friendship of the Jân. Johha strongly advised them to
jump into the sea at midnight on the same day of the week
as that on which they had tried to drown him, and from the
same rock from which he had been hurled. They dis-
appeared.from the village soon afterwards and were never
seen again.

* " A stranger will they not follow, but will flee from him; for they
know not the voice of strangers " (St. John x. 5).

III

EN NEBI DAÛD [1]

A NUMBER of conventional tales, bearing a family likeness to those related concerning the patriarchs at Hebron, are told concerning the prophet David, and his tomb (En Nebi Daûd) at Jerusalem. Here are examples :—

In the reign of Sultan Murad, the Governor of Jerusalem, Mahmûd Pasha by name, was a just and upright man who favoured the Jews. As, however, Government appointments could be purchased by anyone in those days, a worthless Arab, known as Ibn Faraj, succeeded in obtaining the post from the Pasha of Damascus, who was at that time Governor-General of Syria and Palestine. Ibn Faraj proved extremely tyrannical and rapacious, and greatly oppressed the Jews in Jerusalem. One Sabbath day (Elul II. A.M. 5385, *i.e.* A.D. 1625) he attacked the Synagogue during the hours of divine service, and had fifteen of the most respectable Jews cast into prison. They were not released till they had paid 3000 ducats. Such events were of frequent occurrence, and the Jews were, in consequence, greatly impoverished. Many of them sought to flee, but were prevented by guards specially stationed for that purpose. At last, however, they succeeded in letting the Sultan know the state of affairs in Jerusalem. The Padishah was very angry when he heard of all this, and, on Kislev 22, 5386 (December 1626), he sent orders to the Pasha of Damascus to dismiss the unworthy official. Ibn Faraj, however, succeeded in bribing not only the Governor-General, but also the Agha, or Commandant of the troops in the castle. He now raged without restraint, and many Jews languished in prison because they were unable to satisfy his rapacious demands.

[1] See p. 252.

Suddenly, on Tuesday the 12th of Kislev, A.M. 5387, he took to flight, because, as is related in a document printed in Venice in the following year, and attested by all the chief officials of the Jewish community then at Jerusalem, an aged and venerable personage, clad in a purple mantle, appeared to him in a dream, and was going to strangle him. In his terror he asked why? and was informed " that King David wanted to avenge his subjects." Having begged long and piteously to be spared, his life was granted on condition that he left Jerusalem and the Holy Land at sunrise next morning.*

Another Moslem Governor of Jerusalem, being on a visit to En Nebi Daûd, greatly desired to see the tomb itself. He therefore went into the room immediately above it, and looked through a hole in the floor. While so doing a jewelled dagger slipped from his girdle and fell into the vault. Concerned at the loss, he had one of his attendants let down by a rope to search for it. This man remained below so long that the others, growing anxious, pulled in the rope. They brought up his lifeless body. A second and third attempt to recover the dagger failed in like manner; till the Governor, determined not to lose the pretty weapon, bade the Sheykh of En Nebi Daûd himself go down and fetch it.

The Sheykh replied that it was clear the Prophet did not like Mohammedans to enter his tomb; but, since he was known to be fond of Jews, the Pasha would do better to ask the Chief Rabbi. Accordingly, an urgent message was forthwith sent to that dignitary, who at once called the Jews together to fast and pray for deliverance from the anger of the Moslems on the one hand, and on the other from that of King David, whom the Jews believe to be " alive and active." † He begged for three days' grace in which to find a person willing to undertake so desperate an adventure. On the third day a Jew volunteered for the task, in hopes to save the community.

* Rabbi Schwartz, *Das Heilige Land*, footnote, pp. 402–403.
† In the special prayer for the monthly blessing of the moon, these words occur: " David Melekh Israel khai va kayam " (David, King of Israel, is alive and active).

Having purified his soul and body he was lowered into the vault in the presence of all the leading Moslems of the city. Almost immediately he asked to be drawn up again, and appeared alive and well with the dagger in his hand. On reaching the ground he had found himself face to face with a noble-looking old man, clad in robes like shining lead, who had handed him the dagger the instant his feet touched earth and, with a gesture, bidden him be gone.

An old Jewess, a widow, pious and industrious, used to wash for one of the sheykhs of En Nebi Daûd. One day, when she had brought some clean clothes to his house, he offered to show her the sepulchre of David, and she followed him in great delight. Opening the door of a room, he made her enter, and then, locking the door, went straight to the Kadi and told him that a Jewess had slipped into the sanctuary, left open for a few minutes for the sake of ventilation, and he, discovering the sacrilege, had locked her in that she might be punished formally, for a public example.

The Kadi, with other Moslems, went at once to En Nebi Daûd, but when the room was opened, no Jewess could be found. The Sheykh swore solemnly that she had been there when he locked the door. " I know her well," he said; " it was my washerwoman." " That it was not," said one who stood by, " for not a quarter of an hour ago my servant went to her house with a bundle of clothes, and saw her there hard at work." The inquisitors adjourned to the woman's house. There she was, at her washing, and ready to swear that she had been there since daybreak.

Convinced by her earnestness, the Kadi charged the Sheykh of En Nebi Daûd with perjury and had him severely punished. It was not until the woman came to die that she told the true story of her adventure. Then, having summoned the elders of the Jewish community, she confessed that the sheykh had locked her in the dark room, as he had said he did, but that a noble-looking old man, clad in apparel as of shining lead, had straightway appeared to her, saying: " Fear not, but follow me." He had led her by a path that wound through the heart of the earth to a door which opened on a dunghill in the Meydân.* There he ordered her to go home at once and get to work, and on no account to publish what had happened to her.

* The Meydân is in the Jewish quarter, on the north-eastern brow of the traditional Mount Sion. The exact spot where the washer-woman came out was, till the early part of 1905, marked by a large octagonal stone which has now disappeared.

IV

FOUR different sets of traditions are associated with and furnish as many names to the only open gateway (there being others walled up) in the eastern wall of Jerusalem. It is known to the Moslems as " Bâb el Asbât," or Gate of the Tribes of the Children of Israel, which is generally abbreviated to " Birket Israìl," a huge reservoir lying along part of the northern side of the Temple area, and said by learned Mohammedans to have been one of the three constructed by Ezekias,* King of Judah. Amongst the native Christians the gate is called " Our Lady Mary," because just inside it is the traditional site of the birthplace of the Virgin, and also because the road leading through the gate is that by which her supposed tomb, in a great underground church of the Crusading period down in the valley, is reached. For several centuries past, Europeans have called the gate by the name of St. Stephen, because a tradition, not older than the fourteenth century, states that he was stoned on a bare rock which is pointed out by the roadside not far from the above-mentioned church. In Crusading times the gate that stood where the Bâb el Asbât now is was called " the Gate of Jehoshaphat," from the valley that runs past it ; whilst amongst the modern German-speaking Jews it is known as " das Löwentor," from the pair of roughly carved lions built into the city-wall on either side of the entrance.

Now, as it is a rare thing to find " the likeness of anything in heaven or earth " in the ornamentation of Mohammedan buildings, though here and there (as in the case of the very interesting thirteenth-century bridge at Lydda [2]) such representations are met with, one naturally looks for some

* Hazkial aw Hazkia.
[1] See p. 254.   [2] See p. 254.

tradition to explain the unusual ornament. In the case of the Bâb el Asbât the story has been preserved in current folk-lore, and is as follows:—

Sultan Selìm * dreamed a dream in which he imagined he was being torn in pieces by four lions. Awaking in terror, he sent at once for all the learned to interpret this vision. But they could not. He than had recourse to a famous sheykh who dwelt at a distance. This sage, being informed of the matter, asked to know what the Sultan had been thinking about before he slept on the night in question. " I was thinking how to punish the people of Jerusalem," was the reply. " They have refused to pay their taxes, and are quite unmanageable." " Ah ! " said the sheykh, " Allah has sent the dream in order to prevent your Majesty from committing a great sin. El Kûds is the House of the Sanctuary, the city of the saints and prophets. So holy is it that according to the learned it was founded by the Angel Asrafìl, at Allah's command, built by his assistant angels, and then visited by them in pilgrimage fully two thousand years before the creation of our Father Adam, who was buried there. Ibrahìm el Khalìl, En Nebi Daûd, and many other prophets and saints lived and died there; therefore Allah Himself loves the place and will punish all who hate it and would do it an injury. I advise thee, O Monarch of the Age, to put in hand some work that might improve the city."

Struck by these words, the Sultan set out shortly on a pilgrimage to Jerusalem; and in the course of his stay there gave orders for the restoration of the Haram, and the rebuilding of the walls.

The work on the walls was entrusted to the super-intendence of two brothers, who were architects. Each of them had his own party of workmen, and his sphere of labour. They both began at Bâb el Asbât, one party working north-wards and the other southwards. It took seven years † to complete the task. At the expiration of that time both

---

* Sultan Selìm conquered Palestine in A.D. 1517, and planned that thorough restoration of the walls of Jerusalem which was carried out by his son and successor, Suleymân, surnamed the Magnificent, who, on the extant inscriptions, is styled : " King of the Arabs, the Persians, and the Rûm " (Romans, *i.e.* Byzantines).

† This statement that it took seven years is an Orientalism. According to the inscriptions still to be seen, the work was begun A.D. 1536 on the north side of the city, and finished on the south side A.D. 1539.

working parties met again at Bâb el Khalìl. The architect who had been given the duty of enclosing the southern part of the city was, however, beheaded by the Sultan's orders because he had left the Cœnaculum and adjoining buildings outside and unprotected by the new rampart. The lions at the Bâb el Asbât were placed there in order to recall the incident that led to the great work.

The foregoing is not the only legend connected with Bâb el Asbât. Just inside the city, a few yards from the gateway and between it and the historic Church and Abbey of St. Anne, there stood, till the summer of 1906, an interesting old Saracenic bath-house, which has been pulled down in order to make room for a new building. The following legend used to be told concerning it :—

When Belkis, Queen of Sheba, visited Jerusalem, King Suleymân, enchanted by her loveliness, wished to marry her ; but a mischief-maker told him that the queen was not human, but a jinnìyeh, having legs and hoofs like a donkey. The king ordered his informant, a jealous woman,* to hold her tongue on pain of death. But the charge rankled in his mind, and he determined to see for himself that it was untrue. So he caused the Jân to build a spacious hall whose floor was one huge pane of transparent crystal, through which could be seen a stream of running water with fish swimming about in it. At one end he placed his own throne, and beside it that of Belkis, which was made of precious metals, encrusted with the costliest jewels. On leaving her own land the queen, who valued this throne as her greatest treasure, had it locked up inside the innermost of seven chambers, in the most inaccessible of her castles, with guards at the gates day and night, to prevent anyone from getting near it. But all these precautions were in vain, for Suleymân, wishing one day to convince her of the power of the name of Allah, by invoking that name, had the throne transported to Jerusalem in less time than it takes to relate.†

* Some of the learned say it was a junni who came to Suleymân with this tale about Belkis. The Jân feared lest the royal lady, whose mother had been a jinnìyeh, should be converted from idolatry to El Islâm and, on her marriage with the king, blab certain secrets of might to keep them (the Jân) for ever in the servitude to which El Hakìm had reduced them.

† He did this, of course, before her conversion. It is a sin to play tricks upon a woman who is a true believer.

When all was ready he sent for the queen to come and see his fine new building. On entering she was surprised to behold the king upon a throne which seemed to be set, like that of Allah, on the face of the waters. In order to get to her own throne, at his side, she perceived that she would have to wade, so she lifted up her skirts, exposing her feet and legs almost up to the knees. The next moment showed her mistake, but, as shoes and stockings were unknown in those days, Suleymân had seen that her feet were human feet, but yet her legs were covered with shaggy hair like a young donkey's. Having converted her to the true religion, Suleymân called together all the learned for counsel how to remove that extraordinary growth of hair. " Let her shave," was the unanimous suggestion. " No! " roared Suleymân in anger, " she might cut herself, and the hair would only grow again." He drove the learned forth and convoked the Jân, who either could not or would not help him. In despair, he finally asked help from real devils, who told him to build the above-mentioned bath-house for the queen's use, and also taught him how to concoct a depilatory, by the use of which her limbs quickly became as smooth, white and comely as if they had been of cast silver. " Ever since that time," says a famous, learned and veracious Arab historian,* " people have used bathing and depilatories, and it is said that the bath-house is the same that is situated at the Bâb el Asbât, close to the Medresset es Salahìyeh,† and that it is the first bath-house ever built." ‡

* Mejr-ed-dìn, *Uns El Jelìl*, Vol. i. p. 125.
† Now St. Anne's Church.
‡ The new building has now been in use for many years.

V

In the early part of the eighteenth century the learned Rabbinical writer Kolonimos was head of the small and greatly oppressed Jewish community at Jerusalem.

One Sabbath day the Rabbi was at his devotions at the Jews' Wailing-place, when the " Shamash " or verger of the Synagogue came, breathless with haste and fear, to tell him that the town was in an uproar, and that the Mohammedans were threatening to exterminate the Jews, because a Moslem boy had been found slain in the Jewish quarter. He had not finished his tale when a party of Moslems came up and began to beat the Rabbi, dragging him off towards the serai. The Pasha, at sight of him, pointed to the body of the murdered lad, which had also been brought before him, and sternly told the Rabbi that unless he could produce the actual murderer, all the Jews would be massacred.

The Rabbi said that he could detect the guilty party if pen and paper, together with a bowl of water, were given to him. When this had been done, the Rabbi wrote on the paper the tetragrammaton, or unpronounceable name of the Most High, together with certain passages from Scripture, and from the Kabbalistic writings. He then washed the document in the water,* repeating certain magic formulæ all the time. The next thing he did was to apply the wet paper to the lad's lips and forehead, the result being that the murdered boy immediately sat up, and, after gazing about him for a moment, sprang to his feet, seized one of the bystanders by the throat, and exclaimed, " This man, and no other, is guilty of my blood." Then he sank to the floor, a

* For a somewhat similar ceremony in the Mosaic ritual see Numb. v. 23.

[1] See p. 254.

corpse as before. The man, thus charged with the crime, a Mohammedan, confessed and was led away to punishment.

The Rabbi was at once released; but remembering how by writing and using magical arts he had not only profaned the Sabbath but also been guilty of a heinous sin, even though compelled thereto for the preservation of his flock, he spent the rest of his days in doing penance. Nor was that enough. On his death-bed he gave orders that he should not be buried honourably, but that his friends should take his body to the brow of the hill overlooking the Kedron, just opposite the traditional monument of Zechariah the prophet, and throw it down in the same way that the carcases of horses and asses are to this day cast down the same slope. Where it stopped rolling, there it might be buried; but no monument must be erected over the grave, and, for a century after his death, every Jew passing by that spot must cast a stone upon it, as was the custom in the case of malefactors.[2] His friends carried out his instructions till the body was buried, but could not bear to leave his grave without some memorial. They therefore placed a great stone upon it, but the very next morning it was found broken, and the same thing happened every time it was replaced. They saw that he would not be disobeyed. It thus became customary, as Kolonimos had desired that it should, for Jewish passers-by to cast a stone upon his grave, and also to repeat prayers there.[3]

A few years ago an acquaintance of my own happened to be at the house of one of the principal Rabbis in Jerusalem, when a Mohammedan of very good repute came to ask the Rabbi for advice and help. He told how a certain Jew, whom he named, had come to his place of business an hour or so previously, when he was alone, for a few minutes. Soon afterwards he had missed a valuable ring that was lying on the desk in front of him when the Jew entered. No one had been in since. He could produce neither proof nor witness against the Jew in question, but felt sure he had taken the ring. Having questioned the Moslem straitly, the Rabbi saw that he spoke the truth, and bade him wait while he

[2] See p. 254.   [3] See p. 255.

sent for the culprit. The Jew came without knowing why he had been sent for. Before he had time to utter a word of salutation, the Rabbi addressed him in Hebrew, in tones of excited pleading: " I beg you, for the sake of all that is holy, to deny that you know anything about the ring which this Gentile accuses you of having stolen!" " That," said the rascal, quite thrown off his guard, " that is exactly what I meant to do." " Very well," said the Rabbi sternly, " as you have virtually confessed before all these witnesses that you have the ring, hand it over to its owner immediately, and be thankful if he takes no steps to have you punished." The thief gave back the ring and went unpunished.

During the Egyptian occupation of Palestine between 1831 and 1840, Ibrahìm Pasha, Governor of the country, happened to be at Jaffa, when a certain goldsmith came to him, complaining that his shop had been burgled in the night, and demanding justice in a high tone. " While we were under the shadow of the Sultan," he said, " I never lost a thing. But now, with you Egyptians who talk so much about good government, in the first month I lose half my substance. It is a shame to you and a great loss to me; and I think that you owe me compensation for your own honour."

" Very well, I take the responsibility," said Ibrahìm in some amusement. He then sent a crier through the streets calling upon all who loved strange sights to be at the goldsmith's shop at a certain hour next day, with the result that, when the hour arrived, the street in front of the shop was packed with people. Then Ibrahìm appeared, attended by his officers and the public executioner. He first harangued the people on the virtue of trustworthiness, saying that the Egyptian Government was determined to administer the strictest justice, and to punish, without partiality, the slightest breach of trust, even though committed by a senseless and inanimate object. Then, turning to the door of the shop: " Even this door," he said, " shall be punished for failing in its duty, which is to keep out thieves, unless it tell me who it was that passed it the night before last and stole the things out of the shop." The door giving no answer, he bade the executioner administer one hundred lashes with his kurbâj.*

When the punishment was ended, he again exhorted the door to speak, saying that, if it feared to utter the name aloud, it could whisper in his ear. He gave his ear to the door, as one listening, then sprang erect and laughed in scorn: " This door talks nonsense. Executioner, another hundred lashes! "

After this second beating, he listened again to hear what the door had to say, while the people murmured and shrugged shoulders one to another, thinking him mad.

" The same stupid tale," he cried despairingly. " It will persist in telling me that the thief is present in this crowd of honest people and still has some dust and cobwebs from the shop on his tarbûsh." At that a man was noticed hurriedly to brush his fez, and the Pasha, on the watch for some such action, had him arrested. He proved to be the guilty party, and was punished.

Another story of the kind is told of Ibrahìm Pasha. They say that while in Jerusalem he encouraged the fellahìn of the country to bring their produce to the city, assuring them that his soldiers would be punished if they hurt them or took anything from them without payment. One day, a woman from Silwân, with a basket of jars filled with leben,† came and complained of a soldier having seized one of her jars and drunk off the contents without so much as " By your leave." Ibrahìm asked her when this had happened, and if she thought she could identify the soldier. She replied that it had happened just this minute, and she would know the man again among ten thousand.

" We shall see," said Ibrahìm, and called his trumpeter. Soon every soldier in the city was on parade before the castle and the Pasha led the woman down the ranks, asking her to pick out the offender. She pointed to a certain man and stopped before him. Ibrahìm asked if she was sure it was the culprit, and she swore by Allah she was not mistaken.

* A whip of hippopotamus hide.
† Curds, or else buttermilk.

Three times he put the question, and she replied that she was quite sure. Then he drew his sword, and, with a deft stroke, cut the soldier open, releasing the leben, still undigested. " It is lucky for you, you were right," he remarked to the woman, " or your fate would have been far worse than this soldier's."

VI

SCRAPS OF UNWRITTEN HISTORY

ABOUT a quarter of a mile below the "Bir Ayûb" near Jerusalem, on the right-hand side as one goes down the valley, there is a recess in the bank which, if noticed in dry weather, might be taken for a gravel-pit. Here, however, in the rainy season water comes to the surface in considerable quantities. The place is called "'Ain el Lozeh," or the Almond Fountain. Many years ago Sir Charles Warren was told by a peasant that, according to tradition, there was a subterranean passage here approached by a stairway cut in the rock, whose lowest steps were of precious metal, and that the staircase and tunnel had been closed by order of the Egyptian Government, because the Egyptian soldiers had often hidden in the tunnel to waylay women who descended in order to fetch water.*

From 'Ain el Lozeh a pathway runs up the hillside towards the ruins of the village of Beit Sahur, the inhabitants of which fled one night, about eighty years ago, in order to escape the conscription. Since then their descendants have lived as Bedû in the wilderness on the western shores of the Dead Sea.

On the opposite side of the valley, and on the declivity of its northern bank, is a ruin, a monastery, which, though unmistakably that of a cistern, is called by the peasantry "Deyr es Sinneh." [1] Close by, traces of a village and old baths were discovered a few years ago; and some curious stories are related respecting the ancient inhabitants of the convent and village, who figure under the ethnic name of Es-Sanawìneh. They are said to have been such stupid people that Allah was obliged to destroy them. They never cooked food properly, but hung it in a pot from a hole shown in the roof of the cistern above-mentioned, about twenty

* For a description of the wonderful tunnel which Sir Charles discovered at 'Ain el Lozeh, see *The Recovery of Jerusalem*, pp. 257 ff.

[1] See p. 256.

feet above the fire. After burning any quantity of fuel it was raw. Their religion was a worship of the heavenly bodies, of which they knew so little that one night, when the moon was late in rising, they thought the men of Abu Dis, a neighbouring village, had stolen it, and went out against them armed to the teeth.

From the top of the hill, which is between the two villages, they saw the moon rise, whereupon they shouted and danced in triumph, saying one to another: " Those rascals had heard we were coming and have let go our moon."

Whenever they were in difficulties or perplexed as to the course of action they should pursue, they were accustomed, instead of asking the advice of other people, to observe the actions of animals and take hints from them. " All other men but ourselves," said they, " are wicked, and therefore foolish, for which reason they cannot instruct us. The birds and beasts, however, are many of them innocent and wise, and so we may learn from them." So it happened one day that some of them wanted to carry a long beam of wood into a chamber where they wished to put up an oil-press. Try as they would, they could not get it in because they carried it stretching across the entrance instead of taking it through endways. Being greatly troubled, they sent twelve men in different directions to try to get some hint from the methods used by animals. The messengers returned after seven days, but only one had found a solution of the problem. This he got from having noticed a sparrow draw a long straw endways into a hole in which it was building its nest. As a reward for this discovery the man was made sheykh of the community.

Because they would not use the common sense which Allah has given to the sons of Adam that they excel other creatures in wisdom, He decreed that they should all die childless with the exception of one family, possibly that of the aforesaid sheykh, whose descendants still live at Bethany. And even on them there rests a curse, for they never have more than one son to represent them.

In the cliff that towers above the railroad on the northern

side of the savage Wady Isma'in just east of 'Artuf, is a large cave which bears evident traces of having once served as an abode for ascetics. It has, for some years past, been called " Samson's Cave," from the supposition that it was here that the Danite champion found shelter after the exploit of the foxes and the following slaughter. A little further east are several smaller caves which also appear to have been used as hermitages, and are known by the name of " Alali el Benât," or the " Upper Chambers of the Maidens."

The fellahìn of the neighbouring village of 'Akûr say that in the times of the Infidels [2] these caves, too high up to be reached unless by ropes and ladders, were full of beautiful girls who, having vowed to keep single, had retired hither to be out of the way of temptation. The necessaries of life were lowered to them day after day by ropes from the top of the cliff, and their seclusion appeared of the strictest. After some years, however, children were seen running from one cave to another, and it was found that the girls had lowered a rope into the valley and brought up a handsome hunter, whom they had espied from their eyrie. They are said to have been starved to death for their hypocrisy.

High up on the southern side of the Wad er Rabâbeh, the traditional Valley of Hinnom, just where it opens into the Kedron Valley, there is the Greek convent of St. Onuphrius,[3] erected in recent years over a number of rock-cut sepulchres containing many human bones.

Amongst the peasantry of Silwân there exists a very curious tradition that the human remains in the above-mentioned sepulchres are those of Christian hermits massacred during the persecution carried on by the insane Fatemite Khalîfeh El Hâkim bi amr Illah, whom to this day the Druzes worship as a god, and who, in the fifteenth year of his reign (A.D. 1010) compelled his Christian secretary, Ibn Khaterìn, to write the following fatal order to the Governor of Jerusalem:—
" The Imâm commands you to destroy the Temple of the Resurrection, so that its heaven may become its earth, and

[2] See p. 256.   [3] See p. 256.

its length may become its breadth." The order was only too literally executed, and Ibn Khaterìn in his grief and despair, because he had been forced to write this sentence, " smote his head on the ground, broke the joints of his finger and died in a few days." *

The caves in Wad er Rabâbeh were at that time the abode of a population of monks and holy men who spent their time in fasting and prayer. Now it happened that El Hâkim needed money, so he sent orders to the Mutesarrif of Jerusalem to make everybody pay a tax. The Mutesarrif and his Council wrote back to say that it was impossible to do that, since there were large numbers of poor religious men in the land who, though Christians, lived like dervishes in bare caves, and had no means wherewith to pay a tax, however small. On receiving this news the Caliph bade his secretary write : " Number the men."

Whether the secretary was careless in his writing and placed a dot over the second letter of the first word; or whether El Hâkim in his wickedness took the order which his scribe had written and himself put in the dot, Allah alone knows, but when the order reached Jerusalem the dot was there, and the order read, not " Number," but " Mutilate the men." †

This was cruelly carried out, and its victims died in consequence, and were buried where they had lived. The human bones now found in the caves in the Wad er Rabâbeh are theirs.

On a hillside in Gilead is situated the village of Remamìn, inhabited chiefly by native Christians,[1] who account for their preservation in this remote region, during the centuries that have elapsed since the Crusaders, by the following romantic story :— ‡

When the Crusaders first occupied Palestine there were

---

* Renandot, quoted in footnote to Williams' *Holy City*, p. 349.
† [Akhsa er-rijâl instead of Ahsa er-rijâl, the difference in the Arabic being a dot only.—M. P.]
‡ This story was told me by my school-mate, the late Henri Baldensperger, junior.
[1] See p. 257.

beyond the Jordan a great many Christians dispersed in
various old towns and villages, and suffering daily
martyrdom from the Moslems. Many of these migrated
westwards with their families and their cattle, gladly exchanging the wooded mountains, fertile pastures and rich vine-
yards of the country east of Jordan for the less fruitful
western districts and a Christian government. Some, however, chose to remain, amongst them a man renowned for
his integrity, who, when the Bedû entered into possession of
the cultivated lands deserted by the emigrants, consented to
become the *wakil* or overseer of those which fell to the lot of a
great Arab sheykh whose followers scorned to till the lands;
and who was therefore glad to secure the services of a person
competent to overlook the work of his slaves, and such
refugees of the fellahìn across the Jordan as had fled to his
protection.

The arrangement worked well till, on an evil day, the
chieftain quarrelled with the young wife he had lately
married, who was the daughter of an emìr of some distant
tribe. As her father's tents were far away, she fled to the
dwelling of the Christian, and continued there with his family
till reconciled with her husband.

For a time things went smoothly between the couple.
Then a fresh quarrel arose, and the sheykh said sneeringly
to his wife, " Go again and ask for shelter in the kennel of
that Christian dog." " He is no dog," retorted the woman,
" but a man of stock, though a Christian. If anyone is a dog
it is you; " and to these words she added expressions such as
can only fall from the lips of an angry woman. Stung to
fury by her bitter tongue, the chieftain resolved to avenge
himself upon the Christian. He therefore mounted his mare
and galloped to the abode of the latter, who received him with
all courtesy and entertained him. Taking leave at length,
he mounted his mare, the Christian holding the stirrup. As
soon as he was in the saddle the Bedawi suddenly drew a
dagger from his girdle and drove it up to the hilt between the
shoulders of the stooping Christian, who fell to the ground.
The wife and the three little sons of the murdered man
beheld the deed. The sheykh then galloped off.

The Christian suddenly widowed ran to help her husband; to find him dead. She drew out the dagger, which had been left in the wound, and there and then made her children swear upon it that if Allah spared them to grow to manhood they would punish the assassin with his own weapon.

As soon as the murdered man had been buried, his widow packed up her belongings and, accompanied by one or two Christian neighbours whom her late husband had dissuaded from migrating to the district west of the Jordan, she went to live at Nazareth, where she had relatives.

Years passed. The three little boys had become men, when one day their mother told them that was the anniversary of their father's death, recalled to them once more every circumstance of the murder, and, placing the dagger in the hands of the first-born, bade all three go and avenge their father's death, as they had sworn to do beside his lifeless body.

That night, fully armed and well-mounted, they rode noiselessly away, having taken the precaution of tying several folds of *lubbâd*, or thick felt, round the horses' hoofs. Travelling by out-of-the-way routes during the hours of darkness, and hiding, when daylight approached, in some cavern, it took them three days to reach the neighbourhood of the upland plain where, as they had heard at Nazareth, their enemy was encamped.

Their first care was to find some place of shelter for their animals to ensure their having an undisturbed rest before the return journey. Such a place having been found, they lay there concealed until the sun had some time set, and they had reason to think that the encamped Bedû were asleep. The three preceding days and nights had been intensely hot, but now a refreshing west wind bringing dew-clouds had come up. Having left their steeds ready saddled for immediate flight, the avengers of blood drew near the Arab camp. It was buried in silence and darkness, the very dogs asleep, not a sound to be heard.

Approaching, two crouched down behind a boulder, while the eldest, armed with the dagger, crept in among the tents. The sheykh's was easily found. His spear, the tip adorned with a bunch of ostrich feathers, was planted in the ground before the entrance, and the owner's priceless mare was tethered close by. Loosening one of the tent-pegs, the young man lifted the curtain and crawled beneath it into the tent. There lay his father's murderer, now an aged man with a long white beard, asleep on the ground before him. Beside the chief lay his wife and children, all fast asleep. By the faint light of stars shining in through the interstices of the tent-curtains the visitor perused the old assassin's features. Having made sure that it was indeed the murderer he raised the dagger in the act to strike. But at that moment, weakness came upon him; he could not kill thus, in cold blood, an old man lying unconscious. That would be murder. With a prayer to the saints that he might meet his foe face to face, and so punish him openly, he sheathed the dagger and crawled back to the spot where his brothers waited.

Having heard his tale the second took the dagger and crept forward into the camp; to return in due course with the same story. The youngest then advanced. He also entered the enemy's tent and found him sleeping, but could not resolve to kill him on the spot. He therefore crept out of the tent again and went up to the mare. With the foeman's dagger he cut off her beautiful mane and the long locks of hair hanging forward between her ears. He then cut all the hair off her sweeping tail, and, wrapping the dagger in the horse-hair, re-entered the tent and laid the dagger on the chieftain's pillow.

Leaving the tent, he drew his own dagger and cut every other tent-rope, leaving just enough to keep the structure from collapsing. Then, drawing the spear out of the ground, he carried it off, and, returning to his brothers, told them that their father was avenged. The three then returned to the place where they had left their horses, and before day-break were beyond pursuit. Pressing on by day and night, they reached their home in safety.

Great was the consternation in the Arab camp when the terrible insult to the sheykh was discovered. It was clear that the miscreants must be deadly enemies, thus to disfigure the sheykh's mare, cut his tent-ropes, and remove his lance.

It was likewise evident that the chieftain's life had been at their mercy, but why had they refrained from slaying him? Lastly, what did this dagger wrapped in the mare's mane and tail hairs signify? The sheykh himself did not recognise the weapon, nor indeed, as it was passed from hand to hand, did anybody else, till it reached the chief's younger brother, who, after closely examining it, suggested that it was that with which the Christian wakìl had been killed years ago at Remamìn. Then the sheykh remembered, and understood how he owed his life to the magnanimity of his deadliest enemies.

He had known remorse for the murder of their father. Now he resolved to do what he could to get the matter accommodated without its becoming a regular blood-feud.

Accordingly, accompanied by the elders of the tribe, he rode to Nazareth, and got a friend there to act as intermediary. He paid a *dìyeh* or compensation-fine for the murder, and, what was more, assured the family of the murdered man that, in case they chose to return to their father's land at Remamìn, they, their descendants, and Christian neighbours should be allowed to live there respected and unmolested. His terms were accepted, and ever since then there has been a Christian community at Remamìn.

Some four centuries ago, when Sultan Selìm took Palestine, he set a garrison of Kurds at Hebron,* who used the proud inhabitants of the city with great arrogance. The Arabs, disunited by the feud between the Keys and the Yemen factions, could not oppose their tyranny. The Kurds became lords of Hebron, and espousing neither party hectored both. They built fine houses on the hillside north of the Haram, and planted orchards of foreign trees till then unknown. Now, it is a custom in Palestine for anyone passing along a road to pick fruit hanging over an orchard wall without rebuke.† But the Kurds, if they caught a man gleaning from the skirts of their plantations, would cut off

---

* This story was told me by the sheykh of the village of Dûra, south of Hebron.

† For the corresponding provision of the Mosaic Law, see Deut. xxiii. 24 ff.

both his hands. They were hateful in all their ways. At last their tyranny grew so unbearable that the two rival factions were at one in the determination to have done with it, only waiting an occasion for a general rising. On an evening of the feast of Bairam, the Kurds and their Agha were drinking coffee in the market-place, when the Agha suggested that they should send for Budrìyeh, the daughter of a notable of the city, to make fun for them. The men of Hebron flew to arms at this insult, which was soon washed out in blood, for the Kurds were unprepared, having always regarded the townsmen as unwarlike dogs. Most of them were killed. A remnant, including the Agha, fled to Beyt Ummar, Beyt Fejjar, and other villages.

They never came back in force to Hebron, but their leader one day disguised himself as a woman and presented himself at the door of the father of Budrìyeh at nightfall. He called for the master of the house, and, on the latter stepping out to see what was wanted, struck him dead and departed.

It was about the same time that the Kurds were at Hebron that the now ruined castle close to Solomon's Pools, and the aqueduct conveying water from the said pools to the Haram at Jerusalem, were constructed. The people of the village of Artass were entrusted with the care of the pools and aqueduct, and, as a recompense for this service, were exempted by the Government from paying of taxes. In consequence of these privileges the fellahìn of this place grew rich, and their sheykh gained considerable power in the district. So great grew his influence that disputes amongst the peasants were frequently submitted to his arbitration, and in time he even had a prison for offenders in the tower he had erected in the village. Prosperity, however, begat pride and arrogance in a generation or two, and the Artassites became so insolent that their downfall could not be averted.

At that time faction fights between the people of different villages were frequent. When a battle was to take place, the warriors of the respective parties used to go forth accompanied by their wives, daughters or sisters, shouting their respective battle-cries. When the fighting was in progress it was no uncommon thing for a hero to crouch or stand behind his female companion and fire at the enemy over her shoulder or from between her feet, because he knew that his fire would not be returned; it being an understood thing that the persons of women were to be respected. If a woman got killed it was by accident.

Now, one day the people of Idhna, a village west of Hebron, but allied to the Artassites, having been worsted in a fight and forced to retreat to their village, where they were besieged by their enemies, sent some of their women to Artass to ask for succour. The envoys reached the village safely, but instead of hastening to the help of the men of Idhna, the men of Artass insulted the women and sent them home to their husbands.

Justly incensed, the people of Idhna made peace with their enemies, and waited for an opportunity for avenging the dishonour done to them. Hearing that on a certain day a great wedding was to take place at Artass, they quietly mustered their forces and suddenly fell upon the unprepared villagers at a time when they were unarmed and disporting themselves in the gardens. Only a few escaped,* and with their families found refuge in the castle at the Pools, where their descendants continued to live till some fifty years ago, when, the country having become more settled, they returned to the adjacent valley of Artass, and built new dwellings amid the ruins of the former village.

During the early part of last century the Hebron district was misruled by a petty despot named Sheykh 'Abd-ur-Rahman, who committed the most horrible crimes with impunity. The following story is told by the fellahin to describe his character.

A certain fellâh of Hebron had a handsome wife desired of 'Abd-ur-Rahman. In order to attain his object he so intimidated her husband that the latter, to save his life, divorced her. The woman, however, abhorred the tyrant, and absolutely refused to assent to his proposals of marriage. At last, being greatly pressed, she, in a fury, said before witnesses that she would rather have a dog than him for a husband. Now, according to Moslem law, a man who has

* Cf. 1 Maccabees ix. 37–42.

divorced his wife cannot take her back until she has legally been married and divorced again by some other man; and in order to get out of this difficulty, husbands who have divorced their wives and regret having done so get them married to some person who is physically unfit for marriage, but who, for payment, consents to go through a form of marriage followed by divorce. Seeing, therefore, that his suit was in vain, and being full of rage, the despot took the poor woman at her word, and, in order to prevent her from going back to her husband, he had a legal marriage contract drawn up between her and his greyhound Rishân, and signed by witnesses who had heard her imprudent speech, and lacked courage to oppose his will. In consequence of this high-handed procedure, the woman was known till the day of her death as " the wife of Rishân."

When the Turks, in 1840, succeeded after the bombardment of Acre by the united British and Austrian fleets in regaining their power in Palestine, 'Abd-ur-Rahman was deposed, and later on, exiled to Cyprus, where he died.

VII

A WEAVER, closing his shop for the night, left a long needle sticking in his work on the loom.* A thief got in with a false key, and, as he was stumbling about in the dark, the needle put out one of his eyes. He went out again and locked the door behind him.

Next morning he told his story to Karakash, the impartial judge, who sent for the weaver, and eyeing him sternly, asked:

" Did you leave a packing-needle in the cloth on your loom when you shut your shop last night? "

" Yes."

" Well, this poor thief has lost his eye through your carelessness; he was going to rob your shop, he stumbled, and the needle pierced his eye. Am I not Karakash, the impartial judge? This poor thief has lost an eye through your fault, so you shall lose an eye in like manner."

" But, my lord," said the weaver, " he came to rob me, he had no right there."

" We are not concerned with what this robber came to do, but with what he did. Was your shop-door broken open or damaged this morning, or was anything missing? "

" No."

" He has done you no harm then, and you do but add insult to injury by throwing up his way of life against him. Justice demands that you lose an eye."

The weaver offered money to the robber, to the Kadi, but in vain; the impartial judge would not be moved. At last a bright thought struck him, and he said: " An eye for an eye is justice, O my lord the Kadi; yet in this case

---

* This story was related by the late Yuhanna Costa, former dragoman to Bishop Gobat.

[1] See p. 257.

it is not quite fair on me. You are the impartial judge, and I submit to you that I, being a married man with children, shall suffer more damage in the loss of an eye than this poor robber, who has no one dependent on him. How could I go on weaving with but one eye? But I have a good neighbour, a gunsmith, who is a single man. Let one of his eyes be put out. What does he want with two eyes for looking along gun-barrels?" The impartial judge, struck with the justice of these arguments, sent for the gunsmith and had his eye put out.

A carpenter was fitting the doors and lattice-work to a house newly built, when a stone over a window fell and broke one of his legs. He complained to Karakash, the impartial judge, who called the lord of the house and charged him with culpable negligence. "It is not my fault, but the builder's," pleaded the lord of the house; so the builder was sent for.

The builder said that it was not his fault, because at the moment he was laying that particular stone a girl passed by in a dress of so bright a red that he could not see what he was doing.

The impartial judge caused search to be made for that girl. She was found and brought before him.

"O veiled one," * he said, " the red dress which you wore on such a day has cost this carpenter a broken leg, and so you must pay the damages."

"It was not my fault, but the draper's," said the girl. "Because when I went to buy stuff for a dress, he had none but that particular bright red."

The draper was forthwith summoned. He said it was not his fault, because the English manufacturer had sent him only this bright red material, though he had ordered others.

"What! you dog!" cried Karakash, "do you deal with the heathen?" and he ordered the draper to be hanged from the lintel of his own door. The servants of justice

* *Ya mustûrah.* Respectable Moslem and Christian townswomen always go about veiled.

took him and were going to hang him, but he was a tall man and the door of his house was low; so they returned to Karakash who inquired: " Is the dog dead? " They replied, " He is tall, and the door of his house is very low. He will not hang there."

" Then hang the first short man you can find," said Karakash.* [2]

A certain rich old miser was subject to fainting fits, which tantalised two nephews who desired his death; for, though constantly falling down lifeless, he always got up again. Unable to bear the strain any longer, they took him in one of his fits and prepared him for burial.

They called in the professional layer-out, who took off the miser's clothes, which, by ancient custom, were his perquisite, bound up his jaws, performed the usual ablutions upon the body, stuffed the nostrils, ears and other apertures with cotton wool with a mixture of rose-water, pounded camphor and dried and pounded leaves of the lotus tree,† and bound the feet together by a bandage round the ankles, and disposed the hands upon the breast.

All this took time, and before the operator had quite finished, the miser revived; but he was so frightened at what was going on that he fainted again, and his nephews were able to get the funeral procession under way.

They had traversed half the road to the cemetery when the miser was again brought to life by the jolting of the bier, caused by the constant change of the bearers, who incessantly pressed forward to relieve one another in the meritorious act of carrying a true believer to the grave. Lifting the loose lid, he sat up, and roared for help. To his relief he saw Karakash, the impartial judge, coming

---

* [A delightful compound of this and the foregoing story is given as a reading exercise in *A Manual of the Spoken Arabic of Egypt*, by J. S. Willmore. It is called " El Harâmi el Mazlûm " (The ill-treated Robber), and the name of Karakash is omitted. It is the funnier from being written in the kind of baby-Arabic spoken by the Egyptian fellahìn.—M. P.]

† *Zizyphus spina Christi*. This stuffing was in order to prevent demons from entering the body.

[2] See pp. 257–258.

down the path the procession was mounting, and appealed to him by name. The judge at once stopped the procession, and, confronting the nephews, asked: " Is your uncle dead or alive? " " Quite dead, my lord." He turned to the hired mourners. " Is this corpse dead or alive? " " Quite dead, my lord," came the answer from a hundred throats. " But you can see for yourself that I am alive! " cried the miser wildly. Karakash looked him sternly in the eyes. " Allah forbid," said he, " that I should allow the evidence of my poor senses, and your bare word, to weigh against this crowd of witnesses. Am I not the impartial judge? Proceed with the funeral! " At this the old man once more fainted away, and in that state was peacefully buried.

VIII

A few of the Jews resident at Jerusalem celebrate, beside the usual Jewish feasts of Passover, Pentecost, Tabernacles, etc., a yearly anniversary which they call " the Saragossan Purim," in order to commemorate the deliverance of the Jews of Saragossa, the capital of their former kingdom of Arragon, from a great peril. The story of this escape, as recorded in certain small parchment scrolls or Megilloth written in the style and evident imitation of the Roll of Esther, is read in public at each celebration. I had heard of the custom a good many years ago, but on February 13, 1926, having been informed that the festival had been held two days before, I obtained the loan, through a friend, of a copy of the roll. It was, of course, in Hebrew, and on parchment. The narrative is, briefly, as follows:—

About the year 1420, in the reign of Alphonso V of Arragon, there were in the city of Saragossa twelve handsome synagogues supported by as many congregations of prosperous and influential Jews, who were so well treated by the Government that, whenever the king came to Saragossa, all the Rabbis went out in procession in honour of him, each carrying, in its case, the Roll of the Law belonging to his synagogue. People objected that it was dishonour for the sacred Rolls to be carried out to flatter the vanity of a Gentile; and so the Rabbis, possibly glad of an excuse not to carry the heavy manuscripts, got in the habit of leaving the scrolls at the synagogue on such occasions and going out with the empty cases.

Now, a certain Jew, named Marcus of Damascus, turned Christian, and in his zeal as a new convert became the deadly enemy of his own race. When the king one day was praising the loyalty of his Jewish subjects, this renegade, who was among the courtiers, replied that his Majesty was being grossly deceived. The loyalty of the Jews was a sham, he averred, like their carrying empty cases before the king when pretending to bear the rolls of their respective synagogues.

At this the king was angered against the Jews, but would not punish them until he had ascertained the truth of the charge. He set out at once (Shebat 17th) for Saragossa, with Marcus in his train; and the latter was in high spirits, thinking he had ruined the Jews. But that night an aged man roused the servant of each synagogue, and told him how the king intended to surprise the Rabbis. So when the noise of the king's coming went abroad next morning, and they went out to meet him as usual, they were not unprepared. Alphonso did not return their greetings but, frowning, ordered the cases to be opened. His command was obeyed very cheerfully, and every case was found to contain his scroll of the Pentateuch. The king then turned his anger upon Marcus, who was hanged from the nearest tree.

To commemorate this event the Jews of Saragossa instituted an annual feast, observed even after subsequent persecutions had driven them from Spain, and still, as we have seen, celebrated by their descendants on the 17th of Shebat.

IX

ON the southern wall inside the great Mesjid El Aksa at Jerusalem, which stands on the site of Justinian's famous Church of St. Mary, there hangs in a gilt frame a specimen of ornamental Arabic caligraphy. It is the well-known Koranic text concerning Mohammad's night-journey from Mecca to Jerusalem,[1] and the guardians of the sanctuary state that it was penned by Sultan Mahmûd, father of Sultan Abd-al Mejìd, and by him presented to this mosque. Sultan Mahmûd was an excellent writer, and hearing people vaunt the penmanship of a certain scribe, he invited him to a trial of skill. The specimens of handwriting thus produced were submitted to various experts, of whom all but one, being courtiers, decided for the Sultan. But one of the judges managed, without offence to the Padishah, to be just to his more skilful rival. On the latter's paper he wrote, " The handwriting of the best of scribes "; on Mahmûd's, " The handwriting of the best of Sultans and scribes." The Sultan, struck with this uprightness, made him a splendid present, and sent the text which he had written to the Mosque El Aksa.

[1] See p. 258.

X

A CERTAIN Sultan dreamt that all his teeth fell suddenly out of his mouth,[1] and, awaking, was so frightened he woke his servants and bade them summon the learned with all speed.

The sages, gathered in haste, heard the dream, and afterwards kept silence, seeming much embarrassed.

But a young man, fresh from school, stood forth unbidden, and falling at the Sultan's feet, exclaimed:

" O Sultan of the age! The dream be to your enemies, and the interpretation thereof to all that hate you. It means that all your relatives will be destroyed before your eyes in a single day."

The Sultan, furious, ordered the officious wretch to be bastinadoed, thrown into prison, and fed on bread and water for a year. Then, turning fiercely on the trembling herd of councillors, he stamped his foot, repeating his demand to them. For a while they trembled in silence. Then the sheykh of the learned * stepped forward, and raising his hands and eyes to heaven exclaimed: " Praise be to Allah, who has deigned to reveal to your Majesty the blessing which He holds in store for all the nations under your dominion; for this is the interpretation of that Heaven-sent dream; that you are destined to outlive all your kindred."

The monarch filled the old man's mouth with pearls, hung a gold chain round his neck, and put on him a robe of honour.

* Sheykh el 'Ulema.
[1] See p. 258.

SECTION III

CONTAINING STORIES AND ANECDOTES ILLUSTRATING
SOCIAL IDEAS, SUPERSTITIONS, ANIMAL AND
PLANT LORE, ETC.

I

FOLKS GENTLE AND SIMPLE [1]

AHMAD AL-MUTTAFAKHIR, ibn Al-muttashakhia, sheykh of
the Fasharìn Arabs,* was unduly proud of his noble ancestry
and constantly boasting of it.† One day, when with a
caravan on its way from Tadmor to Akka, he was speaking
on his favourite theme when he saw a derwìsh by the roadside staring intently at a white object which he had in his
hands. Being of an inquisitive turn of mind, Ahmad
galloped up to him in order to see what it might be. It
turned out to be a human skull. The sheykh asked the
derwìsh why he was examining it so closely. "Ah!" said
the holy man, who evidently knew his man, "I found this
skull lying at the door of a cave which I passed this morning,
and am trying to discover whether it belonged, when alive,
to some great man, or whether it was only the brainpan
of some ordinary mortal like yourself or me." Ahmad
galloped off offended, and for that day said no more about
his noble forefathers. Subsequently, however, as the caravan
was passing a village cemetery he noticed that the roof of a
burial vault ‡ had fallen in, and that the bones of the dead
were exposed. Of the skulls, some were black and brown,
others white. "See!" he cried, "even after death there
is a difference between persons of good stock and those of
meaner birth; the skulls of the former are all white, and
those of the latter of a darker colour." Some days after he
had made this remark the travellers approached their
destination. Fixed over the city gate were the heads of

* This story was told by the late Elias Donghan, a Protestant native
from Es-Salt in Transjordania.

† [Ahmad the Conceited, son of the Vainglorious, sheykh of the
Boaster Arabs.—M. P.]

‡ Fûstikìyeh.

[1] See p. 260.

men who had been put to death for hideous crimes. Birds
of prey, insects and the action of the sun and rain combined
had completely bleached the skulls. "Look up, O Emìr,"
shouted one of the company, "those skulls up there must
each of them have belonged to a person, like yourself, of
noble family."

A certain Sultan had two wazìrs, a Jew and a Christian,
who were jealous of one another. The Sultan one day
questioned whether it were better to be humbly born, but
well educated, or to belong to some good family, however
poor. The Jew stood up for race, while the Christian took
the side of education, saying that he himself had trained a
cat to do the work of a good servant. "If your Majesty
will let him show his cat," said the Jew, "I shall demonstrate,
in my turn, that good birth is above training."

The trial took place next day, when, at a signal from the
Christian wazìr, a beautiful cat came on its hind legs into
the Imperial presence, bearing a small gold tray of re-
freshments. But the Jew had got a mouse in a little box up
his sleeve and, just as the cat was offering the tray to the
Sultan, he released that mouse. The cat, at once becoming
conscious of the presence of its natural prey, hesitated for a
moment, then let go the tray and dashed off in pursuit.

The Jew then asked that a well-educated gipsy from the
Sultan's harìm might be called into the presence. The
girl was brought, and he put a question to her: "Suppose
that, after midnight but before daybreak, you awoke from
sleep, how would you be able to tell when dawn drew near?"
She said, "I should listen for a donkey's braying, because
at the approach of dawn they bray like this;" and she gave
an imitation of the sound.

"Your Majesty will please observe," said the Jew, when
she was gone, "that she answered from her ancestry and
not her education. Now let us ask some girl of good descent,
but poor and uneducated, the same question." A girl
answering these requirements was brought into the presence.
She had but newly joined the harìm, and her manner was
of graceful shyness. When the Sultan asked her how she

would perceive the approach of dawn, she faltered: "May it please your Majesty, my mother has told me that the light of a diamond grows dull when dawn approaches." The Sultan and all present applauded her answer and gave to good birth the palm over education.

A certain Emperor of China,* a land of idolaters and infidels, was once visited by a famous traveller who related the marvels which he had witnessed in different countries, and, among other things, informed his Majesty that the Shah of Persia had a lion so tame that it would follow its master about everywhere like a well-trained hound; that the Emìr of Cabûl had a tiger; the ruler of Cashmere a leopard; and, in short, every potentate he had visited or heard of possessed some wild beast which had learned to be companionable. It made the ruler of the Chinese feel small to think that he alone, among the sovereigns of the earth, had no strange pet. As wisest of men and chief of monarchs, he scorned to ape such inferior mortals as either the Shah of Persia or the Czar of Muscovy, and determined to adopt some creature that no human being had ever dreamt of taming.

Having, after much deliberation, made his choice, he summoned his councillors and laid upon them his commands to devise some means to tame that foul and fierce animal the pig, so completely that it should become as clean, gentle and well-disposed as a lamb.

The assembled sages and courtiers told their master that what he asked of them was feasible, and, in fact, so easy that they would set about it at once. "All that has to be done," said they, "is to give orders that a sow in pig be closely watched, and, as soon as she litters, one of her young ones be snatched away before it has had time either to smell her or to taste her milk. It must be suckled by a ewe, carefully washed every day, and trained in cleanly habits. If this course be adopted the vilest of beasts is sure to grow up as mild and unobjectionable as a lamb."

* Tale told at Sunday-school (1862) by the late Armenian Protestant, Rev. Stephen Garabed of Diarbekir.

The monarch ordered all this to be done. An official of high rank was appointed guardian of the Emperor's sucking-pig. He had under him a special staff of washers and feeders, and the ruler of China awaited with Imperial patience the result of his servants' labours. The sucking-pig was duly obtained; washed in frequent baths of rose-water and other perfumes; and brought up in the manner directed by the learned. In time the officials in charge had the honour to present to their lord a pigling elegant and lamb-like.

The monarch liberally rewarded all concerned, and made the tame pig his constant companion. It followed him about everywhere, to his great delight.

One day, however, the Emperor took it into his head to extend his walk beyond the palace grounds. His pig, wearing a gold collar set with jewels, followed at his heels. All of a sudden the animal forgot its manners. It began to sniff the air and grunt in most unlamblike fashion, and, before anything could be done to prevent it, left its master, and scampering across fields and scrambling through hedges, rushed headlong into a morass in which a number of swine were wallowing. The courtiers in attendance were horrified and ran as fast as they could, forgetting all dignity, zealous to save their lives. But in vain every effort. When they reached the edge of the slough, no one could tell which of the unclean beasts rolling about in it had been the royal pet. They suspected indeed that one particularly filthy creature might be he, but could not be sure, seeing that there was no trace of any collar; so they returned in fear and trembling to their sovereign, who threatened to do terrible things. Orders were given that all the absent members of the Council and all the wise men in the capital should immediately appear before him. When everyone of the frightened grey, black and brown beards had come into the presence, they were told that their master felt sorely tempted to have their heads chopped off that very instant; but since it pleased him to remember that he was the fount of mercy as well as retribution, he would give them grace

of three days in which to find some infallible means of
turning a pig into a permanent lamb.

Grateful for the respite, the wazìrs, the old men, and the
learned discussed the momentous question in all its aspects.
At the close of the last hour of the third day they returned
to the hall of audience and prostrated themselves before the
throne. " O mighty monarch of this golden age," said
their spokesman, "your humble and obedient servants
and slaves have very carefully considered and discussed
the matter graciously entrusted to them, and have found a
solution of the difficulty. The achievement is, indeed, a
hard one, but just for that cause worthy of so great a ruler.
Therefore, if it please your Majesty, let orders be sent to
all your ambassadors and representatives in foreign parts
to promise great rewards to that skilled surgeon who shall
undertake the operation of cutting both a live pig and a live
lamb open at the same time, and, extracting the heart of
the former, of inserting the lamb's heart in its place. When
the wound is sewn up and the swine has recovered, it will
be found a perfect lamb, and the achievement will be one
to add lustre to the wonderful annals of your Majesty's
most glorious reign." So pleased was the Emperor of
China with the suggestion that he at once issued an Iradé
commanding that orders should be immediately forwarded
to his envoys abroad. However, though advertisements
may have appeared in all the leading gazettes of Belâd el
Afranj, I have not heard that any surgeon applied in
response to the invitation.

II

IN a town not far from the capital there lived, years ago, a young man noted for his learning.* He had completed his studies at the great University of El Azhar at Cairo, and was a master in all the seven sciences and an owner of the seven tongues, a beautiful caligraphist, a poet so accomplished that his verses were said by his friends to deserve to be affixed to the gates of the Ka'aba [1] at Mecca, and a scholar so erudite that none grudged him the right to wear the wide formal and much-respected shape of turban called *mûkleh*.[2] But, despite these advantages, he could not get on in the world, having no influential relative to push him forward. Nothing discouraged, however, he resolved, being ambitious, to gain the notice and approbation of the Sultan himself, and, as a result, position and wealth, for he was poor although of stately presence.

He therefore wrote a magnificent poem in praise of the great Khan and mighty Khakan, the Commander of the Faithful, our Sovereign Lord the Sultan Fûlân,† ibn-es-Sultan Fulân, Sultan of the Arabians, the Persians, and the Rûm, whose fame and influence extended over the seven continents and across the seven seas. When the ode was finished he forwarded it to the potentate, having sold nearly everything he possessed in order to gain the favour of the various officials through whose hands the document would have to pass before it could be laid at the foot of the couch whereon reposed the Sovereign of the Age.

Great were the hopes this young man founded on his verses,

---

* Tale told by a Christian native of Beit-Jalu near Bethlehem. [This, from internal evidence, I judge to be a Christian fable.—M. P.]
† [Fulân = " So and so." Cf. Span. Don Fulano.—M. P.]
[1] See p. 261.   [2] See p. 261.

but yet greater was his disgust when the " Sheykh el Hara " (or headman of the street in which he lived) one day sent for him and called upon him to sign a receipt for fifty dinârs out of the Imperial treasury, and when he had done so, coolly told him that forty dinârs had gone to pay the fees of various officials between the throne and himself, that he himself must keep five for his own fee, and three on some other pretext, leaving the poet a balance of two only. Thoroughly disgusted with his want of success, but being of a persevering character, our hero wrote a second ode yet more beautiful than the former, and then started on foot for Stambûl, resolved not to trust to intermediaries but to lay his work himself at the feet of the well-spring of all earthly bounty. He reached the capital on a Thursday evening and took a lodging at a khan. The next morning, having been to the bath, he arranged his turban and robes in such a manner as to make a good impression, and then took up a position near the entrance of the mosque in which the Padishah was wont to perform his public devotions week after week. As soon as the Sultan appeared the poet rushed forward and, falling at the Sovereign's feet, presented his poem. The paper was graciously received by the monarch, who immediately afterwards passed into the mosque. The poet awaited his return, and when the Sultan came out and saw him standing, he graciously commanded him to follow him to the palace. On reaching it the Sultan read the poem, and, being pleased with it, went to his private money-chest, and taking out ten dinârs gave them to the young man. Noticing the look of disappointment on the latter's face, and being himself in a very good humour, the Padishah told him to say why he was not pleased, and to speak frankly without fear or reserve. On receiving such encouragement, the poet fell at his Sovereign's feet, told him of his aspirations, his disappointments, and how he had spent the whole of his property in striving to achieve success and attain a high position. " My son," said the benevolent ruler, when the poet had stopped speaking, " be content with what I now give you. For you to receive more at present would only be a cause of trouble to you, for it would be sure to excite the attention and rouse the envy and hatred of your neighbours. I will, however, add to it something of greater worth than all the talents and learning which you already possess. I will tell you what is the secret of success in life. It is expressed in one Arabic word, *Heylim*.* "Make *Heylim* your rule in life and you will be sure to attain eminence." With these words the scholar was dismissed. Walking home, he pondered on his Sovereign's strange advice. Suddenly a bright idea struck him. Meeting a well-dressed Greek priest in the lonely road, he accosted him. "O Nazarene, son of a dog, change clothes with me." The priest objected at first, but finally he yielded to the Moslem's threats, and was glad to be allowed to go his way unharmed, as a Mohammedan 'âlim or savant, whilst the poet, as a Greek priest, returned to Istanbûl, took a room in a quiet khan, and remained in retirement till his hair was grown so long as to enable him to pass for a priest of the Orthodox Church.[3]

Having attained this object he called on the Sheykh el Islâm and desired a private interview, which was granted. "Three nights ago," said the impostor, "I had a dream which greatly troubled me. It has been repeated on the two succeeding nights. I dreamt that a venerable man, who had such and such features, and wore such and such a garb" (here he gave a description which would remind learned Moslems of the traditional appearance of the Founder of Islâm), "appeared to me and, declaring that he had been sent to teach me the true religion, made me repeat the following prayer after him several times till I knew it by heart. When I could do this, he told me to come to you, repeat what he had taught me, and ask for further instruction." He then, to the Sheykh's great surprise, repeated the "Fatha" or first chapter of the Koran with great unction. The Sheykh el Islâm cross-questioned his visitor shrewdly but failed to disconcert him. It appeared he was in truth a Christian priest to whom Mohammed

* The English expressions "flatter, insinuate, ingratiate yourself, and dissimulate" hardly express the full significance of this one word.
[3] See pp. 261–2.

himself had taught the first rudiments of Islâm, a most interesting convert. The highest religious official in the Moslem world, therefore, vouchsafed him the desired instruction, and received him into his house. Next day he informed his host that he had again dreamed that he was visited by the venerable person, and that the latter had taught him a second set of texts, which he was to ask the Sheykh to expound to him. He then repeated the second sûra of the Koran, entitled " The Cow," and containing 286 verses, without making a mistake in a single vowel-point or accent. The Sheykh was astonished beyond measure, and not a little flattered at the thought that the Prophet should have singled *him* out to be the religious instructor of so miraculous a disciple. What would his enemies say when it became known that his authority was not only upheld by the Khalìfeh, but by Mohammed himself?

During the next night the pseudo-Christian was taught, as he stated, the third sûra, and the following morning he repeated it correctly to his host, who then expounded it. Next night the fourth sûra was revealed, and so on, till the Sheykh could no longer abstain from inviting the learned of his acquaintance to come and witness the marvel. They came, saw, heard, questioned and cross-questioned, but found more than their match, and retired greatly mystified, if not convinced. In the meantime the case of conversion was spoken of openly throughout Stambûl. The Christians dared not gainsay the exultant Moslems, who boasted of the wonderful conversion of a great Christian theologian which had been effected by the Prophet himself assisted by the Sheykh el Islâm. The fame of the latter went up by bounds. His *fetwahs* or legal decisions were humbly accepted. Gifts came to him from all sides, and being a generous man, he shared them with his pupil.

The supposed Christian, however, retained his clerical habit, asserting that the Prophet had bidden him not to lay it aside nor be admitted into the pale of El Islâm by circumcision till his instruction was complete. In due time news respecting the extraordinary case reached the Commander of the Faithful, who, being a wise man, first inquired about the time when this remarkable Nazarene first applied to the Sheykh el Islâm for instruction. His suspicions roused, he commanded that the supposed Christian should be brought to him privately. The Sultan knew him at a glance, in spite of his disguise and long hair, and sternly inquired what was meant by this mummery. " O Ruler of the Age!" replied the scamp, falling at his feet, " your Majesty advised me to *Heylim* and I, obeying the precept, have found it profitable." He then told his story, which greatly amused the Sultan, who sent word to the Sheykh el Islâm that he himself would be responsible for the further progress of that interesting convert, who would remain in the palace as his guest. After this, having commanded the palace barber to attend the rogue, and dressed him in robes be-fitting a true believer, he made him one of his private secretaries, and by degrees advanced him to higher posts in the Government. Ever since that time the plain rule " *Heylim* and you will live," or in other words, " Kiss a dog on his mouth till you have got what you want from him," * has been well observed in the East.

* [Bûss el kelb ala fummo hatta takdi gharadak minno; in the dâraji (common) Arabic of Palestine.—M. P.]

III

A WEALTHY merchant had three sons.* He himself was growing old and felt in doubt how to arrange for the management of the property after his death; because, although his sons were grown-up men, industrious and dutiful, he feared that they were too good-natured, and having from their childhood been brought up in comfort, might not have sufficiently realised the value of money. He therefore tried by a trick to find out which of his sons was gifted with most common sense.

He feigned to be very ill, and sent word to his sons, employed in different branches of his extensive business, that they must take turns in nursing, for his days were numbered.

The eldest came at once. When he reached his father's bedside the old man complained that his feet were very cold. Noticing that they were uncovered the young man drew the *ilhaf* or quilted cotton coverlet, which in the East takes the place of blankets, over them. A few minutes later the father complained that his shoulders were cold, so the son drew the *ilhaf* upwards, and observing that it was too short to cover both feet and shoulders at the same time, wanted to fetch a long quilt, of which there were plenty in the house. The old fellow, however, angrily refused to let him do this, and said that he could not bear a heavier weight of covering, and preferred the quilt he had to all others. Unwilling either to disobey or to provoke his father, the eldest son dutifully spent a whole day and night in drawing the scanty covering now over his shoulders, now over his bare feet. He was quite worn out when the second brother came to relieve him. The second endured the same experiences. In spite of coaxing and remonstrance, the old merchant refused to let a

* Tale told by a Christian Bethlehemite lad.

longer quilt be brought to cover him, and yet was constantly
crying out, now that his shoulders, now his feet, were cold.
It came to the turn of the third and youngest son. He also
tried in vain to persuade his father to let him fetch a longer
quilt. Then on a thoughtful observation of his parent,
seeing him enjoy his meals, and troubled with no special
pain, he suspected a game of some kind. He left the bedside
for a minute, cut a good and supple rod from a pomegranate tree in the garden, and straightway returned to
the sick-room, where he was greeted with the usual complaint
of cold in the extremities. He suddenly brought down the
stick within an inch of the ancient's feet, saying, "Very well,
father! Stretch your legs according to your coverlet."

The effect was magical. The old man jumped out of bed,
completely cured. He made arrangements that at his death
the supervision and management of the estate should devolve
on his youngest son, who, without failing in duty, had
proved himself too shrewd to let himself be imposed on
even by his own father. This incident is said to have given
rise to the proverb: "Stretch your legs according to the
length of your coverlet."

An *afrit*[1] who had grown old, feeling that his term of
existence was drawing to a close, resolved by way of turning
over a new leaf to go on a pilgrimage. He therefore called
his friends together, informed them of his conversion, and
bade them farewell. Now, among them was a couple who
had a son for whose future they were anxious. They considered that it would be of the greatest advantage to their
young devil to travel under the wing of one so good and
venerable. They therefore begged leave for their son to
accompany him. He at first objected, but finally yielded
to the solicitations of his friends, only stipulating that his
companion should swear by the seal of Solomon that while
travelling he would do no harm to man, beast, bird, or creep-
ing thing. To this condition the young devil and his parents
readily agreed.

The penitent then set forth with his young disciple, but

[1] See p. 262.

the latter soon began to find the journey intolerable without the recreation of a little mischief. The *afârìt* * always journey by night and sleep in the day. One dark, moonless night the couple reached a large encampment of Bedû.† Everything was silent, and it was clear that the whole tribe was asleep. The two devils passed through the camp without disturbing a soul; but a little later the young one begged leave to return and walk once more through the camp, declaring that he wanted to go from pure curiosity and without any mischievous intention.

He was gone but a minute, and they proceeded on their way. But they had not made many steps before there arose a din to wake the dead in the camp behind them—horses neighing, dogs barking, women shrieking, men shouting. The elder *afrìt* turned fiercely on his pupil, crying, " Perjurer! you have broken your solemn oath! " " You lie," replied the youngster, " I have done no harm to any living thing." " What, then, is the meaning of that noise? " " I cannot think; unless it be that the Sheykh's stallion has got loose. He was tethered to a tent-peg, and I thought I would see if he was securely fastened. Perhaps I loosened the peg a little." From this answer comes the saying, when someone does much mischief indirectly: " He only moved the tent-peg."

Karakoz and 'Iweyz [2] were two rogues who had long lived on terms of the closest amity, sharing the toils and dangers as well as the fruits of rascality. But a time came when they spoke no more to one another.

'Iweyz was sitting one day in his dwelling, cudgelling his brains for some new trick by which to fill his empty purse, when there came to him one of his acquaintance, a youth whose father had just died. After the usual salutations, the visitor told 'Iweyz that his father had left him one thousand dinârs, but that he had not yet made up his mind what to do with them. Meanwhile he was anxious to find some

---

* *Afârìt* (pl. of *afrìt*) = a sort of devils.
† Bedû (pl. of Bedawi) = the desert Arabs.
[2] See p. 262.

honest person who would take charge of them for him till he, the owner, could decide upon a line of business; and he asked 'Iweyz whether he could do him the favour. Though inwardly delighted at the offer, the rogue assumed the greatest aversion, crying, " No! no! no! go and find someone else to take charge of your money, I cannot be troubled with so great a responsibility." On hearing this emphatic refusal the young man became more importunate. " My father told me on his dying bed," said he, " not to trust anyone who showed an eagerness to accept the offer of having the money given into his charge, but, on the other hand, to leave it with full confidence in the hands of anyone who showed a dislike of the responsibility. As you are such a person, I beseech you to take it from me." " No! no! no! " repeated 'Iweyz, with yet greater vehemence, " do what you like with your money, bury it, throw it in a well, but do not leave it in my keeping." " I shall leave it here," said the youth, producing a bag of money. And though 'Iweyz yelled at him to take it away, he placed the bag on the diwân without having taken receipt or summoned witnesses. When the young man was gone, 'Iweyz took the bag, locked it up safely, and felt very happy. An hour later, Karakoz came in, and, struck with his friend's unusual gaiety, inquired the cause. " I have secured uncontrolled possession of a thousand dinârs," said 'Iweyz, and related what had happened. " That is very fine," remarked Karakoz, " but you cannot ' eat up ' the money, even though it has been placed in your hands without either receipt or witnesses, for you may be forced to take your oath concerning it at the *mazâr* or shrine of some saint, who will torment you in case you swear falsely. What will you give me if I show you a way out of the difficulty? "

" My dear friend," answered 'Iweyz with some warmth, " you know that we are comrades and share equally in all that En Nusìb * sends us. I shall, of course, let you have half the money, that is five hundred dinârs."

" Very well," said Karakoz; " the expedient I would recommend is a simple one. Whoever asks you about the

* *i.e.* luck.

money, whether the fool who left it with you, or the Kadi, or anyone, be sure in every case to answer: ' Shûrûlûb.' "

" Your advice is good, and I shall follow it," said 'Iweyz. Several months passed, and at last one day the young man to whom the money belonged came to 'Iweyz and asked him for it, as he had the intention of starting business.

" Pth, tth, th," said the rascal 'Iweyz, stammering and spluttering, " pth, tth, th, sh, th, shûrûlûb."

His visitor was surprised, but explained again that he wanted the money.

" Pth, tth, th, sh, th, shûrûlûb," answered 'Iweyz gravely.

" My money, give me back my money! " shouted the youth.

" Pth, tth, th, sh, th, shûrûlûb," replied the hypocrite with a look of surprise and deprecation.

" If you do not give me back my money at once," angrily said the owner, " I shall accuse you to the Kadi."

" Pth, tth, th, sh, th, shûrûlûb," retorted 'Iweyz, assuming an air of the greatest indifference.

Finding that all entreaties, expostulations and threats were useless and that the only answer he could get was the spluttering and stammering, ending with the meaningless expletive " shûrûlûb," the injured youth went and complained to the Kadi.

'Iweyz, on being summoned, appeared promptly and in silence, but the only answer he gave to all questions and cross-questions, even when they were emphasised by a severe flogging, which he bore without flinching, was " Pth, tth, th, sh, th, shûrûlûb."

So absurd did the case become that at last the Kadi and his court were in fits of laughter, and dismissed the accused, after severely blaming the plaintiff for having neglected the simple precaution of depositing the money in the presence of witnesses, if, as he confessed he had done, he insisted on leaving it with a man who refused all responsibility.

'Iweyz went home and was chuckling over his success, when Karakoz came and asked for his share of the booty.

" Pth, tth, th, sh, th, shûrûlûb," said 'Iweyz.

" Now, 'Iweyz," pleaded Karakoz in surprise, " don't

play the fool with me after I have shown you the way to secure this great fortune. You surely are not going to cheat an old friend and comrade!"

" Pth, tth, th, sh, th, shûrûlûb," replied 'Iweyz with a mocking gesture.

The common expression " to swallow trust-money shûrûlûb " is said to be derived from this incident.

IV

WHEN out riding one day, the Caliph Harûn er Rashìd noticed a very venerable-looking old fellâh planting a fig tree.* Accosting him, the Commander of the Faithful asked why he was taking the trouble to plant a tree of the fruit of which he could hardly hope to taste.

"O Emìr el Mûmenìn," replied the greybeard. "Inshallah, I may be spared to taste the fruit of this tree, but if not, my sons will do so, even as I have eaten the fruit of trees planted by my father and great-grandfather." "How old are you?" asked the monarch. "One hundred and seven," exclaimed the husbandman. "A hundred and seven!" exclaimed the Caliph in astonishment, and added, "Well, in case you really do live to eat fruit from this tree, be sure and let me know."

Several years passed, and Harûn had quite forgotten the incident, when one day he was told that an aged peasant desired an audience, saying that by the Caliph's own command he had brought him a basket of figs. Having ordered the man to be admitted, Harûn was surprised to find that it was the same fellâh he had once seen planting a fig tree, who now brought him some choice fruit from that very tree. The Commander of the Faithful received the gift most graciously, making the old man sit beside him on the diwân, and commanding a robe of honour to be put on him; he gave him a gold dinâr for each fig, and then dismissed him with honour.

When the old fellâh had left the Presence, the Caliph's son El Mamûn asked his father why such grace had been shown to an illiterate peasant. "My son," replied Harûn, "Allah Himself had honoured him, so I was bound to do the same."

* Tale told by a Moslem from Jaffa.

The old fellâh returned to his village in high glee, and there extolled the liberality and condescension of the Prince of Believers. Now next door to him lived a jealous and avaricious woman, who, envious of her old neighbour's good fortune, resolved to outdo him, and therefore worried her husband till, for peace, he filled a large basket with figs and presented himself with them at the door of the Khalifeh's palace. When asked what he wanted, he answered that as the Commander of the Faithful was famed for his impartiality and had so richly rewarded his neighbour for a few figs, he had also brought some and hoped to receive a similar reward. On hearing this reply the guards reported the case to Harûn, by whose orders the foolish man was pelted with his own fruit. Angry and hurt, he went home and divorced the wife whose folly had exposed him to such shame.*

A certain Sultan was one day struck with the difference between the cries of two beggars in the street near his palace. One of them was shouting, " O Allah, Thou Bountiful One," whilst the other bawled, " O Allah! give victory to the Sultan!" The monarch, flattered by the interest which the latter showed in his welfare, called his wazìr and said, " See to it that that beggar who keeps praying for me gets a roast fowl stuffed with gold pieces; but to the other give a fowl cooked in the usual way."

The wazìr obeyed, and the man who had called Allah bountiful was gratefully turning away to carry the fowl to his wife, when the other said to him, " Buy this fowl from me. I have neither wife nor children. What I want is money, and not rich food." " I have only a *bishlik*," † was the reply, " and that is nothing like the value of a roast fowl." " You shall have it for that," said the other; and so it happened that the beggar who praised Allah got not only a good dinner but also a small fortune.

This man now gave up begging, and opened a little shop.

* [Variants of this story are legion in Syria and Egypt, but the greater number could not fitly be ranged under the headline, " Moral Tales."—M. P.]

† A coin worth a little less than sixpence.

His companion, however, having spent his *bishlik*, returned to the palace gate and cried, " O Allah! give victory to our Sultan." The monarch commanded a second fowl stuffed with gold to be given to him. On receiving it he hurried to his former comrade and offered it for another *bishlik*, which was promptly paid.

When the cry, " O Allah! give the Sultan victory!" was again heard near the palace the Sultan cried, " What is this? I have made that fellow rich twice over and he still must beg. Bring him in to me." When the beggar was brought in, the Sultan, frowning on him, asked, " Why do you go on begging when I have made you rich?" " Alas, O Sultan of the Age," answered the beggar, " all that I have received at your Highness's gate were two fowls, which I sold to another beggar who used to cry, ' O Allah! O Thou Bountiful One!' but who has since grown rich and taken a shop." " Wallahi! Allah has shown that it is better to praise His bounty than to pray for my prosperity," cried the Sultan in amazement.

A certain Sultan once had a dispute with his wazìr as to what constitutes true kindness. He said that it might be found among the poorest of the people, while the wazìr maintained that it was impossible to show kindness, or to feel it, unless one were well-to-do. When the Sultan thought enough had been said, he summoned the Sheykh el Islâm, and ordered a record of the debate and of the arguments of both sides to be made and deposited in the public archives.

Some time afterwards the Sultan one afternoon sent secretly for the Sheykh, and the two disguised themselves as derwìshes and went out to settle the question. In the city they found much to interest them but nothing bearing on the problem which they wished to solve. By the time they reached the outskirts of the town the sun was setting, and as they advanced into the country it drew dark apace. They were glad to behold a light shining in a field beside the road, and went towards it. It came from a little mud-roofed hut, the abode of a poor goatherd. The man was himself out at work, but his wife and mother bade the strangers welcome in his absence. A few minutes later he came home, bringing with him four goats, which were all his substance. Having assured the guests that his house was theirs, he asked to be excused for a minute, and going to the owners of the flock he tended, begged two loaves of wheaten bread, as he could not set coarse dhurrah * bread before his guests. The two loaves with some eggs, curds † and olives, made a tempting meal. " But pardon us," said the Sultan, " we are under a vow not to eat anything but bread and kidneys for a year and a day." Without a word, the host went out, killed his four goats, and broiled their kidneys. But the Sultan, when they were set before him, said, " We have a vow to eat nothing until after midnight. We will take this with us, and eat it when our vow has expired. And now, I grieve to say, we must be going." The goatherd and his family begged them to stay till morning, but in vain.

When the masqueraders were once more alone on the highway, the Sultan said, " Now let us try the wazìr!" They reached his house, from which streamed light and music; he was entertaining. The humble request of two derwìshes for food and lodging was promptly refused; and when they still persisted, the wazìr was heard shouting, " Drive away those dogs, and thrash them soundly. That will teach them to plague their betters." The orders were so well obeyed that the twain escaped with their bare lives. Bruised and bleeding they reached the palace about midnight. When they had put off their disguise, the Sultan sent privately for a dumb physician to tend their wounds. He then called together his council of ministers, and, having described the whereabouts of the goatherd's dwelling, told them all to go and stand near it, but without disturbing the inmates. " When the lord of that house comes out in the morning, greet him with the utmost respect, and say that I request the favour of a visit from him. Escort him hither honourably, and, between you, bring the bodies of four goats which you will find near his door."

The goatherd feared for his life in the morning, when he found his hut the centre of a crowd of courtiers and soldiers.

* _Sorghum Annuum._   † Ar. _leben._

Nor was his alarm diminished by the respectfulness of their manner towards him as they invited him to the Sultan's palace, nor by their inexplicable conduct in picking up the dead goats and carrying them as honoured corpses. When the procession reached the palace, the Sultan made the goatherd sit beside him and ordered the record of his dispute with the wazìr to be read aloud for all to hear. The recital ended, the Sultan told the story of his adventures on the previous evening. Then turning to the wazìr, he said, "You have betrayed your own cause! No one in this realm is in a better position than you to show kindness to his fellow-men! Yet you show nothing but cruelty! You are no longer my wazìr, and your wealth shall be confiscated. But this goatherd, who begged better bread than he himself could afford to eat, for the greediest and most ill-mannered guests that ever came to man's house, and who sacrificed his whole substance rather than disappoint them, he shall be my friend and sit beside me." Thus was kindness rewarded and churlishness dishonoured.

There once lived in Jerusalem twin brothers who, even after they were grown up, lived and worked together, sharing the produce of their fields.*

One night after threshing their corn and dividing it, as was their custom, into two equal heaps, they slept out on the threshing-floor to prevent theft. In the night one of them awoke and thought to himself: "My brother is a married man with children to look after, whereas I—praise to Allah—am single. It is not right that I should receive a share equal to his from the produce of our toil."

So thinking he rose, and noiselessly took seven measures from his heap and put them on his brother's; then went back to sleep. A short while afterwards his brother woke and, as he lay blinking at the stars, said within himself, " I, by the blessing of the Highest, have a good wife and four lovely children. I know joys to which my brother is a stranger. It is not right that I should receive a share equal

* This tale was told by the late Moslem Sheikh Mahmoud of Neby Daûd about 1864.

to his from the produce of our toil." Thereupon he crept
to his heap and transferred seven measures thence to his
brother's portion; then went back to sleep. In the morning
each was amazed to find the heaps still equal; till Allah
sent a prophet who informed them that their unselfish love
was pleasing to the Almighty; and that threshing-floor *
was blessed for evermore.

The Kadi " Abdullah el Mustakìm," [1] some of whose
descendants are said to reside at Jaffa at the present day,
lived at Baghdad during the reign of El Mansûr, one of the
Caliphs of the dynasty of Abbâs, and is alleged to have
obtained his honourable surname, which means " the
honest or upright One," from the strict impartiality with
which he administered justice. The following story is told
of him :—

As the upright Judge was leaving his house one morning
he was met by a woman of the lower classes, who, accompanied by a boy, her son, was driving a donkey and weeping
bitterly. On beholding her distress the Kadi, who was as
kind-hearted to the poor and afflicted as he was stern to
wrongdoers, stopped her and asked the reason of her sorrow.
" Alas! my lord," said the woman, " have I not reason to
weep? My husband died a few months since, after making
me swear on his death-bed not to sell the small piece of land
by the cultivation of which we had supported ourselves, but
take care of it for our son, this boy, and teach him to till it
as his ancestors had done for generations. But the Caliph
sent one of his servants and offered to buy the land from me,
because it adjoins an estate belonging to him, on which he
intends building a palace. He says that he must have my
piece of ground in order to carry out his plans. I refused to
sell, for the reason which I have told you, and after thrice
pressing me to dispose of it and being refused, he, this
morning, had me and my son driven away from our lawful

* It was on the hill traditionally known in Zion—the rock-hewn
base of a tower which once formed the south-west corner of the city
wall. It is now part of the foundation of Bishop Gobat's school. My
authority for alleging it to be the scene of the above incident is the
late Sheykh Mahmûd of Nebi Daûd, who used to tell this story of the
twin brothers in connection with it.

[1] See p. 262.

possession, inherited from our forefathers, and told us that
as I would not sell the land, it should be taken from me without a recompense. We have thus lost everything, except
each other and this ass with an empty sack on its back, and
know not to whom to look for help, seeing that there is none
greater than the Khalìfeh." "Where is your land situated?"
asked El Mustakìm. "In such and such a place." "And
you say that you have just come from thence, and that
Commander of the Faithful was there when you left?"
"Yes, my lord." "Very well, you remain here in my
house till I return, and in the meantime let me have your
donkey and its empty sack for a few hours. Inshallah, as I
am somewhat known to the Emìr el Mumenìn,* I shall
succeed in persuading him to alter his plans and restore your
property."

On hearing these words the poor widow at once consented
to his proposal, and the Judge departed, driving the ass
before him. He soon reached the place, and found the
Khalìfeh on the spot, giving various orders to the architect
who was to erect the new palace. On beholding the ruler
of El Islamìyeh,† the Judge, prostrating himself before him
with every reverence, begged for a private audience without
delay. The Khalìfeh, who had a great respect for the
Kadi, granted his request, and Abdullah, acting as the
widow's advocate, earnestly pleaded with his master on her
behalf. Finding the monarch relentless, Abdullah said:
"Well, O Prince of Believers, you are our ruler and may
Allah prolong your rule, but, as your Highness has seized
the widow's and orphan's property, I beg, in their name, to
be allowed to take one sackful of this earth for them."

"Ten if you like," laughed the Khalìfeh, "though I fail
to see what good it can do them."

The Kadi seized a pickaxe that lay near, loosened the
earth with it and filled his sack. Then, turning to the
Caliph, he said, "I now adjure your Highness, by all that
we Muslimûn hold sacred, to help me to place it upon the
back of this ass." "You funny man," replied the ruler,
greatly amused, "why not call some of those slaves to lift
it?" "O Commander of the Faithful," answered the
Kadi, "the earth in the sack would altogether lose its
virtues were your Highness to command others to lift it;

---

* [Prince of Believers, the phrase commonly translated, "Commander of the Faithful."—M. P.]

† [The whole region of El Islâm. Cf. Christendom.—M. P.]

and your Highness would be the greatest sufferer by the loss." "Well, so be it," said the Caliph, growing curious. With that he took hold of the sack, but could not move it. "I cannot," said he, "it is much too heavy." "In that case," said the upright Judge, "as your Majesty finds that the weight of one sack of earth, which you are willing to restore to its rightful owners, is more than you can bear, you will pardon me for asking how you will bear the weight of this whole piece of land which you have taken by violence from the widow and fatherless, and how will you answer for your injustice at the Day of Judgment?"

This stern but faithful reproof provoked the Caliph; but on a minute's reflection he said, "Praised be Allah, Who has given me so conscientious a servant. I restore the land to the widow and her son and, to compensate her for the tears she has shed through my fault, I remit all dues and taxes payable on this piece of land."

A herd of camels happened to be passing an orchard, the owner of which was seated upon the *sinsileh* or rough stone fence.* One of the animals, a very fine male, caught hold of the overhanging bough of a fruit tree and broke it off with his teeth. Hereupon the owner of the orchard snatched up a stone and threw it at the camel. The aim was unexpectedly true, and the beast fell dead. Its owner, stung to fury by the loss of his property, snatched up the same stone and threw it with as deadly accuracy at the owner of the orchard, who, struck on the temple, was instantly killed. Horror-struck at his rash act, and realising what the consequences would be, the frightened camel-herd leapt on to the swiftest of his beasts, and leaving the rest to shift for themselves, fled as fast as he could. He was, however, promptly followed by the sons of the slain man, and forced to return with them to the scene of the tragedy, which happened to be close to the camp of the Caliph Omar ibn el Khattâb. The sons of the dead orchard-owner demanded the life of the man who had slain their father, and, though the latter explained that he had not done the deed with malice aforethought, but under the influence of sudden

* Story related by the late Arsaad Effendi El Jamal, a native Protestant.

provocation, yet, as he had no witnesses to prove that he was speaking the truth, and as the sons of the dead man would not hear of a pecuniary compensation, the Caliph ordered the man-slayer to be beheaded. Now in those times it was customary for the execution of a criminal to take place almost immediately after he had been condemned to die. The mode of procedure was as follows: a skin or hide called *nut 'a* was spread in the monarch's presence, and the person to be beheaded was made to kneel upon this hide with his hands bound behind him. The *Jelád* or executioner, standing behind him with a drawn sword, then cried aloud, " O Commander of the Faithful, is it indeed your decision that Fulân * be caused to forsake this world? " If the Caliph answered " yes," then the executioner asked the same question the second time, and if it were answered in the affirmative, he asked it once again for the third and last time, and immediately afterwards, unless the potentate instantly revoked the fatal order, he struck off the prisoner's head. Now, on the occasion of which we are speaking, the condemned, finding that his life was irretrievably forfeited, earnestly besought the Caliph to grant him three days' respite that he might go to his distant tent and arrange his family affairs. He swore that at the expiration of that term he would return and pay the penalty of the law. The Caliph told him that he must find a surety to die in his stead in case he should break his word. The poor man looked around him in despair upon the crowd of utter strangers. The *nut 'a* was brought and the executioner advanced to bind his hands. In despair he cried out, " Has the race of the manly † perished? " Receiving no answer, he repeated the question with yet greater emphasis, where-upon the noble Abu Dhûr, who was one of the *Sohaba* or companions of the Prophet, stepped forward and asked the Caliph's permission to become his surety. The monarch granted his request, but warned him that his own life would be sacrificed in case the man did not return within the time

---

* *Fulân* = " So and So."

† Or " virtuous," *Ahl el merowah* ; lit. the family, or race, of manly virtue.

stipulated. Abu Dhûr having agreed to this, the condemned was set free. He started off at a run and was soon
out of sight.

The three days had passed, and as the man-slayer had not
returned and nobody believed that he would do so, the
Caliph, yielding to the dead man's relatives, gave orders that
Abu Dhûr should pay the forfeit. The hide was brought
and Abu Dhûr, his hands tied behind him, knelt upon it
amid the lamentations and tears of his numerous friends and
relatives. Twice, in a voice that was heard above the
noise of the assembly, had the executioner asked the ruler
of Islâm if it was indeed his will that the noble man should
quit this world. Twice had the monarch grimly answered
" yes," when, just as the fatal question was to be put for the
third and last time, someone cried out, " For Allah's sake,
stop: for here comes someone running!" At a sign from
the Caliph the executioner remained silent, and, to everyone's astonishment, the man who three days previously had
been condemned to die ran up out of breath and, with the
words, " Praise be to Allah," sank exhausted to the ground.
" Fool," said the Caliph to him, " why didst thou return?
Hadst thou stayed away, the surety would have died in thy
stead and thou wouldst have been free." " I returned,"
replied the man, " in order to prove that not only the race
of the virtuous has not yet died out but also that of the
truthful." * " Then why didst thou go away at all? "
asked the monarch. " In order," said the man, who was
now kneeling with bound hands upon the hide from which
Abu Dhûr had arisen, " in order to prove that the race of
the trustworthy † has not yet perished." " Explain thyself,"
said the Commander of the Faithful. " Some time ago,"
said the man, " a poor widow came to me and entrusted
some articles of value to my keeping. Having to leave our
camp on business, I took the things into the desert and hid
them under a great rock in a spot which no one but myself
could find, and there they were when I was condemned to
die. Had my life not been spared for a few days, I should

* _Ahl es sidk._
† _Ahl el amâny_ ; lit. " the family of the pledge-acknowledging."

have died with a heavy heart, as the knowledge of the hiding-place would have perished with me; the woman would have been irretrievably injured; and my children would have heard her curse my memory without being able to clear it. Now, however, that I have arranged my household affairs and have restored her property to the woman, I can die with a light heart." On hearing this Omar turned to Abu Dhûr, and asked, " Is this man any friend or relative of thine? " " Wallahi! " replied Abu Dhûr, " I assure thee, O Emìr el Mumenìn, that I never set eyes on him till three days since." " Then why wast thou such a fool as to risk thy life in his stead? for had he not returned, I was determined that thou shouldst die in his place." " I did so in order to prove that the race of the manly and virtuous had not yet died out," replied Abu Dhûr. On receiving this answer the Caliph was silent for a while; then, turning to the kneeling man, he said, " I pardon thee, thou canst go." " Why so, O Commander of the Faithful? " asked an aged and privileged sheykh. " Because," answered Omar, " as it has been proved that the races of the manly, the virtuous, the truthful and the trustworthy have not yet perished, it only remains for me to demonstrate that the races of the clement * and the generous † are also still alive, and I therefore not only pardon the man, but shall pay the 'dìyeh (blood money) out of my own private means."

* *Ahl el 'afu* ; lit. " the race of pardon."　　　　　　† *Ahl el kurrum.*

V

THE ANGEL OF DEATH [1]

THREE mighty angels were standing before the throne of Allah with the most profound reverence, waiting to fulfil His high behests, and Allah said to one of them, " Descend to the Earth and bring hither a handful of its dust." On receiving this command the messenger, with swift wings and cleaving the atmosphere, descended to the Earth, and gathered a handful of its dust in obedience to the Most High. No sooner, however, had he begun to do this, than the whole world shuddered and trembled from its centre to its circumference and groaned most pitifully; and, moved and startled by the distress and anguish which his attempt had caused, the gentle angel let the dust which he had gathered fall back, earth to earth, and returned weeping and ashamed to the Presence of Him that had sent him. And Allah said, " I blame thee not, it was not written on the tablet of destiny that this should be thine office. Stand now aside for other service." Then Allah said to the second of the three angels, " Go thou, and fetch a handful of Earth's dust." He, too, flew swiftly down to Earth and tried to gather up a handful of its dust, but when he saw how the Earth shook and shuddered, and when he heard its groans, the gentle angel could not do the deed but let that which he had gathered fall, dust unto dust, and lifting up himself, he returned ashamed and weeping to the Presence of Him Who had sent him. And Allah said, " This task was not for thee. I blame thee not, but stand thou too aside, and other service shall be thine." Then Allah sent the third angel, who descended swiftly, and gathered up the dust. But when the Earth began to groan and shudder in great pain and fearful anguish, the sad angel said, " This so sore task was

---

[1] See p. 263.

given me by Allah, and His Will must be done, even though hearts break with pain and sorrow." Then he returned and presented the handful of Earth's dust at Allah's throne. And Allah said, "As thou the deed hast done, so now the office shall be thine, O Azrael, to gather up for me the souls of men and women when their time has come, the souls of saints and sinners, of beggars and of princes, of the old or young, whate'er befall; and even though friends weep, and hearts of loved ones ache with sorrow and with anguish, when bereft of those they love." So Azrael became the messenger of Death.*

Azrael had done some wrong in heaven, to expiate which he was obliged to live a man's life on earth, without, however, neglecting his duties as Angel of Death; so he became a physician, and, as such, attained wide celebrity.† He married and got a son, but his wife was a dreadful shrew, and it did not increase his happiness in her society to know that she was destined to outlive him.

When Azrael had grown old, and the time for his release drew near, he revealed his real character to his son under oath of the strictest secrecy. "As I am shortly to depart," he said, " it is my duty to provide for your future. You know all that can be known of the science and procedure. I shall teach you to be a doctor. Whenever you are called to a bedside, I shall be present, visible to you alone. If I stand at the head of the bed, be sure the patient will die in spite of all your remedies; if at the foot, he will recover though you gave him the deadliest poison." Azrael died, as was predestined; and his son, following his instructions, soon grew rich and famous. But he was a spendthrift, and laid by nothing out of all he earned. One day, when his purse was quite empty, he was called to the bedside of a rich notable, who lay at death's door. On entering the sick-room, he saw his father standing at the head of the bed; so, after going through a form of examination and delibera-

---

* This account of the appointment of Azrael was given by a Moslem lady of rank to comfort my wife, who was mourning the death of her brother.
† Tale told by a native dragoman, Ibrahim el 'Araj, a Jewish Christian.

tion, he pronounced the patient's case quite hopeless. At that the poor rich man, beside himself with fear, clasped the doctor's knees, and promised him half his possessions if he would save his life. The son of Azrael was sorely tempted. " Well," he said at length, " I will see what I can do, if you will make it three-fourths of your wealth, to be mine whether I succeed or no." The patient in fear of death consented, and a contract was drawn up, signed and sealed and witnessed. Then the physician turned to his father, and by frantic gestures implored him to move to the foot of the bed, but the Angel of Death would not budge. Then, having called in four strong men, he bade each take a corner of the bed and, lifting all together, turn it round so quickly that the sick man's head should be where his feet had been. This was done very cleverly, but Azrael still stood at the head. The manœuvre was oft repeated, but Azrael always moved with the bed. The son was forced to rack his brains for some new expedient. Having dismissed the four porters, he suddenly fell atrembling and whispered, " Father, I hear mother coming." In a trice fear flamed in the grim angel's orbs, and he was gone. So the sick man recovered. But from that day forth Azrael ceased to appear to his son, who made so many mistakes in his practice that his reputation fast declined.

One day he had been at the funeral of a Jew, his victim, and was strolling down Wady-en-Nâr,* in sad thought of his father, when he saw Azrael standing at the door of a cave. " In a few minutes you are going to die," said the father sternly. " For thwarting me in my duties, your life has been shortened." The youth implored his mercy, falling at his feet and kissing them, till Azrael said more kindly, " Well, come into my workshop, and see if your wits can find a way out of the difficulty. Though I myself am powerless now to help you, it is possible that you may yet help yourself." They passed through a suite of seven chambers, the sides of which looked like the walls of an

* Hell has seven gates, one of which is in Wady-en-Nâr; and the Angel of Death has his workshop in one of the caves in that gloomy valley, as appears in this story.

apothecary's shop, being covered with shelves on which were all sorts of bottles, urns and boxes; each of which, as Azrael explained, contained the means of death for some human being. Taking down a vessel, he unscrewed its metal lid, and it seemed to the son as if some air escaped. " A certain youth," he explained, " has to die within a few minutes by a fall from his horse, and I have just let loose the ' afrit ' who will scare that horse." Of a second vessel he said, " This contains eggshells of the *safat*, a strange bird, which never alights, even when mating. Its eggs are laid while on the wing and hatched before they reach the ground. The shells only fall to the earth, for the young are able to fly as soon as they leave the egg. These shells are often found and devoured by the greedy and bloodthirsty *shibeh*,* which goes mad in consequence and bites every creature that comes in its way, thus spreading hydrophobia and giving me plenty of work."

Thus they passed from room to room till they came to a mighty hall, where on rows upon rows of tables were myriads of earthen lamps of various forms and sizes; some of which burned brightly, others with a doubtful flame, while many were going out. " These are lives of men," said Azrael. " It is Gabriel's place to fill and light them; but he is rather careless. See! he has left his pitcher of oil on the table next to you." " My lamp! where is my lamp? " cried the son feverishly. The angel of Death pointed to one in the act of going out. " O father, for pity's sake, refill it." " That is Gabriel's place, not mine. But I shall not take your life for a minute, as I have got to collect those lamps at the end of the hall, which have just gone out." The son, left standing by his dying flame, grasped Gabriel's pitcher and tried to pour some oil into his vessel; but in his nervous haste he upset the lamp and put it out. Azrael came and took up his son's empty lamp, carrying it back through the rooms to the mouth of the cave, where the dead body of the physician was found later. " Silly fellow," he thought to himself.

* *Shibeh* (lit. " the leaper ") is one of the names of the leopard. But in folk-lore it is described as a creature combining the characteristics of the badger and the hyæna.

" Why must he interfere in the work of angels? But at any rate he cannot say I killed him." Azrael always finds an excuse, as the saying goes.

Among the soldiers of Herod there was an Italian named Francesco, a brave young man who had distinguished himself in the wars and was a favourite with his master as with all who knew him.* He was gentle with the weak, kind with the poor, and except in fair fight had never been known to hurt a living thing. Children especially used to delight in his companionship. He had but one vice: he was an inveterate gambler, and all his spare moments were spent at cards.

Not only did he gamble himself, but he seemed to take a special delight in persuading others to follow his example. He would waylay boys and lads on their way to school, and apprentices sent running upon errands, and entice them to try their luck at a game. Nay, so infatuated did he become, that he is said to have ventured to accost some respectable Pharisees on their way to and from the Temple and invite them to join him at his loved diversion. At last, things went so far that the Chief Priests and Rulers betook themselves to Herod in a body and demanded his punishment. But card-playing happened to be a pastime in which Herod himself delighted, so he did not take the charge against Francesco very seriously. Only, when the Jewish rulers kept on worrying him, he gave the Italian his discharge, and bade him leave Jerusalem and never again be seen within its walls.

Francesco entered on a new course of life. Gathering round him certain of his former comrades whose time of service had expired, he became the leader of a band of armed men whose business it was to waylay travellers on their way to and from the Holy City. Their principal haunt was a large cave on the road a little to the north of El Bireh, the ancient Beeroth. In no case were they guilty of violence and they always let the poor go unmolested. Their mode of procedure was singular. They used to stop and surround travellers who seemed wealthy and invite them to their cave

* Story told by the late Henri Baldensperger, junior.

to play a game with Francesco. The travellers dared not refuse so courteous an invitation when delivered by a band of armed brigands. They were politely welcomed by the gambler, treated to wine, and made to stake at cards whatever valuables they had with them. If they won, they went undespoiled; if they lost, they were compassionated and begged to come again with more money and try their luck a second time.

This went on for a long while, till, on a certain day, the sentinel on the look-out announced that a party of pedestrians was in sight. " If they are on foot," said the leader of the outlaws, " they are not likely to have with them anything worth playing for; still, let us see. How many of them are there? " " Thirteen," was the answer. " Thirteen," said Francesco musingly, " that is a curious number. Now where was it that I met a party of just thirteen men? Ah! now I remember; it was at Capernaum, where the Carpenter-rabbi of Nazareth cured the servant of one of the centurions belonging to our legion. I wonder whether by any chance he and his twelve pupils can be coming this way. I must go and see for myself." So saying he came out of the cave and joined the watchman at his point of vantage. The travellers were now near enough for Francesco to know them for Our Lord and His Apostles. He hastily called his men together, and told them that this time a really good man and a great prophet was coming, and that they must hide away the cards [2] and all else that was sinful, for this was quite a different person from the hypocrites of Jerusalem. Leaving them to prepare for the coming guests, he hurried down the road and, saluting the Saviour and His companions, pressed them, seeing evening was at hand and a storm threatening, to honour him and his comrades by spending the night with them. The invitation was accepted, and Jesus and His followers became the guests of the outlaws, who did their best to make them comfortable and, after supper, gathered round the Divine Teacher and, drinking in His gracious words, wondered. Although in all He said there was not a word that could be construed into blame of their way of life,

[2] See p. 263.

yet a sense of guilt fell on them as they listened. The brigands made the guests lie down on their own rough beds, whilst they themselves wrapped their 'abâyehs around them and slept on the bare ground. That night it was Francesco's turn to keep the watch. It chanced to strike him that the Saviour, lying fast asleep, had not sufficient covering, so he took off his own 'abâyeh and laid it over Him. He himself walked up and down to keep warm, but could not help shivering. Next morning, having breakfasted with the outlaws, Jesus and His Apostles departed, Francesco and some of his own men setting them on their way. Before parting, the Saviour thanked Francesco for his hospitality and that of his comrades and asked whether it were in His power to gratify any special wish he might have. " Not one, O Lord, but four," replied the gambler. " What are they? " asked Jesus. " First," said Francesco, " I am fond of playing cards, and I beg Thee to grant that whoever I play with, whether human or otherwise, I may always win. Next, that in case I invite anyone to sit upon a certain stone seat at the door of our cave, he may not be able to get up without my permission. Thirdly, there is a lemon tree growing near the said cave, and I ask that nobody who climbs it at my request may be able to descend to the ground unless I bid him. And lastly, I beg that in whatever disguise Azrael may come to take away my soul, I may detect him before he come too near, and be ready for him." On hearing these strange petitions, the Saviour smiled sadly and answered, " My son, thou hast spoken childishly and not in wisdom. Still, that which thou hast asked in thy simplicity shall be granted, and I will add thereto the promise, that when thou shalt see thy error, and desire to make a fresh request, it shall be granted. Fare thee well."

Years passed away and many of Francesco's comrades had left him, when one day the Angel of Death, disguised as a wayfarer, was seen approaching. Francesco knew him from afar, and when Azrael came to the door of the cave, the gambler invited him to sit down on the stone seat without. Having seen the angel fairly seated, Francesco cried, " I know thee. Thou hast come to take my soul, or the soul of

one of my comrades, but I defy thee! I entertained the
Lord of Life in this cave years ago, and He gave me power
to forbid anyone who sits on that seat to rise from it without
my leave." The angel at once struggled to get up but found
himself paralysed. Finding rage of no avail, he humbly
begged to be released. Francesco extorted from him a
solemn oath not to seek his soul nor that of his comrades for
the space of fifteen years, then let him go.

The fifteen years passed, and Francesco now dwelt alone
in his cave as a godly hermit, when the Angel of Death drew
near once more. The recluse at once withdrew into the
cave and lay down on his bed, groaning as if in agony. This
time Azrael entered the cave dressed in a monk's habit.
" What ails thee, my son? " he asked. " I have fever and I
thirst," came the reply. " I beg you to gather a lemon for
me off the tree which grows close to the cave, and to mix a
little of its juice with water that my thirst may be slaked."
As it wanted yet some minutes to the time appointed, Azrael
saw in the request a good excuse for administering a mortal
draught, so he climbed the tree to reach the fruit. But, no
sooner was he up in the branches than he heard a laugh and,
looking down, beheld Francesco in the best of health. He
strove to descend but could not move without Francesco's
leave, which was not granted until he pledged his word to
keep away for another fifteen years.

That term elapsed and Azrael came a third time. " Do
you intend to play any more vile tricks on me? " he inquired
of Francesco, now an aged man. " Not if you will grant me
one favour," answered Francesco, " and allow me to take
my pack of cards into the other world." " Will my giving
you the permission lead to some fresh practical joke at my
expense? " " No, I most solemnly assure you," replied the
old man. Hereupon the Angel of Death snatched up
Francesco's soul and his pack of cards and went with them
to the gate of Paradise where St. Peter sits to admit the souls
of the righteous. Francesco was told to knock at the gate.
He did so and it was opened, but when the porter saw who
it was, and that he had brought his cards with him, he
slammed the door in his face. So Azrael lifted the poor soul

up again and descended with him to the gate of Hell where Iblìs sits, eager to seize and torment dead sinners. On beholding who it was that the Angel of Death had brought, he said in great glee, " Here you are at last, my dear. I have waited long for your arrival, and so have many others with whom you played cards on earth. They all hope to see you beaten at your own game, for, as you did not allow travellers to reach the Holy City till they had played with you, so shall I not allow you to roast on the red-hot coals till you have played a game with me. You have your cards, I see, so we will begin at once." So Francesco and the Evil One began to play, and to the surprise of both, Francesco won the game. Satan insisted on a fresh trial of skill, and when he was once more defeated, he would insist on another trial, till at last, when he had been beaten seven times, he lost his temper and drove out Francesco, saying that he could not have anyone in hell who excelled him in anything even though it were a game. On hearing this, fresh hope was roused in the poor sinner's heart, and recalling the Saviour's pledge to grant him one more boon, he begged Azrael, who had stopped to watch the game, to take him back to the gates of Paradise, as he felt sure the Saviour would not treat him as harshly as the Prince of Saints and the chief of lost spirits had done. So Azrael took the poor soul to Heaven's gate and it once more knocked thereat, and when St. Peter opened, and would have driven it away, it pleaded the Saviour's promise to grant one more boon. So St. Peter called his Master, Who, when Francesco asked admission, confessing that his life had been one great mistake and offering to throw away his pack of cards, told Mar Batrus to let him in, and so the lifelong gambler entered Paradise.

A story told by His Beatitude the late Gregory IVth, Orthodox-Greek Patriarch of Antioch, resident at Damascus.

A very wealthy baker who was a widower, and without kith or kin, was wont to supply bread gratuitously, and every day, to a hundred worthy people known to be in need. This had been his practice for many years, and, by Allah's blessing, his business was marvellously prosperous.

One day a holy hermit descended from his cave in the

mountains and visited the good baker to inform him that he
(the hermit) had been granted a vision in which the
Archangel Gabriel directed him to tell the baker that his
deeds of charity were acceptable to the Most High, Who, as
a reward, would, before the year ended, remove him from
this world of sin and sorrow to live with Him in Paradise.

On receiving the message the baker humbly gave thanks
to God, and made arrangements that from that day forward
two hundred poor but worthy people should be supplied
daily, and without payment, with loaves from his bakery;
and also that when he died, all his wealth should be used to
endow a continuance of this charity. He himself devoted
every moment of his time to attending to the details of the
matter.

To his thankful surprise the year came to an end, was
followed by several more, and he was still alive.

The hermit, however, as year after year passed and he was
told that the charitable baker was still alive and thriving,
became very angry because his own predictions had been
discredited. He became morose and bad-tempered so that
people ceased gradually to come to him for advice and comfort. This loss of appreciation grieved him sorely; till, at
last, another vision was vouchsafed and the angel rebuked
him for his evil thoughts. " Of such saints as you are," said
the celestial visitant, " there are scores who fast, pray and
spend sleepless nights longing for heaven, and despising
others who, though they fear God and strive to please Him,
remain amongst their fellow-men, having patience with their
infirmities and doing their best to help them. The baker
is such a man, and in these evil times, God cannot spare him
from His service. Hadst thou delivered the message to
another that thou didst to him, he would have given up
business and spent the short span of his life allowed him in
self-indulgence. The baker, however, never thought of
himself but lives day by day as if it were his last, and uses it
for the benefit of others. By grieving because God has
prolonged His servant's life, and caused thy fame as a holy
recluse to be diminished, thou hast incurred grievous sin. I
have been sent to admonish thee to go to the baker and beg
him to allow thee to work as an unpaid servant in his bakery,
thus, like him, ' serving God in the bread.' "

The hermit took the rebuke to heart, obeyed the advice
given him by the angel, confessed his sin openly and in all
humility, and to the end of his life became a faithful assistant
to the baker.

VI

THE people of Palestine, Christian as well as Moslem, believe
in the existence of a race of beings of preadamite origin,
called by the general name of " Jân." * Whilst the angels
dwell in the heavens and have various offices and forms
differing according to their respective abodes (those in the
lowest heaven, for instance, being shaped like cows; those
in the second like falcons; in the third like eagles; in the
fourth like horses, and so on), the Jân are said by the learned
to be created out of the fire of the *simûm*, which they describe
as a fire lacking both heat and smoke.† They are said to
dwell chiefly in or amongst the Jebel Kâf, the range of
mountains which surrounds the earth. Some of the Jân
are good Moslems, and do not injure their human co-
religionists, but the greater number of them are unclean
infidels who take up their abode in rivers, fountains, cisterns,
ruined buildings, baths, cellars, ovens, caves, sewers, and
latrines. Some of them choose as dwellings cracks in the
walls or under the doorsteps or thresholds of inhabited
houses, so that it is very dangerous for people, especially
females, to sit on a doorstep in the evening when these night-
prowling evil spirits may do them grievous bodily injury.
The Jân are believed to be able to assume any shape they
please and to change it at pleasure. Among the peasantry
there is current another story as to their origin. It is that
our mother Eve, on whom be peace, used to bring forth forty
children at a birth, but being unable to nurse more than half
that number, she picked out the twenty best ones and threw

---

* Genius. Under the name of Shedim the orthodox Jews also
believe in their existence and general character as here described.
† Mejr-ud-din, *Uns el Jelîl* (Cairo edition), Vol. I. p. 15.

the others away. She told Adam on each occasion that she had borne only twenty; but he did not believe her. He therefore asked Allah to let any children she had thrown away live underground and go abroad at night when all men sleep. Thus the Jân came into being.

The Jân are envious of us men and women, always on the watch for a chance to injure; and unless we say " Bismillah " whenever we begin any work, or take anything out of our stores, they succeed in robbing us. There is, at the present day, a man living at Ain Kârim who has experienced this to his cost. He had a silly, forward daughter, who, in spite of frequent warnings from her parents and neighbours, would not invoke the Name. He was a man of substance, and brought home provisions in plenty, yet the blessing of Allah did not rest upon his property. At length, perplexed and discouraged, he had recourse to a great sheykh, who asked, " Whom have you in the house? " " My wife and daughter." " Does your wife invoke the Name of Allah? " " I would not have married her if she had not done so." " Does your daughter also ' name '? " " I regret to say she does not." " Then," said the sheykh, " don't let her touch anything about the house, and get rid of her at once! "

The father acted on the sheykh's advice; and no sooner had he disposed of his daughter in marriage than the Jân ceased to trouble him ; but the bridegroom, till then a thriving man, has not now enough money to buy oil to keep a lamp burning through the night.*

Not only are the Jân men and women like ourselves, but they can, and sometimes do, intermarry with other sons and daughters of Adam, often against the will of the latter, when these have neglected to ask the protection of Allah. In proof of this I will relate an incident that occurred some years ago.

There was a man of the village of El Isawìyen, in the valley north of the Mount of Olives, who, going down to reap his harvest in the neighbourhood of Ushwan, near Artûf, was not heard of for nine years. It was said he had been devoured by a hyæna. But in the end he reappeared

* None but the very poorest will sleep without a night-light.

and told his story. He was sleeping one night on the threshing-floor to protect his store of dhurra when he was awakened about midnight by a sound of voices drawing near. Supposing it to be the tax-gatherer and his assistant *khayâleh,** he lay quite still for fear of being beaten. But it was a party of the Jân, and, as at lying down he had neglected through weariness to invoke the protection of Allah, so now, sudden fear kept him from using that simple precaution, and left him at the mercy of the demons. He did not realise who they were till it was too late and he had become their victim. All he knew at first was that a woman came and smote his forehead, and the blow bereft him of all strength of will. She bade him follow her, and he obeyed blindly.

When they had gone some distance from the threshing-floor she told him she was his wife, and that, unless he submitted to her desire, her brothers, who had seen him follow her, would kill him horribly. Soon afterwards her brothers came up, when he saw that they were jinnis. They told him he had become one of themselves, and would thenceforth be invisible to the eyes of men.

Nine years he belonged to the Jân, and took part in all their depredations, till one day, when they were lying hid among some ruins, he noticed how his companions kept away from one of the walls on which was a luxuriant growth of *feyjan* [1] or rue, and himself, out of curiosity went towards it. At a shriek from his jinnìyeh of " Don't go near those plants!" he ran and plucked whole handfuls from the wall. Then, looking round, he saw that the Jân had vanished and he was free to return to his human family. When the fellahìn, his neighbours, disbelieved this story, he asked after a woman named " Ayesha," and was told that her husband had repudiated her because she robbed him and gave his goods to her brothers; there was no other supposition that could account for the way things vanished from his house. Thus, one day, he had filled a large *khâbieh* or mud-built bin with barley, but when he opened it on the morrow it was empty, and, in spite of his wife's protestations, he believed her to be

---

* Irregular cavalry.
[1] See p. 263.

the thief. The man who had been with the Jân explained that he had asked for the woman on purpose to prove her innocence and his own truthfulness. He had been present when the barley was carried off by the Jân, who knew that the Divine Name was not habitually called upon in that house. Other things that had been missed from the village while he was away had been carried off in like manner. Since that time everyone has been careful to gather handfuls of the plant known as rue, and to keep it in his house; and no good man will begin a piece of work without invoking Allah, the Merciful, the Compassionate; and no respectable woman will take even a handful of flour from its receptacle without likewise calling on the Most High.

A certain young married couple, though hard-working and economical, could not achieve prosperity, because one thing after another kept disappearing from the house. Did the wife put a bag of wheat beside the hand-mill overnight, in the morning it had vanished; and if she put aside cooked meats or preserves, they were sure to be spirited off. Her husband had a mare which he greatly prized. Every night, before going to bed, he fed the mare himself, carefully locked the stable door, and kept the key under his pillow till the morning. One morning, when he unlocked the door, the mare was gone, and, believing her to have been stolen by some human enemy, he trudged to the nearest towns in which cattle-markets were held, in the hope to recover her; but in vain. At last he concluded that the Bedû of the Belka had somehow gained possession of a false key, and used it to rob his stable, so he set out for the country east of Jordan, hoping to find his missing steed in some Arab camp.

At nightfall of the first day he found himself in a narrow gorge, in the sides of which were many caves. Seeing light in one of them, he supposed some shepherds or camel-drivers were putting up there for the night, and hastened to join them. But on entering the cave he saw it was full of the Jân. Afraid to give offence by a retreat he saluted them with as cheerful a voice as he could command. They replied politely in the common formula: " Our house is thy house, our dwelling and all it contains belongs to thee."

The demons, on the point of sitting down to supper, invited the guest to share the meal with them; and he nervously accepted the invitation. Among other dishes there was one of rice and lentils mixed, of which, at the entreaty of the Jân, he partook, though sparingly. " We have already told you that everything here is yours." Then, looking around him, the man fancied a resemblance between the furniture of the cave and things which had mysteriously disappeared from his own house. There followed a conversation in the course of which he told his hosts about the loss of his mare, and whither he was going in the hope to find it. They told him he need go no further, for the mare was there with them, and he could have her for the asking. He managed to frame the demand, and the mare was brought to him at once. Dark as it was, he would have mounted then and there and started homeward, but his hosts invited him to stay the night, and, as he feared to offend them, he tied up the horse and remained. When he arose next morning he found the cave empty, but his mare still tethered in the same place where he had put her before lying down to sleep.

Without mishap he rode back to his home, where his wife welcomed him with the news that all the things which had been missing had reappeared in the night as miraculously as they had vanished. Her joy was increasd by the sight of the mare. Her husband, who had no breakfast, asked for food; when she at once produced a dish of lentils mixed with rice, explaining, as she did so, that she had cooked it the day before, but not being hungry herself, had put it by for his return. Thereupon she uncovered the dish, to start back in surprise. " What is this? " she exclaimed. " When I put this dish away yesterday, it was full and carefully covered, and yet, as you see, somebody has had a taste of it. It cannot have been the cat, for, though she might have moved the cover, she could not possibly have replaced it." The young man was himself surprised when his wife said this, till, examining the dish, he knew it for the same from which he had eaten at the request of the Jân. This fact threw a new light on this strange experience. " My dear wife," he cried, " I know now the secret of our late misfortunes. It is that we have neglected a pious custom of our fathers, to name the name of Allah at all seasons. Our things were stolen by the Jân through that neglect. Let us amend our ways henceforth." Needless to say, from that day forward the couple were very careful to ask the blessing on all they undertook, and thus, to the end of their days, enjoyed the protection of the Most High.

Not only is it held foolhardy to sit on the doorstep or the threshold of a house, especially about sunset, but it is dangerous to call any animal, even the smallest insect, without at the same time pointing at the object; because many of the Jân and other demons are named after animals and other things in nature, and should the name be used without a gesture, some jinni will think that he is called and will take advantage of the mistake to harm the person calling him. A perfect multitude of the Jân may thus be summoned inadvertently, for among them, as among men, some names are common. For instance:—

A certain woman who had no children, but who longed for offspring, sat one evening on her doorstep, ignorant of the danger, when she noticed a black beetle crawling along the road. " I want a child," said the woman, " even though she be only a girl and as black as a beetle. O Khûnufseh ! * won't you come and be my daughter? " With that she rose and went into the house. Some time later, to her vast surprise, she actually gave birth to a whole swarm of black beetles. " O Lord ! " said she, " I only asked for one. Whatever shall I do with all these hundreds? I will sweep them up into the basket where I put dry dung,† and carry them to the *tabûn* and burn them all." She did so, but, on the point of returning to the house, she noticed that one of the creatures had escaped destruction by clinging with its feet to the wickerwork. " Well," she considered, " I did ask for one. I will make a pet of this beetle, which, after all, is my child." So she took the insect home and made a pet of it. It grew bigger and bigger, and in time, to the

* Black beetle. † Fuel for the *tabûn* or hovel-oven.

mother's joy, developed into a dark maiden whom she
named Khûneyfseh.* The creature, however, was a *ghûleh*,
one of the most dreadful enemies of the human race; and
she was rapidly growing big and strong. At length, upon a
day, her mother bade her take four loaves of bread and a
plate of *leben* to her supposed father who was ploughing.
The monster ate up the bread and the *leben* on her way, and
when she came up to the ploughman she swallowed him and
his yoke of oxen. Then she returned and said to her mother,
" I have devoured the four loaves and the *leben*, as well as
the ploughman and his oxen; shall I also swallow you and
the dough which you are kneading? " " Do so," replied her
mother, who thought her precious child was only jesting.
The *ghûleh* at once gobbled up her mother, the dough, and
the kneading trough. She went next to her grandmother,
who was spinning, and said, " Grandmother, I have eaten
the four loaves and the *leben*, the ploughman and his yoke of
oxen, the troughful of the dough with its kneader. Shall I
eat you? " " Do so, my child, if you like," said the old
woman, and was instantly devoured together with her
spinning-wheel. Then Khûneyfseh went out of the village.
Seated upon the dunghill, after the manner of village elders,
she found an old, wise man, who, though she knew it not,
happened to be armed with a two-edged dagger. Accosting
him, " O sheykh," she said, " I have devoured the four
loaves and the *leben*, the ploughman with his yoke of oxen,
the kneader with the troughful of dough, and the old woman
with her spinning-wheel. Shall I devour you? " Now the
old man was wise and the owner of experience. From the
manner of the dark girl's speech he guessed with what he
had to deal, and so he answered, " Very well, my daughter,
devour me if it please you." But when she came near, he
struck with his dagger and killed her. Then he cut her
open, when lo! there came forth from her belly, whole and
unhurt, the four loaves and the *leben*, the ploughman and his
oxen, the kneader with her troughful of dough, and the old
woman with her spinning-wheel. Since then people have
learnt not to sit on doorsteps† in the evening, and not to
speak to any living creature, except it be human, without
pointing to it.

* Little black beetle.
† It is not uncommon among the natives of Palestine for a man or
a woman to bury a charm under the threshold over which some enemy
is bound to pass. A woman known to me, who was a servant in an
English family, thus buried the shoulder-blades of a sheep covered
over with curses at a gate through which another servant had to go.

Another story illustrative of the danger people run by calling animals by their names without at the same time pointing to them is often heard.

A young peasant woman had one day so much to do that it was not till evening that she found time to knead the bread. By the time it was ready night had come, and it had grown so dark that she was afraid to go, unaccompanied, to the village oven.* She begged her husband to escort her; but he ridiculed her fears, and just when she was setting out called to a he-goat tethered in the yard, " Hear, O he-goat! take her! take her! " He meant it as a joke, and was surprised when she did not return. He went to the oven, she was not there. No one in the hamlet had seen her. He inquired at every house, searched the whole district, but in vain. Unable to believe that she had gone off with another man, since he knew her heart was his, he could not account for her disappearance to himself or to his neighbours, who began to suspect that he had killed her for infidelity.†

One day, when the bereaved husband was ploughing, an aged derwìsh came up and entered into conversation with him. The peasant bemoaned the loss of his wife. " How much will you give me if I tell you how to recover her? " asked the derwìsh. " You shall have this yoke of oxen," replied the peasant eagerly. " They would be useless to me, said the recluse, laughing, " but give me something to eat and I shall be satisfied."

The peasant took the derwìsh to his house and set before him the best he had. When the guest had done eating, he said, " I am certain that your wife has been abducted by some jinni to whom your foolish jest gave power to harm her. I therefore advise you to go this evening to such and such a cave in such and such a wady, the usual trysting-place of the Jân in this district. As soon as you see the cave lighted up after sunset, enter boldly and demand your wife from those within."

The peasant did as he was told. That same evening he took up his station near the cave described to him, and, as soon as he saw light stream from it, called Allah to aid and boldly entered. Within, the king of all the Jân was holding

---

* Ar. *tabûn*.

† As every husband has a right to do, unless he prefer to hand her over to her brothers, or nearest male relations, that they may themselves put her to death for her sins.

court. The peasant, undismayed, demanded his wife. The demon-king seemed neither surprised nor offended by his tone of authority, but quietly inquired of his subjects present whether anyone knew where the woman was. " I saw her in our own country, the Jebel Kâf, a short time since, in such a place," said one. " How long will it take you to fetch her, O Camel? " asked the monarch. " Jebel Kâf is a long way off, and I should need three years to go and return," was the reply. Then the ruler of the Jân asked another demon named " Horse " how much time he would need to fetch the woman, and he said, " Three months." A third jinni named " Wind," being asked the same question, replied, " Three weeks." All the rest of the Jân answered in turn, each naming the time he required to do the errand. At last the king asked the man to detail the circumstances under which he had lost his wife, especially the words which he had used at parting from her. The peasant then confessed that he had thoughtlessly handed his wife over to " He-goat." On hearing this the king ordered the jinni thus named at once to restore the woman to her rightful husband; which he did.

A shepherd once, after folding his flock for the night, went to sleep in a cave. He awoke about midnight to find himself in the presence of a large party of the Jân. Afraid to give offence, and being curious, he lay still with half-closed eyes, pretending to sleep.

The leader of the party sent out some of his followers to forage for provisions. These soon returned with plenty of all kinds of food and the Jân fell to with a relish.

Among the delicacies was a large tray of *bakláweh*,[2] round which the whole party gathered. Just then a young female suggested that they should wake the sleeper and make him join them at the meal. The others, however, objected on the ground that he might ask a blessing on the food, and thus compel them to disperse and leave behind them all that they had brought together out of the houses of people who were not used to name the Name. " We will put a large portion on a tray beside him, for him to eat when he wakes up. By that time we shall have gone, and his blessing, if he ask one, will not hurt us."

[2] See p. 263.

Hearing this, the shepherd sat up suddenly and exclaimed, " Bismillah er Rahman er Rahìm " (in the Name of Allah, the Merciful, the Compassionate), as one awaking, startled, in strange company. At the Name, the Jân all vanished, screaming. The shepherd then slept undisturbed till morning, when he found the cavern stocked with provisions, sufficient to last his family for a whole year. He accepted them as a gift from Allah, and had them conveyed to his own house.

It is of the utmost consequence to remember that the Jân should always be treated with respect. On entering an empty room, a cellar, cave, or even when sweeping a room which has for some time stood empty, one should never forget to say " Dustûrkum ya mubârakin " (by your permission, blessed ones),* or, for short, "Dustûr" (permission). The same formula should be used whenever one is carrying fire or water, so that the spirits may get out of the way, and not run the risk of a wetting or of getting burnt by accident. The safest way, however, is habitually to invoke the Name and protection of Allah.

English people are often shocked at the frequency with which Easterns use the Name of Allah, regarding it as a breach of the third commandment; but not realising that they are merely following a practice, which from their infancy they have been accustomed to look upon as belonging to the very essentials of religion, and the object of which is protection from the powers of evil.† The importance attached to the practice has been already explained, but is further illustrated by the following tales :

There was once a good woman whose husband was so

* " Thou blessed one! " are the words with which you should address a serpent, if you have the misfortune to meet one unexpectedly.
† [The devil once had a bet with someone that he would obtain a meal in a certain city renowned for piety. He entered house after house at dinner-time, but was always frustrated by the name of Allah, till, by good luck, he happened on the dwelling of a Frankish consul who, when Iblìs entered, was at table wrestling with a tough beefsteak. " Devil take this meat," said the consul, and the devil took it.—M. P.]

poor that when their only knife was broken, he could not buy her another. Want of a knife caused her great inconvenience as her neighbours were not always willing to lend their things. Thus, one day when her husband brought home a sheep's lights and liver for her to cook, and she went to a neighbour whose husband was very rich, and begged for the loan of a knife, she was refused it, and returned home greatly hurt and very angry. For want of a knife she was compelled to tear the raw flesh asunder with her teeth and nails, just as if she had become a *ghûleh*, for the *ghûls* do not know the use of iron. In her vexation she forgot to " name," and the Jân at once took advantage of the omission. A sudden whirlwind swept her off her feet and down through a crack in the floor. When at last the motion ceased, and she had recovered her senses sufficiently to look about her, she was in a large, well-furnished room, which seemed empty save for a handsome Persian cat.* Noticing that the creature was soon to have kittens she stroked her, saying, " The mention of Allah be upon you! Allah grant you full recovery! " The animal seemed to understand, and showed great pleasure by purring and rubbing up against her. Suddenly sounds were heard as of a crowd approaching, when the cat observed in Arabic, " Get under that chair and fear nothing." The visitor had just time to obey before a number of the Jân trooped in, sniffing the air and saying, " We smell the smell of a human being. If it is an old man, he is our father; if an old woman, she is our mother; if it is a young man or a young woman, he or she shall be our brother or sister; if a boy or girl, they also shall receive fraternal treatment. Show yourself and fear not, for we honour guests, and they are perfectly safe in our company."

On this the woman left her hiding-place, and greeted the new-comers, who used her kindly and set good food before her. After the lapse of a decent interval, she humbly begged to be sent home. The whirlwind which had brought her there, itself a jinni, was called and asked if she had come of her own free-will. The wind acknowledged that it had brought her against her will, because, in a moment of worry, she had not " named." " In that case she may go home again," said the leader of the Jân. But before she went he made her loosen the string of her *libás*, and filled that sack-like garment with onion-peels. Then the whirlwind caught her and she was at home again.

---

* For Moslem ideas about cats, see the chapter on animal folk-lore.

It suddenly struck her that the contents of her pantaloons were very heavy for mere onion-peels. She could not move for the weight of them, so made haste to take them out, when, to her amazement and delight, she found they were all gold pieces. Being a prudent woman, she said no word of her good fortune to the neighbours, but hid the money away till her husband came home, when she told him what had happened to her, and showed him the treasure. The couple kept their own counsel, and purchased cattle and land so gradually that their neighbours believed their prosperity to be the result of industry.

One person could not credit this, and that was the woman who had refused to lend the knife. Envy made her suspicious, and she gave her friend no peace till she had found out the secret. Having learnt it, she went straight home and made her husband bring the lights and liver of a sheep, which she tore to pieces with her teeth and nails, at the same time omitting to "name." The immediate result of her deliberate and studied action was the same as of her neighbour's inadvertence. A whirlwind whisked her down into the bowels of the earth, and she found herself in the room where sat the Persian cat. But her behaviour was the very opposite of that of the good woman. She abused the cat, and even dared to say she hoped it would not live to see its kittens. When from her hiding-place under the chair she heard the Jân assuring her of her safety, she rudely neglected to salute them when she came forth. Having devoured the food set before her with great greediness, she demanded to be sent home.

The Jân, who took no notice of her rudeness, then inquired of the whirlwind whether she had come of her own free-will. "Yes," was the answer. Then the chief of the Jân bade her loose her trousers, filled them with gold coins, and had her carried home. But when she got there, and had closed the doors and windows, she found her trousers full of spiders, scorpions and centipedes, which soon put at end to her wicked life.

Noticing that a native milkman, a fellâh from Siloam, was always in the habit of invoking the Name of Allah before measuring milk which he handed over to our servant every morning, I one day asked him why he did so. "Oh," said he, "it is always good to 'name,' and we fellahin always do so when we put our hands into a vessel or commence work of any kind." I said, " I quite agree with you that we ought always to ask God to bless us in anything we undertake, but, supposing you were to omit this precaution, what do you think would happen? " " We should most certainly fall into the power of the Jân," replied the man very earnestly, adding, " Ism illah hawwaleynah " (the Name of Allah be around us). " How? " I inquired; when, setting down his pitcher of milk, he told me the following story:—

The son of a great Arab sheykh, a most accomplished youth, was sent forth by his father to travel and see the world. One day, arriving at a certain city, he chose a site for his tent, and bade his servants pitch it while he went and strolled through the markets. He had never before been within the walls of a city, and was so much interested in what he saw that he spent more time than he had intended, and when he at last thought of returning to his camp it was night, and he could not find the way. Coming by chance upon a large open space, he resolved to sleep there till morning; so, wrapping himself in his 'abâyeh he lay down upon the bare ground, saying: " In the Name of Allah, the Merciful, the Compassionate, I place my confidence in Allah, and commend myself to the protection of the owner of this field."

Now the Jân were celebrating a wedding-feast that night, and invited the jinni of that particular field to the feast. He refused, saying that he had a guest and could not leave him. " Bring him too," said the merrymakers. " That is impossible," was the reply, " because he ' named ' as well. I am therefore responsible for his safety." " Well, this is what you can do," said the Jân. " The Sultan has a lovely daughter shut up in the castle. Take him to her in his sleep, and leave him with her while you come to the wedding. Before daybreak you can put him back again. So he will be quite happy, and no harm will befall him." The host was pleased with this suggestion and at once acted upon it. The youth awoke towards midnight to find himself lying in a luxurious bed by the side of a beautiful maiden, on whose sleeping form the tapers in tall golden candlesticks shed a subdued light. He was lost in wonder and delight, when her eyes opened on him; and he saw the like rapture dawn in them. They held loving converse, exchanged their seal-rings, and then sank back to sleep. When the youth awoke the second time, to find himself on a piece of waste land near the wall of the city, he was at first inclined to regard his night adventure as a blissful dream; but when he saw on his finger the signet-ring which his lady had placed there he had no doubt of the reality of that strange experience, and made up his mind to not leave the city until he had solved the mystery.

The princess was equally astonished, when she awoke, to find only a ring to confirm her recollections of the night. In time she became with child; but the Sultan, her father, being passionately fond of her, could not make up his mind to kill her,[3] as was his duty, since she had no brothers. Her strange story, and the sight of the signet-ring which her unknown lover had given her, made him resolve to spare her life; for he knew the power and malice of the Jân, and saw their hand in the matter. So when his daughter had been safely delivered of a son, he sent her and the child into exile without other attendants than one aged nurse.

Now the town to which she was sent happened to be the same in which her lover still dwelt in the hope of obtaining news of her. She abode there in obscurity, devoting herself to the child, who would let no one but his mother carry him, and cried whenever anyone else tried to take him out. One day when she was tired of fondling him she told her female attendant to take him out of doors in spite of his crying. Whilst obeying these orders the woman chanced to pass a place where the young Bedawi was sitting listlessly. Something in the child's crying touched his heart, and he asked the woman to let him take the little man. The moment the transfer was made the child stopped crying as if by magic and began to laugh, which so pleased the unconscious father that, before handing him back to the nurse, he bought him loads of sweetmeats from a passing vendor.

The woman, going back to her mistress, extolled the beauty and goodness of the youth who had quieted the baby for her. A hope at once flashed upon the mother's mind. She commanded the nurse to take her to that young man.

The couple, meeting, knew one another, and the signet-rings confirmed their intuitions. They were married forthwith, and with the Sultan's favour; and it is said that they lived happily ever after.

When the milkman had finished his story, I said, " Would

[3] See p. 264.

it not have been better for the young man to have invoked
the Name of Allah without putting himself under the protection of the jinni? Had he trusted in Allah alone, all
this would not have happened." "No," was the answer,
"Allah only does good. Had he omitted to claim protection
from the owner of the field, the jinni would have hurt him,
if not carried him off while he slept. By claiming hospitality
he prevented anything of that sort, and so nothing but good
resulted to him."

A fellâhan of El Welejeh * lost an eye a few years ago
under the following circumstances, related by another fellâhan.

She was returning from Jerusalem, and as she was passing
the fountain named " Ain El Haniyeh," she heard a frog
croak. Looking round she noticed close to the stream a
female frog much advanced in pregnancy, and she thoughtlessly but ill-naturedly said to the creature, " Allah grant
that you may not be delivered of your child till I be called
to act as your midwife." Having uttered this unkind speech,
the woman went her way. In the evening she retired to rest
with her children, whose father had died in the war, around
her; but what was her terror when, awaking during the
night, she found herself in a cave surrounded by strange and
angry-looking people, one of whom sternly told her that
if she ventured to " name " she was a dead woman. " If
we who live below," said he, " come to you who live above-
ground, then it is a protection for you to ' name '; but if,
as in your case, one of you intrudes needlessly and officiously
on us, ' naming ' will not help you. What harm had my
wife done you that you should curse her as you did this
afternoon?" " I do not know, nor have I ever seen your
wife," replied the woman in terror. " She was the pregnant frog you spoke to at Ain El Haniyeh," was the answer.
" When we who live underground want to go abroad by
day-time we generally assume the form of some animal.
My wife took that of the frog you saw. You cursed her
and mentioned the ' Name.' She was in the pangs of labour

* A village about nine miles S.W. of Jerusalem, and on the
Jerusalem–Jaffa railway line.

but, in consequence of your cruel malediction, cannot be relieved till you assist her. I warn you, therefore, that unless she give birth to a boy, it will go hard with you." He then led her to where his wife lay, with females round her. The woman from El Welejeh, though almost frightened out of her wits, did her best for the uncanny patient, who soon gave birth to a fine boy. When the father was informed of the happy event he handed the human midwife a *mukhaleh* or kohl-vessel and told her to apply some of its contents to the infant's eyes, in order that they might become dark and bright. When doing this she noticed that the baby's eyes, like those of the other Jân around her, differed from those of ordinary men and women, in that the pupil was longitudinal and vertical. When she had applied the kohl to the little one's eyes, she took the bodkin which she had used and put some kohl to one of her own eyes, but before she had time to put kohl to the other the female Jân, who noticed what she was doing, angrily snatched the *mukhaleh* from her. They then bade her loosen one of her long flowing sleeves, in which, like other Syrian peasant-women, she was wont to carry things, and filled it with something, though she did not know what. They next blindfolded her and led her out of the cave. When they told her she might uncover her eyes, she, on looking around her, found herself standing alone at Ain El Haniyeh. Being curious to know what was in her sleeve she opened it and found a quantity of onion-peels, which she promptly threw away. A few minutes later she reached her home, where she found her children still asleep. As she was preparing to lie down, something fell out of her sleeve. She picked it up and found it was a piece of gold. Realising the true nature of the supposed onion-peels she had thrown away, she at once hurried back to the fountain, and sure enough found the onion-peels lying untouched, but all of them turned into gold pieces. Gathering them up eagerly she returned home, and as there were still some hours till daylight, lay down and went to sleep. On awaking next morning, she thought that she must have dreamt all that had been narrated. When, however, one of her children told her that one of her eyes had kohl in it and the other not; and, above all, when she saw her store of gold coins, she was convinced that she had not been dreaming but was now a wealthy woman.

Some time afterwards she went to El Kûds to *howij*, *i.e.* to do some shopping. As she was standing close to the draper's shop—you know the Jewish draper whose shop is just in front of the wheat-bazaar—she saw the being whom she had assisted in her confinement, mingling with the crowd and pilfering as she went from shop to shop. The woman from El Welejeh went up to her, and, touching her shoulder, asked her why she did so. Being frightened by the jinnìyeh's angry look, she stooped and kissed the baby. The people who stood by thought her mad when, as they supposed, they saw her kissing the air, for, as they had not the Jân's kohl applied to their eyes, they were unable to see what was going on. The jinnìyen, however, said angrily, " What! are you going to disgrace us? " and straightway poking a finger into the poor woman's eye—the eye which had the kohl in it—she blinded it on the spot. What misfortune might have happened had she applied Jân's kohl to both eyes, Allah only knows; but this seems certain, namely, that by reason of their having such curiously-formed eyes, the Jân can see and know many things which ordinary mortals cannot; and their kohl helps them to a sort of second-sight which we do not possess. You very rarely meet people with such eyes. There is perhaps scarcely one in ten thousand, but that one sees and can do things which other people cannot, and therefore the Mûghâribeh (Arabs of North Africa), who by the powers of magic know where hidden treasure may be found, are always on the look-out for such persons, in hopes of obtaining their assistance.

A mason, nearly related to one of my neighbours, rose very early one morning to go to his work. As the full moon was shining he did not realise how early it was. Going along, he was overtaken by a wedding procession, all bearing torches, the women uttering their *zaghari̇t*. As they were going the same way, he kept up with them out of curiosity, noticing only that the men looked grim and fierce. One of the women gave him a lighted taper, which he accepted. He now realised the true character of these people whom he had taken for Circassians; but, having the presence of mind instantly to invoke the aid of Allah and all the saints (he is a member of the Orthodox Greek Church), his dread companions vanished; and he found himself alone in the street with a donkey's leg-bone in his hand. Terribly frightened, he went straight home and was very ill for a long while afterwards.[4]

4 See p. 264.

VII

ALLAH had given a certain woman seven sons, and she was
very thankful for them, but for all that she longed to have a
daughter and asked Allah to let her have one. One day,
as she was passing through the market, she saw some fair
white goat's-milk cheese exposed for sale; and the sight so
moved her that she exclaimed, " O my Lord! O Allah!
give me, I entreat, a daughter as white and lovely as this
cheese, and I will call her ' Ijbeyneh.' " † Her prayer was
heard, and in due time she became the mother of a beautiful
girl with a complexion like goat's-milk cheese, the neck of a
gazelle, blue eyes, black hair, and a rose on either cheek.
The child was named " Ijbeyneh," and everyone who saw
her loved her, with the exception of her cousins, who were
very jealous.

When Ijbeyneh was about seven years old, these cousins,
at her own request, took her with them on an excursion
into the forest,‡ where they were in the habit of going in
order to pick the fruit of the Za'rûr.§ The child, having
filled her square linen head-veil (tarbî'ah) with the berries,
laid it at the foot of a tree and wandered picking flowers.
When she returned to the place where she had left her head-
veil, she found bad berries instead of the beauties she had
gathered, and her cousins gone. She wandered hither and
thither through the hìsh calling to them, but received no
answer. She tried to find her way home, but went further

* Tales told by a Christian (Roman Catholic) female of Bethlehem.
The story of Khûneyfseh, which properly falls under this heading,
was told in the foregoing chapter in connection with the Jân, as illus-
trating some of the ideas in vogue concerning them.
† The diminutive for jibn = cheese.
‡ The hìsh, thick brushwood, is dignified with that name in Palestine.
§ Crategus Azarolus; the berries are edible and make a delicious
jelly.

astray. At last a *ghûl*, out hunting, came up and would have devoured her, but Ijbeyneh being Allah's gift to her parents, and so protected, instead of eating her up the monster pitied her. She cried, " O my uncle: tell me which way my cousins have gone." He answered, " I do not know, O beloved, but come and live with me until your cousins come back and seek you." Ijbeyneh consenting, he took her to his house on the top of a high mountain. There she became his shepherdess, and he grew very fond of her, and daily brought choice game for her to eat. For all that she was most unhappy, weeping often for her home and parents. Now the doves belonging to her parents, which she had been used to feed, missed Ijbeyneh very much, and made search for her upon their own account. One day they espied her afar off, and came to her, showing their joy by settling on her shoulders and nestling to her cheeks, as they had been used to do. And when Ijbeyneh saw them she wept tears of joy and said to them :

> " O ye doves of my mother and father,
> O greet ye my mother and father,
> Tell them that Ijbeyneh, the dear one,
> Tends sheep upon the high mountain." *

Ijbeyneh's naughty cousins had gone home and reported her as lost, without saying that they had purposely deserted her. Her father and her brothers sought everywhere; her mother wept herself almost blind, exclaiming that Allah had punished her for not being content with seven sons; and it was noticed that the very doves seemed mournful and did not coo as of old. One day, however, the behaviour of the birds changed suddenly. From mournful they became lively and seemed anxious to make their owners understand something. Their dumb efforts were apparent to the neighbours, one of whom suggested that the parents of Ijbeyneh should try and discover which way the birds went every day, and follow them. The father, the brothers, and a number of sympathisers set out on the quest. They found

---

* " Ya Hammâm ummi wa abi,
  Sallimû 'ala ummi wa abi,
  Kûlû an Ijbeyneh el ghâlieh
  Ibtir'a ghanam fi el Jebel el 'alien."

that the doves flew straight to the summit of a certain mountain and there settled. Climbing forthwith, they found the missing girl, who was full of joy to see them. They then took all the goods, cattle, poultry, and everything else belonging to the *ghûl*, who was out hunting, and returned. When the *ghûl* came home to find Ijbeyneh gone and his house looted, he burst asunder from grief and died. But when Ijbeyneh had told her story and it was known that her cousins had taken away her berries and left her alone in the wilderness, people were furious. A crier was sent through the district, crying, " Let everyone who loves justice bring a fiery ember! " So a great fire was made, and the wicked little girls were burnt to ashes as they deserved. But Ijbeyneh grew up and eventually the son of the Sultan saw and married her.

There once was a clever man named Uhdey-dûn [1] who lived in a strong castle * on the top of a steep rock. He was at enmity with a dreadful *ghûleh*, who devastated the country and lived with her three daughters in a gloomy cave in a wady near the desert. In those days fire-arms were unknown, and so Uhdey-dûn could not shoot either the ghûleh or her children, but he had a sharp hatchet and a long packing-needle † as well as other things. The ghûleh had nothing but a copper cauldron in which she cooked the food for herself and her children. But they very often did not take the trouble to cook, and ate their food raw. As they had no knife, they used to tear the flesh with their teeth, and break the bones by hammering them with a stone.

However, the ghûleh had one advantage over her adversary in this respect, that she could change her form at will.

Well, one day the ghûleh came in the guise of an old woman to the foot of the rock on which Uhdey-dûn's house stood, and called out: " O Uhdey-dûn, my uncle, won't you accompany me to the forest ‡ to-morrow that we may get some wood? " Now Uhdey-dûn was sharp and he knew

* Or palace; Ar. *kusr*. † Ar. *umsulleh*.
‡ [Ar. *hìsh.* In Syria, a kind of brushwood, like the " maquis " of Corsica, is so named.—M. P.]
[1] See p. 265.

that if the ghûleh got hold of him all alone she would kill and eat him. So, not to offend her, he answered, " Do not take the trouble to come here for me, for I will meet you in the forest to-morrow morning." Next morning, very early, Uhdey-dûn, who knew of a very short way to the forest, took his hatchet and long needle and a sack and went there. He was there long before the ghûleh reached the spot, and he at once cut down a great deal of wood and filled his sack, leaving a hollow place in the middle into which he crawled. He then tied up the sack and remained perfectly quiet till the ghûleh appeared. How he managed to tie up the sack when he was inside it I do not know, but he was a clever man. In time the ghûleh came, and when she saw the sack and smelt Uhdey-dûn, she looked about for him, but could not find him. At last, tired of hunting for him, she said, " I shall carry this sackful of wood to my cave, and then come back to kill my enemy." So she lifted the sack and put it on her back. As soon as she had gone a few steps, Uhdey-dûn gave her a stab with his long needle. The ghûleh thought it must have been the end of a piece of wood that had hurt her, and she therefore moved the sack into a different position. As soon as she started off again with her burden, Uhdey-dûn gave her another dig with his needle, and so on till, by the time she had reached her cave, she was bleeding from countless wounds. " Mother! " cried her daughters, when she appeared, " have you brought us Uhdey-dûn for dinner as you promised? " " I did not find him, my dears," replied the mother, " but I have brought his sackful of wood, and I am now going back to find him and kill him for our dinner." She put down her load, placed a cauldron filled with water on the fire, and departed. As soon as Uhdey-dûn thought she was beyond recall, he began to make a noise like somebody chewing gum, and said quite aloud, " I've got chewing-gum, I've got chewing-gum! " " Who are you? " asked the ghûleh's daughters. " I am Uhdey-dûn, and I've got chewing-gum." " Oh, please give us some," begged the little ghûlehs. " Open the sack and let me out," said Uhdey-dûn. The little ghûlehs did as he wished, but when he got out he took his hatchet and killed all three of them and cut them to pieces and put them into the great copper cauldron which had been placed on the fire full of water for Uhdey-dûn. Their heads he hid under a *tabak* or straw tray. Then he left the cave and went to his home on the great rock.

In the meantime the ghûleh sought Uhdey-dûn in the forest, but in vain. She returned to her cave, and not finding her little ones, but noticing the scent of Uhdey-dûn, and also of cooked meat, she said, " Oh, I am sure that my enemy has been here and my darlings have killed him and put him into the copper to be cooked, and now they are gone in order to invite their cousins to the feast. However, as I am hungry, I shall take some out of the cauldron and eat it." She did so and was rather surprised to find the flesh so tender. She did not suspect that she was feeding on her own offspring. When she was satisfied, she began to look around her, and noticed that some blood was trickling from under the straw tray. So she lifted it up and to her consternation found the heads of her three daughters. In grief and despair she began to bite the flesh off her own arms, and swore to revenge herself on her crafty foe. Now some days later Uhdey-dûn was invited to the wedding of his cousin, and as he was sure the ghûleh would try to kill him on that occasion, he kept sharp watch from the corner whence he could see all comers, himself unnoticed. After some time he saw a great, fierce-looking bitch approach and prowl about the house, and observed how the other dogs slunk away from her. He knew her for the monster that was seeking his life. The wedding meal, which, as usual, consisted of pieces of meat cooked with rice, was served, and Uhdey-dûn sat down to eat. He took a large bone, and having eaten the meat off it, went to the house door and called the dogs. The ghûleh ran towards him and he threw the bone at her with so true an aim that it hit her on the forehead and cut it so that the blood began to flow down her face. As it did so, she licked it with her tongue, saying " Oh, how sweet is the dibs * in my uncle's

* Grape syrup or molasses.

house!" "Ah!" said Uhdey-dûn, as he brandished his hatchet, "do you think that I can't see through your disguise? It was I who destroyed your children, I who poked you with my needle while you carried that sack of wood, and I'll kill you yet. Come near me if you dare!" Now the *ghìlan* (plural of *ghûl*) are afraid of iron and so, when the ghûleh saw that her enemy was armed and on the alert, she slunk away disappointed.

Some days later she thought of a device to tempt him to expose himself unarmed. In the form of a peasant woman she came to the foot of his rock, and called up to him for the loan of a sieve. "Come up and fetch it," said Uhdey-dûn. "I cannot climb the rock," replied the ghûleh. "I will lower a rope for you," said Uhdey-dûn. He did so, but noticing that his visitor was coming up with unusual skill, he observed her more closely and recognised her. He therefore let the rope go, and so the monster fell down the precipice and was dashed to bits. This was the way in which Uhdey-dûn delivered the country from the ghûleh and her brood.

There was once a poor wood-cutter,* who had a wife and three daughters dependent on him. One day, while he was working in the forest, a stranger passed that way and stopped to talk with him. Hearing he had three daughters the stranger persuaded him to let him have the eldest girl in marriage for a large sum of money paid in advance.

When the wood-cutter went home at dusk, he boasted of the bargain to his wife, and next morning took the girl to a certain cave and there gave her over to the stranger, who said his name was Abu Freywar. As soon as the woodman was gone, Abu Freywar said to her, "You must be hungry, eat these." So saying, he took a knife and cut off both his ears, which he gave her together with a nasty-looking loaf of black bread. The girl refusing such food, he hung her up by the hair from the ceiling of a chamber in the cave, which had meanwhile become a magnificent palace. Next day,

---

* Tale told by a Turkish (Moslem) girl. This story seems to be a version of Bluebeard.

Abu Freywar went again to the forest and found the wood-cutter. "I want your second daughter for my brother," he said. "Here is the money. Bring her to the cave to-morrow." The wood-cutter, delighted at his great good fortune, brought his second daughter to Abu Freywar, and directly he had gone, Abu Freywar gave the girl his ears, which had grown afresh, to eat. She said she was not hungry just then, but would keep them to eat by and by. When he went out of the room she tried to deceive him by hiding his ears under a carpet on the floor. When he returned and asked if she had eaten them, she said "Yes," but he called out, "Ears of mine, are you hot or cold?" and they answered promptly, "Cold as ice, and lying under the carpet." Whereupon Abu Freywar in a rage hung her up beside her sister.

He then went and asked for the youngest daughter whose name was Zerendac, saying that he wanted her for another brother. But the girl, a spoilt child, refused to go unless she might take with her a pet kitten and a box in which she kept her treasures. Hugging those, she went with Abu Freywar to the cave.

She proved wiser than her sisters. When her husband's back was turned, she gave his ears to the cat, which devoured them eagerly, while she ate some food which she had brought from home. When the ogre returned and cried as of wont, "Ears of mine, are you hot or cold?" he received the answer, "As hot as can be in this snug little stomach," and this pleased him so that from that time he began to grow very fond of Zerendac.

After she had lived some days with him, he said, "I must go on a journey. There are forty rooms in this palace. Here are the keys with which you may open any door you please except that to which this golden key belongs," and with that he took his departure. Zerendac amused herself in his absence with opening and examining the locked-up rooms. On entering the thirty-ninth, she happened to look out of the window, which opened on to a burial-ground, and was terrified to see her husband, who was a *ghûl*, devouring a corpse that he had just dug out of a grave with his long claw-like nails. She was so fascinated with the sight that (hidden behind the window curtain) she watched him at his horrible repast. A few minutes later she saw him start and hide himself behind a monument in the cemetery. He had been disturbed by the approach of a funeral. As the procession approached, she heard one of the bearers say, " Let us be off as soon as possible, lest the *ghûl* which haunts this place get hold of us," and she could see that the whole company seemed very anxious.

This discovery caused the girl great uneasiness. She was anxious to know what was in the fortieth room, and the discovery she had made as to the real character of her husband prompted her to solve the mystery at any cost. She took the golden key and opened the door. She found her two sisters still alive and dangling from the ceiling by their hair. She cut them down, fed them, and as soon as their health was restored, sent them back to her parents.

Abu Freywar returned next day, but not for long. He left home a few days later, telling his wife she might invite any of her relations whom she cared to see. Accordingly, she invited many of her friends and relatives, who came to see her, but heard nothing of her troubles. It was well for her that she did not complain, for her visitors were not the persons they seemed to be, but simply her husband in various shapes assumed in order to entrap her. He succeeded at last in the form of her grandmother, to whom she was beginning to tell all her sorrows, when the old woman became Abu Freywar and, taking a poisoned nail, drove it into her breast. The wound did not kill her, but it caused her to swoon away. No sooner was she unconscious than the monster put her into a chest and sank it in the sea.

Now the son of the Sultan of that land was fond of boating and fishing, and this prince happened to cast a large net from a boat close to the place where the chest in which she was lay at the bottom of the sea. The net, happening to enclose the chest, was hauled in with the greatest difficulty. The Sultan's son had it drawn into the boat, and, before opening it, said to his attendants, " If it contains money or jewels, you may have them all; but should it contain anything else, it is mine."

He was greatly shocked when he saw its actual contents, and mourned the sad fate of that lovely girl. He had her body carried to his mother's chamber, to be honourably prepared for burial. During the process,* Zerendac sneezed and came to life again, as soon as the nail was removed.

She married the prince, and in course of time bore him a daughter. But one day, when she was alone with the child, the wall of her room suddenly split open and Abu Freywar appeared. Without a word to the mother, he snatched up the infant and swallowed it, disappearing as suddenly as he had come. Zerendac was so bewildered by this fresh misfortune that, when asked where the baby had gone, she could only weep despairingly.

Her second child, a son, and the third, another daughter, were torn from her in the same horrible manner. On this last occasion, the cruel ogre smeared the poor mother's face with her child's blood. She washed it off, but in her hurry and anguish missed a slight stain beneath her lip. Her husband and her mother-in-law, already very suspicious, judged, of course, that she was a ghûleh and had devoured her offspring.

Zerendac told her story, but no one would believe it. Her husband, being loth to put her to death, ordered her to be imprisoned in a small underground chamber, and, at his mother's suggestion, sought another bride. Hearing of the beauty of the daughter of a neighbouring Sultan, he went to ask for her. But before setting out he sent for the mother of his lost children, and asked her what she would like him to bring her when he came back. She asked for a box of aloes,† for a box of henna,‡ and a dagger. Her request was granted, and when the prince returned from the betrothal to the Sultan's daughter, he brought with him these things for Zerendac. She opened the boxes, one by one,

---

* Described in one of the Karakash stories.
† Ar. *sebr*, also meaning " patience."
‡ The same word means " tenderness."

saying, " O box of *sebr*, you have not in you more patience than I have shown. O box of henna, you cannot be gentler than I have been," and was just going to stab herself with the dagger, when the wall of her prison opened and Abu Freywar appeared, leading a handsome boy and two lovely girls. " Live! " he cried; " I have not killed your children. Here they are." He then by his magic made a secret staircase connecting her dungeon with the great hall of the palace. Having done this he seized the dagger and slew himself.

When the festivities in connection with the prince's marriage began, Zerendac sent the three children, richly dressed in clothes which Abu Freywar had left with her, up the staircase, telling them to amuse themselves without respect for the guests or the furniture. Accordingly, they did all the damage they could think of; but the mother of the prince was slow to punish them, because they were pretty and reminded her of her son at their age. But at last, losing patience, she was going to strike one of them when they all shouted at once, " Ya sitt Ubdûr, shûfi keyf el kamr btadûr," which means, " O Lady Full-Moon, look how the moon is turning round." Everyone rushed to the window, and while their backs were turned the children vanished.

On the actual wedding-day the children appeared again when their father was present, ran about, breaking china and glass, and did all the damage they could think of. The prince forbade them. They replied haughtily, " This is our house, and everything here belongs to us and to our parents." " What do you mean by that? " inquired the prince. The children answered by leading their father down the secret staircase to Zerendac, who explained who they really were and how they came there. The prince, greatly moved, embraced her tenderly and swore to be true to her till his life's end. The Sultan's daughter was returned, with excuses and a satisfactory present, to her father; and the prince and Zerendac lived happily ever after.

One snowy day, a woman who had just given birth to a girl named her " Thaljìyeh " (" Snow-Maiden "), and straightway expired.* The motherless babe was tended by her grandmother, who kept her father's house, till she could walk about and play with other children. But then Thaljìyeh's father took to wife a widow with two daughters, and her grandmother left the house in disgust. The new wife made her step-daughter a household drudge. Thaljìyeh had to carry jars of water on her head from the distant spring. She had to rise at midnight to help grind the corn for next day's bread and when she was old and strong enough to do this by herself, her stepmother and sisters lay abed till sunrise. It was also her duty to go out with other girls and gather fuel, brushwood, thorny burnet, or dried cows' dung from the hillsides, then to heat the village oven † and knead and bake bread; and when, as rarely happened, there was nothing to do at home, she was sent out to gather potsherds to be crushed into *hamra* for cistern cement. Whenever there was a wedding or other merry-making, she was not allowed to go, though she sat up late the night before, embroidering many-coloured breast-pieces ‡ to deck the festal gowns, of her unkind relatives. But Allah had given Thaljìyeh a sweet nature. She found comfort in singing at her work, and was always ready to help others at theirs. But to see her thus cheerful did not please her stepmother and the daughters of the latter, whose own voices were as harsh and unmelodious as those of screech-owls; and they forbade her to sing in the house.

One day when the rest of the family had gone to a wedding, Thaljìyeh was left alone in charge of the vineyard tower, for it was summer-time. Just outside the vineyard gate, by the roadside, there was a cistern for rain-water, from which she was wont to draw water for the house and to fill the drinking trough § for thirsty wayfarers. On this day Thaljìyeh had lowered her bucket into the cistern when the rope broke and the vessel sank to the bottom and was lost. She was obliged to go to a neighbour and borrow a well drag.¶ Having

* Tale told by the Roman Catholic female servant from Bethlehem.
† Ar. *tabûn.*   ‡ Ar. *kubbeh.*   § Ar. *sebîl.*
¶ Ar. *khuttâfeh.* This instrument consists of a flat iron ring from which iron hooks hang by short chains attached to its circumference.

obtained one, Thaljìyeh tied it to a rope, and having said
*dustûr,** to warn any spirits that might be in the cistern to get
out of the way, she lowered the drag while she sang :

" O well drag! gather, gather,
And all that you find sweep up, sweep up." †

Now, though she did not know it, these words were a spell,
and as there happened to be a jinnìyeh in the cistern who
liked Thaljìyeh, the latter immediately felt the drag catch
hold of something heavy, and when she drew it up there was
her bucket full of the most lovely jewellery—rings, massive
gold bracelets, anklets, chains for tying the headdress round
the neck,‡ and gold chains for the head-tie. Full of joy at
her good fortune, the girl took the pretty things into the
tower, and when her relations came home she gave them
into their keeping. They, however, pretended not to want
them, and, having been told how Thaljìyeh had come by
them, said they would get some for themselves. They
therefore each in turn dropped the bucket into the cistern,
and in loud arrogant tones of command uttered the words of
the spell which Thaljìyeh had sung so sweetly. Try as they
would, they always brought up the bucket full of mud,
stones and loathsome crawling things. So, in their disappointment, they took Thaljìyeh's jewels, continued to
treat her with great unkindness, and one evening, after
her father's death, actually turned her out of doors.

It was raining, and the poor girl did not want to spoil
her pretty shoes made of red Damascus leather, which had
been her dead father's gift. She tied them together and
threw them over her shoulder, one hanging in front of and
the other behind her.§ It was now dark, and Thaljìyeh
knew not where to go. Seeing a light glimmering from the

The whole is suspended from a ring in the centre of the two curved
cross-bars fastened over the flat ring.

* Lit. permission = By your leave.

†   " Ya khuttâfeh, hûshi, hûshi,
           Shû ma lakeyti, kûshi, kûshi."

‡ Ar. *Iznâk.*

§ As the fellahìn in Palestine always do whenever it is raining, and
they go barefoot in order to save their shoes.

open door of a cave-dwelling, she went towards it, hoping to obtain shelter for the night. Seated at the door of that humble abode was an old woman spinning. It happened to be Thaljìyeh's grandmother, though the girl did not know her, she had been so young when her father married the widow. The old woman, however, recognised her grand-child and gladly granted her request for a night's lodging. " Your mother's daughter," she said, " should not be out of doors at this time of night, so, of course, you may stay here. My own daughter died at the time you were born, and if you like it you shall take her place in my dwelling." She then set the best food she had before her guest, who gladly agreed to remain with the old woman when the latter disclosed their relationship.

It so happened that one of Thaljìyeh's shoes had been lost on her way to the old woman's cave. The string with which the pair were tied had given way, and the shoe which was hanging behind her shoulder had fallen off, while its fellow, by a curious chance, caught on a knot or hook which was on her gown, so that it was not till she had found shelter with her grandmother that she discovered her loss. It was then too late for her to go and look for the missing shoe, but she meant to do so the first thing in the morning.

Now the old woman was spinning woollen thread to make an 'abâyeh for the son of a wealthy sheykh. The young man was very handsome, and many a mother, including Thal-jìyeh's unkind stepmother, had been plotting and planning, quite unsuccessfully, to obtain him for a son-in-law. Whilst Thaljìyeh was having her supper, he approached the cave-dwelling, having, as it happened, noticed and picked up the girl's shoe on his way. Hearing a man's step, the girl sprang up hastily and hid herself in a dark corner of the cave, where she could see and hear without herself being seen. " My aunt," said the youth, addressing the old woman, " have you got all the thread spun ready for my new 'abâyeh? " " I shall have it finished by to-morrow at noon," answered the old woman; " but what have you got in your hand? " " It is a girl's shoe which I have just picked up," answered the youth, " and it is so small and pretty that its owner must be a

very pretty maiden, and therefore—Wallahi! Wallahi!
Wallahi!—I shall search for her, and when I have found her,
she, and no other, shall become my wife." The old woman
was pleased with this impetuous speech; but, being wise,
she said nothing to the young man, but laughingly bade him
meet her at the dyer's next day.

Next morning, having finished her task, the old woman
left Thaljìyen alone in the cave, having enjoined her to
keep the door closed and not to answer the young man,
should he, as she suspected he would, come again to ask if
the thread was all ready. Things fell out as Thaljìyeh's
grandmother thought they would. The young man, who
had thought she was putting him off with the promise that
the thread would be ready that day, came to the cave
instead of going to meet her at the dyer's shop. He found
the door closed, and received no answer when he called to
the old woman to ask whether her work for him was done.
Hearing Thaljìyeh singing as she turned the spinning-wheel,
he peeped through a crack in the door in order to see who
it was that sung so sweetly; and finding that the maiden
was alone, he went away, sorry for his rash vow of the
previous evening, to the dyer's, where he found the grandmother. She handed him the thread, and when he asked
her who was the maiden singing in the cave, she answered,
"Your bride." "What do you mean?" replied he in
surprise. "It is the girl to whom the shoe which you picked
up last night belongs, and whom you swore thrice by Allah
that you would marry," said the old woman. The youth was
delighted. His father made no objection to the marriage,
seeing that Thaljìyeh was of good family. By the kindness
of the jinnìyeh in the cistern, all the jewellery belonging to
the bride was found one morning at the head of her bed in
her grandmother's cave; and the cruel stepmother and her
daughters had the bitterness of listening to the *Zaghárìt* *
and the shouting as the veiled bride, the beautiful Snow-

* [Cries of joy by the bride's female friends; properly zalâghit
(sing. zal'ghateh, zarghateh or zaghrateh). The zaghrateh is a very
shrill fluttering sound peculiar to Eastern women, made by rapid
revolution of the tongue in the mouth.—M. P.]

maiden, whom they had so despised and ill-treated, seated upon the bridal camel, was led in joyful procession to her husband's house.

It is not likely that any reader will fail to recognise in this tale a local version of " Cinderella."

VIII

SATIRE

On the mountain-top above a Mohammedan village stood a wely or saint's tomb, of which the guardian was one Sheykh Abdullah, a genial old man and well-beloved in the neighbourhood. Accompanied by an orphan boy named Ali, his disciple, and mounted on an ass which he had brought up ever since it was a foal, he used to ride from village to village, prescribing for the sick, and selling amulets and charms written by himself, which were warranted to preserve their wearers from the evil eye and other strange adversities. He would also draw up horoscopes, and discover secrets in the magic mirror [1] of ink or by the sand table.*

When Ali was grown up, the old man said to him: " My son, I have taught you all I know. There are few khatìbs † with half your learning. All you have now to do is to become a Haji by pilgrimage to the Holy Places. Then, in sh'Allah, you will find it easy to obtain a post, like mine, of honourable ease. As a derwìsh, you need no money. Take my old 'abâyeh, this mahajaneh [2] and the ass to ride on, and start to-morrow with the other pilgrims."

Ali, though reluctant to leave his adopted father, followed the sheykh's advice, and, having obtained his blessing, set out next day. By the mercy of Allah he journeyed in safety for many months, till on a day he found himself in a barren plain, with a hot wind blowing, far from any well or human habitation. He was walking to save his donkey's failing strength, when suddenly the poor beast stopped, rubbed its

---

* For an account of " Land divination " see No. 2 of *The Moslem World*, Vol. XVII, April 1927, pp. 123–29.
  † The *khatìb* is the Moslem village preacher and schoolmaster.
  [1] See p. 265. [2] See p. 265.

nose against his arm, and died. He could not bear to leave the body of so old a friend to the vultures and hyænas, so he set to work to dig a grave. This was no easy task, yet he performed it before sunset, and prepared to sleep beside the mound thus raised. All at once he heard the sound of horses galloping, and looking up beheld a troop of riders. He could hear their leader call to his companions, " Look! there is a holy derwìsh mourning on a newly-made grave. Death has overtaken the companion of his travels, and he has piously buried him in this lonely spot. How sad to die in so forlorn a place, where one cannot find even water to wash a corpse! I must go and speak to him." So saying he galloped up, and, saluting, asked the name of the departed. " 'Eyr," replied Ali, using a poetical and uncommon word for " ass." " Ah! poor Sheykh ' 'Eyr,' " sighed the tender-hearted chief. " The ways of Allah are most mysterious. Do not, however, let this death deject you. His memory at least shall live. To-morrow morning I shall send men to build a splendid shrine over his grave "; and, ere Ali had time to explain matters, the impulsive nobleman galloped off with his men.

Ali could not sleep that night for thinking of his strange predicament. Next morning, soon after sunrise, he descried moving dots on the horizon, which presently resolved themselves into camels laden with lime and donkeys carrying cut stone, driven by a company of masons and builders who had received orders to build at once the *makâm* of Sheykh 'Eyr. Ali could only watch the work, which was begun without delay. First of all they built a cenotaph over the grave and enclosed it in a room of the right shape and size. Then they made an open hall * with a prayer-niche,† to mark the *kibleh*. On the side of the hall opposite the tomb-chamber, a second room was erected for the accommodation of the guardian of the shrine. Last of all they built a little minaret, dug a well, and surrounded the whole with an enclosure-wall, thus forming a large courtyard with cloisters along its four sides. All this work took time, but Ali, having heard from the Emìr that he was to be sheykh of the shrine with a

---

* *Iwân.*   † *Mihrab.*

good stipend, patiently watched its completion and entered with content upon his new duties.

Placed at a convenient halting-place for travellers who had to cross the desert, the new shrine soon grew famous, and was visited by hordes of pilgrims yearly. Presents were showered upon its sheykh, who began to show his wealth in dress and bearing.

News of this new popular shrine came at last to the ears of the old Sheykh Abdullah, who had visited most holy places in his youthful travels, but could not remember even to have heard of this one. Out of curiosity, he determined to make the pilgrimage to Sheykh 'Eyr and find out for himself its origin and history. On the last day of its season of pilgrimage,* ³ he reached the *makâm* and was astonished at the endless crowd of pilgrims. In the guardian of the shrine he was still more surprised to recognise his pupil Ali. The pair embraced one another with cries of joy, and went into Ali's house to feast together. After supper Sheykh Abdullah fixed his gaze on Ali and said solemnly, " My son, I adjure you by the saints, the prophets, and all we Muslimìn consider holy, to hide nothing from me. What is it that is buried in this place? " The young man told his story without reserve, and, when it was finished, said, " Now, father, tell me what saint lies buried at your shrine at home? " The old man looked down shamefacedly, but, pressed by Ali, whispered, " Well, if you must know, he is the father of your donkey."

There once lived at Jerusalem a pious old widow named Hanneh, who belonged to the Orthodox Eastern Church.†
She was poor, yet dispensed wide charity, and she had the love of all who knew her. There was only one person in the world for whose faults she could see no excuses, and that was the Patriarch, an exemplary if somewhat humorous prelate. Years ago she had been nurse in the family where he, an only child, lively and spoilt, had made her life a

* *Maûsam.*
† Tale told by the late Asaad El Jamal, an Arab Protestant.
³ See p. 265.

burden with his tricks; and she could not be rid of the notion that he played tricks still. In his childhood she had no doubt but that he would come to grief; but at school, instead of being punished and expelled, as she expected him to be, he acquired some fame for diligence, and was a favourite both with boys and masters. " Ah," she thought to herself, " some day they will find out their mistake! "

His school days ended, he was ordained deacon; at which Hanneh * shook her head more solemnly, and said in her heart, " Alas! our pastors must have been struck with spiritual blindness to admit that scamp into holy orders." Her astonishment and horror grew when, as time passed, he became a priest, an archimandrite, a bishop, and at last ascended the patriarchal throne. She felt bitterly the humiliation, when she met him in the street, of having to bend and kiss his hand, although she could see in his eye that mischievous twinkle which she had learnt to associate with his tricks. However, she said to herself, " Here on earth, naturally, mistakes are made, but in heaven they will be corrected."

Hanneh died in the odour of sanctity, and her soul was wafted to the gate of heaven, where Mar Bûtrus † sits with the keys to admit the worthy.

" Who is there? " said Mar Bûtrus, looking out of the machicolated[4] window above the gate. " Ah! Another redeemed soul! Your name, my daughter." " Your servant Hanneh," was the meek rejoinder. Mar Bûtrus opened the door at once and bade her welcome, assigning to her a place among the heavenly choir. Here she was secure at last, and for ever, from her aversion, the Patriarch.

Suddenly three great knocks at heaven's gate startled the happy songsters. Mar Bûtrus jumped up and ran to the window to see who it was. He gave one look and then, in wild excitement, sent attendants hurrying in all directions. Presently regiments of cherubs and seraphs marched down to the gate and formed up on either side of the street leading

---

* Ar. for Hannah.   † St. Peter.
[4] See p. 265.

from it. Two of the Archangels came and stood by while
Mar Bûtrus, with unusual ceremony, slipped back the bolt.
All the blessed stood agog to see who it was that had deserved
this grand reception. To Hanneh's chagrin and dismay,
it was the Patriarch. He strode in amid loud acclamations,
and his eyes meeting hers for a twinkling space, she could see
that he was still at his tricks. He was led up to a high seat
near the throne, while his old nurse burst into a flood of
tears.

Now tears are not allowed in heaven. When, therefore,
the other saints beheld her weeping, they thought she was
one of the damned who had got in by mistake, and drew
away from her. She was thus left alone in a circle of the
blessed, all huddled together like scared sheep and neglecting
their parts in the heavenly choir. Mar Bûtrus noticed the
interruption, and came to see what was the matter. Seeing
a saint in tears, he said severely, " Who are you? " " Your
servant Hanneh," was the reply, and he looked up the name
in his register. " It seems all right," he said to himself;
and, turning once more to Hanneh: " Don't you know that
tears are forbidden here? Tell me why you are crying in
this happy place." Then Hanneh sobbed out her story:
how the Patriarch as a child had pinched and teased her,
objecting to be washed and dressed, and so forth, until she
felt quite sure that he would come to grief; how he had
afterwards deceived his schoolfellows and masters, and the
authorities of the Church, and how Mar Bûtrus himself had
now destroyed her sense of justice by giving the rogue a
triumphal entry into heaven. Mar Bûtrus burst out
laughing, and patted her on the back, saying: " There,
my daughter! go back and take your part in the singing.
He's not so bad as you think him. And as for the triumphal
entry, why, there are hundreds of saints like you, thank God,
admitted every day, but only once in a thousand years do
we get a Patriarch."

There was once a young priest who, besides committing
to memory the regular liturgies, learned to read a chapter
of the Bible in Arabic, which he was fond of reciting to his

congregation.[5] It began, " Then the Lord said unto Moses."

The first time he read it the people were delighted and astonished at his learning; but they soon wearied of hearing the same lesson Sunday after Sunday, and one morning, before service, one of them went into the church and moved the book-mark. When the priest came to that point in the service where he usually introduced this lesson, he opened the book and began with confidence, " Then the Lord said unto Moses." But presently, needing to refresh his memory, he looked at the page before him. It was strange to him. Then he realised that his mark had been moved, and began to turn the leaves frantically, hoping to light upon his own chapter. More than once, thinking he had found it, he began, " Then the Lord said unto Moses," but could go no further. At last an old man in the congregation, puzzled by the repetition of this phrase, inquired, " Father, what did the Lord say unto Moses? " To which the priest replied angrily, " May Allah destroy the house of the man who moved my book-mark! "

A certain priest had learned by heart the list of fasts and festivals of the Orthodox Church, with the number of intervening days. To keep a tally of the days as they passed, that he might give due notice of the fasts preceding certain festivals, he put in one of his pockets a number of peas equal to the number of days he wished to remember, and every morning transferred one of them to another pocket. Thus, by counting the peas still in the first pocket, he could always tell how many days remained.

This priest had a wife * who did not know of this arrangement. One day, when tidying his clothes, she found peas in his pockets, and concluded that he was fond of them. So, for love, she filled all his pockets with peas. Soon after, the priest was seen in distress of spirit, beating his forehead

* [The Greek parish clergy are obliged to marry, and, if their wife dies, to retire to a monastery, as it is forbidden them to marry again.— M. P.]

[5] See p. 265.

and exclaiming: " According to the peas there will be no feast."

One day during a fast,* a monk who was strolling through the market came upon a peasant woman with some eggs for sale. Sick to death of eating nothing but vegetables, he bought a few of them, carried them secretly to his cell in the convent, and there hid them till late at night, when all the brethren had gone to bed. Then he got up and prepared to cook and eat them. Having nothing to boil them in, he took one of the eggs in a pair of tongs and held it over the flame of a candle till he judged it done. Presently, as he thus treated one after another, a smell of burning eggshells spread through the monastery. It reached the cell of the Abbot, who at once arose and, candle in hand, repaired to the convent kitchen. It was empty. He then went up and down the passages, sniffing at door after door, till he reached the culprit's cell, where, peeping through a keyhole, he beheld the monk in the act of roasting the last of his eggs.

Still with his eye at the keyhole, he knocked at the door. The monk caught up the eggs, hid them under his pillow, blew out the light, and snored loudly. The Abbot knocked again more loudly and called for admission. At last the snoring ceased and the brother sleepily asked, " Who is there? " " It is I, your Abbot! " The door was speedily opened.

Taking no notice of the monk's excuses, the Abbot accused him of cooking food in his cell. The charge was warmly denied, and the smell explained by the fact that the candle in the cell had burned longer than usual without being snuffed, because the monk had forgotten himself and it in his devotions.

The Abbot then went to the bed, and feeling under the pillow, produced the sooty eggs. Unable any longer to maintain his denial, the monk acknowledged his guilt, but begged for mercy because he had been tempted to sin by the

* The fast days of the Orthodox Eastern Church amount to more than a third of the whole year. Abstinence is enjoined from all animal food, including eggs, milk and butter, and everything cooked with those ingredients.

devil himself. Now, the Father of Evil happened at that moment to be present in a corner of the cell, and on hearing the monk's excuse, he sprang forward, crying, "That is a foul lie! I never tempted this monk. There was no need. I spend my days, it is true, in tempting laymen, but at night I come to convents as a humble scholar."

A monk, one day in the market, saw two fowls for sale. It was not till after he had agreed upon a price with the woman to whom they belonged that it transpired that he was without ready money. The woman offered to keep the fowls for him while he went for his purse; but he objected, preferring to take one bird only, leaving the other with her as a hostage. The woman refused, pointing out that she did not even know his name, in case she had to make complaint to his Abbot. "Oh," said the monk, "that is easily remedied. We all go by Scripture names in our convent. Mine is ''Ufûr lina Khateyâna.' * You have but to inquire for 'Ufûr lina Khateyâna, and I should be called at once." "Ah, that's a beautiful name," said the woman, "but I have a better one: 'La tadkhilna fi et-tajribat wa-lakin najì dajajâti min esh-sharìr.' " †

There once lived at Damascus a rich man, Hâj Ahmad Izreyk by name, whose property consisted of great herds of camels, from which he supplied the caravans from that city.

When this man's time came to die, instead of quickly departing, he lay so long at the last gasp that his friends were sure he must have injured someone who had not forgiven him. They therefore summoned all his acquaintances to come and declare that they had no grudge against him. Even his enemies, moved by this prolonged agony, came to his bedside and begged Hâj Ahmad to forgive them as they forgave him any wrong he might have done them. But in vain. The gates of death remained closed to the dying man.

At last someone imagined that it might be some animal

* Forgive us our trespasses.
† Lead us not into temptation, but deliver my fowls from the Evil One.

he had offended. As he had had most to do with camels, it
was decided to ask his camels to forgive him. Camels are
disobliging creatures, and these flatly refused to come until
a whole day's holiday had been given them in which to
discuss the matter. This was granted, and the next day
thousands of camels assembled on the plain beyond the
gardens of the city. The grunting, groaning, gurgling,
snuffing, puffing, wheezing made a volume of noise that was
heard at Mazarìb. The debate was long and angry, but
by dark they had come to a decision, which their sheykh
was to communicate to Hâj Ahmad.

This sheykh of camels was so huge that he looked like a
mountain moving. Hair hung from his sides like the tassels
from a pair of saddle-bags. At every step he raised a cloud
of dust that darkened the air, and his foot left a print as
large as a kneading-trough.* All who passed him exclaimed, " Mashallah! Praised be the creator! " at the
same time spitting to right and left against the evil eye.

When this beast arrived before the house of Hâj Ahmad, he
proved too big for the doorway. He was asked to give his
message through the window. But, as a deputation from
the most noble of all animals, he was indignant at the
suggestion and threatened to go away again. The friends of
Hâj Ahmad then besought him to have patience while they
pulled down one wall of the house. At last the camel
came to the death-bed of his master, and, kneeling down,
pronounced :

" O Hâj Ahmad, be at rest, the camels forgive you; but
they have sent me to tell you why you need their forgiveness.
It is not for our burdens nor for the blows we daily receive
at your servants' hands. Those are from Allah, and belong
to our lot in life. But, after loading us heavily and stringing
us together by the score like beads on a rosary, to oblige us to
follow the lead of a wretched little donkey—this it is we find
insufferable." †

* Circular wooden dishes are used as kneading-troughs by the Syrian
fellahìn.
† This story, before the expulsion of the Turks from Palestine, was
often related as a covert criticism of the Government, the " wretched
little donkey " being the Sultan.

IX

A CERTAIN man was living with his wife and her bedridden mother in a two-storeyed house when the house caught fire. The man having thrown all the furniture of the upper storey out of the windows, was looking round for anything else worth saving. He espied his wife's mother. Seizing her in his arms, he carried her to a window and threw her down into the street. Then, rolling up her bed with care, he carried it downstairs. When he emerged, his neighbours asked him what he was hugging so tenderly. "My mother-in-law's bed," he replied. "And where is your mother-in-law?" "Oh," said the bewildered man, "I dropped her from the window." It was agreed that he had done wisely.

There is nothing craftier and more to be feared than an old woman. A person of this description, walking out one morning, met Iblìs, and asked him where he was going. "Oh," he replied, "about my usual business, getting people into trouble." "There is nothing in that," said she, "any fool can do that." "So I have often been told," said Iblìs. "I have heard that not only fools, but old women like yourself can beat me at my own trade." "Well," she said, smiling, "let us have a match." The devil agreed, and offered her first innings; but she declined, saying that, as he was the acknowledged author of evil, he should have the precedence.

Near to where they stood champed a fiery stallion fastened to a tent-peg. "See," said Iblìs, "I just loosen this peg, without drawing it from the ground; now mark the mischief." The horse, tugging at his tether, at once pulled up the peg and rushed off, trampling all he met, so that before he was caught he had killed two men and injured several women and children.

"Well," said the old woman, after reckoning up the damage, "that was a villainous piece of work. But now undo it!" "What!" cried the devil. "That is something I never attempted." "Then I am the more skilful," chuckled the woman, "for I can repair what harm I do." "I should like to see you," sneered Iblìs incredulously. "You have only to watch me," was all she took time to say as she proceeded to make good her boast.

She hurried home to get some money, and then went to the shop of a dealer in silk stuff, a man newly married. "A happy day, O my lord," she said, stopping before the bench where he was sitting. "I want the most beautiful dress you have for sale." "For your daughter?" said he. "No, for my son." "He is going to be married, then?" remarked the merchant. "Alas! no," said the woman plaintively, "but is in love with a young woman recently married to another man, and she asks a rich dress as the price of her favour." The merchant, astonished at the confession, said, "A respectable old woman like you should not countenance such wickedness." "Ah, my lord," she moaned, "he has threatened to beat me unless I do his will." "Well," said he, "here is the dress, but the price is five hundred dinârs, and after what you have told me, my conscience will not allow me to sell it at a lower price." After a deal of haggling he accepted two hundred dinârs, and the old woman took the dress and went her way.

Iblìs, who witnessed the transaction, exclaimed, "O foolish woman, you have harmed no one but yourself by paying two hundred dinârs for a dress that is not worth half that amount." "Wait and see," was the reply.

The old woman went home again, and changed her apparel for that of a derwìsheh, throwing a green veil over her head and hanging a great rosary with ninety-nine beads around her neck. It was noon when she again set out, taking with her the dress she had just bought, and went to the private house of the merchant from whom she had bought it. She arrived just as a muezzin of a neighbouring mosque was calling a prayer. She knocked, and, the door being opened, begged for leave to enter and say her prayers there, giving as the reason for the request that she could not reach home in time. She was, she explained, a devotee of mature age, ceremonially clean, and no longer subject to the infirmities of women. The servant told her mistress, who, happy to receive so venerable a visitor, herself came to greet her, and showed her up to a room where she might perform her devotions.

But the old woman was not easy to please. "My dear," she objected, "the men have been smoking in this room. Now, I have just bathed myself and am perfectly pure, but if I took off my yellow boots here my feet would be defiled."

She was taken to a different room. "Ah, my daughter," she complained, "meals have been eaten here. My mind would be distracted by carnal things. Have you not some quiet chamber?" "I am sorry," answered the hostess: "there is no other chamber except our bedroom." "Take me there," said the old woman.

When shown the bedroom, she professed herself satisfied, and asked to be left alone at her prayers, promising to include in them the petition that her hostess might bear a son.

As soon as she was alone, the old woman hid the parcel containing the silken dress under the pillow of the bed, waited long enough to have said her prayers, and then took her leave, with blessings on the house and its kind owners.

The merchant came home as usual, supped, smoked his pipe, and went to bed. Finding the pillow uncomfortable, and trying to put it right, he felt the parcel, and, opening it, found in it a dress he knew. Recalling what the crone who bought it of him had said about the destination of that dress, he jumped out of bed, seized his wife by the arm, dragged her to the door, and, without a word, thrust her forth half-dressed into the street, bolting the door behind her. Fortunately it was a moonless night and no one saw her disgrace, except the author of it, the old woman, who was on the watch. She found the unhappy lady crouching, terrified, in the darkness, and asked with assumed horror what was the matter. The poor soul replied that her husband had suddenly gone mad. "Never mind, my daughter," said the old woman soothingly. "Allah has sent me to help you. Come to my house for the night, and trust me to arrange matters."

The old woman's dwelling consisted of a single room, in which her son was already fast asleep upon a mattress spread upon the floor. His mother fetched two other mattresses and as many cotton quilts out of the alcove, and spread them on the floor beside her son's bed. She then lay on the bed next to her son, and invited her guest to rest on the other. Thus the old woman lay between her son and the guest, who was soon wrapped in slumber. The old woman, however, lay awake, listening to the noises of the night. At length she caught the sound for which she was waiting, the tramp of the watchmen going on their rounds, when she sprang up, and flinging open the window, cried, " Come, O true believers! Come and see the disgrace that has befallen my old age. My son has brought a harlot into the house, and I am obliged to sleep in the same room with them." The watchmen, hearing the clamour, entered the house, seized the innocent young people, and took them off to prison.

Next morning, as soon as it was light, the old woman, wrapped in a long veil, repaired to the prison. Having got leave from the keeper, a man well known to her, to speak with the young woman who had been arrested during the night, she said, " Fear nothing; I will set you free. Change dresses with me, and cover yourself with this veil. So you can pass the guard and reach my house unrecognised. I will join you there." The young wife did as she was told, and escaped without difficulty. The old woman waited until the prison-keeper made his round, and then began to shriek for justice. The official, seeking the cause of the uproar, was surprised to find that it came from an old acquaintance. The night watchman must have been drunk, she screamed, to enter her house and take her and her son to prison without a pretext. The gaoler saw clearly the trick played on him, but he had broken the regulations by admitting a visitor so early, and was averse to any fuss about the matter; so he ordered the couple to be set free.

The young man went to his work as usual. The old woman waited till the city was astir, and then set out to visit the merchant she had bedevilled. He saluted her with an imprecation, but she motioned him to be silent, and, taking him aside, explained how, after visiting the shop, she had been hospitably entertained by his wife and permitted to perform her devotions in their bedroom, how she had carelessly left the parcel she carried under the pillow of one of the beds in that room, and how his lady, whom she had now the honour to entertain in her humble dwelling, was quite guiltless of the intrigue ascribed to her.

The merchant was stupefied, but at the same time vastly relieved, to hear all this. He loved his wife, and, moreover, now that he had no evidence against her, feared to be called to account by offended relatives. Presenting the old woman with the price of the dress, he besought her to intercede for him. She consented graciously, and invited him to her house. He came there, met his wife, confessed his error, and was forgiven. Thus the pair were united as before, and none but the old woman ever knew that they had been separated. The lady, in delight at the reconciliation, gave the old woman a handsome present. And only Iblìs had cause to grumble, being convinced of the truth of the saying, " The devil is no match for an old woman."

The ladies of King Solomon's harìm, jealous of his favourite for the time being, paid an old woman to make mischief between her and the king. The crone, after praising the charms of the favourite till the latter was wax in her hands, declared that the king ought to manifest his love for her by granting some extraordinary request. As Suleymân knew the language of birds, and had power over all things living, it would be easy, the old woman suggested, to build for his love a palace of feathers floating in the air. The favourite took the hint, and when next the king came to her she sulked with him and pouted as one aggrieved. By dint of coaxing, Suleymân learnt her grievance. He at once ordered all the birds to come before him and devise some measure to content his love. All obeyed except the owl, who flatly refused. But Suleymân sent word that if she persisted in disobeying him he would cut off her head; and when she changed her mind, and asked forgiveness for her first refusal, the king promised to overlook it, but only on condition of her answering aright some questions he was going to put to her.

The Hakìm asked her why she had not come when he first called her. The reply was, " Because a wicked old hag has turned your fair one's head and egged her on to ask an impossible thing, for who can build a palace without foundations? " Pointing to the thousands of birds there present, the king asked, " Which of all these birds do you think the handsomest? " " My son," replied the owl. " Which are more numerous, the living or the dead? " " The dead," said the bird. " How do you prove that? " " All who sleep are dead, as far as the business of life is concerned." " What is more abundant, day or night? " " Day." " How so? " " Because when the moon shines it is daylight and people travel." " Only one more question," said the king. " Which are the more numerous, men or women? " " Women." " Prove it." " Count up all the women, and then add all the husbands who are governed by their whims," replied the owl. At that the wise king burst out laughing and told the owl that she might go in peace.

Whenever King Solomon went abroad, the birds of the air, by his command, hovered in flocks over his head like a vast canopy. On the occasion of his marriage he commanded his feathered slaves to pay the like honour to his bride. All obeyed but the hoopoe,*[1] who, rather than flatter a woman, went and hid himself.

The king, on his wedding day, missing his favourite bird,

* *Upupa epops.*
[1] See p. 266.

ordered the rest to go and find the hoopoe. The birds flew
north, south, east and west; and at length after many
months the fugitive was discovered crouching in a hole in
the rock on an island in the most distant of the seven seas.
"You are many, and I but one," said the hoopoe; "there
is no escape now you've found me. I go with you against
my will to Suleymân, whose folly in asking us to do homage
to the most worthless of creatures exasperates and disgusts
me. But before we start, let me tell you three stories of the
nature of woman that you may judge in your minds between
the king and me."

A certain man had for a wife a most beautiful woman of
whom he was consumedly fond; and she was even fonder of
him, for he was very rich.

"Were I to die," she would sometimes sigh in his ear,
"you would soon dry your eyes and take a better wife;
whereas, if you die first, I should end my days in grief."
"Nay, by Allah," replied the man fiercely. "Were you
to die, I would renounce my business and weep on your
grave seven years."

"Would you?" she cried, enraptured. "Oh, I would do
more than that for your sweet memory!"

The woman, as it was decreed, died first, and the man,
true to his vow, gave up his business and mourned at her
graveside night and day for seven long years, subsisting upon
scraps of broken meat thrown to him by the charitable.
His clothes turned to rags; his hair and beard hung about
him like the fronds of maidenhair; his nails grew as long as
eagle's talons, and his body became as emaciated as that
of the leaf insect.*

At the end of the seven years El Khudr, being sent that
way, saw the strange mourner and inquired his story.

The saint asked him whether he really believed that his
wife, had she outlived him, would have done as much. "Of
course," was the reply. "Do you think that, if she were
now alive, she would still love you?" "Of course I do."
"Well," said El Khudr, "we shall see." He struck the
grave with Moses' rod and bade it open, when the woman
arose in her shroud, young and lovely as ever. El Khudr,
having hidden behind a monument, the woman saw only her

---

* *Mantis religiosa*, called by the natives of the Jerusalem district
"St. George's mare," or "The Jew's mare."

husband. Horrified by his appearance, she cried, "Who are you, dreadful creature, more like a beast than a man? Why am I here in the graveyard? If you are a *ghûl*, I pray you not to eat me."

She shuddered still more when she learnt that the frightful creature was her faithful husband, and deferred going home with him till nightfall, saying that people would talk if she went through the streets in her grave-clothes. He sat down beside her, laid his head on her lap, and in the relief of again possessing her, fell sound asleep.

A Sultan, journeying by that way, saw the couple near the open grave, and, struck by the woman's beauty in her shroud, he invited her to be his love. She laid her husband's head on the ground and stepped into a litter that was in readiness.

When the cavalcade was gone, El Khudr came and woke the husband, telling him how his wife had been carried off, and suggesting that they should follow her. They started in pursuit, and reached the palace soon after the Sultan's arrival there. El Khudr demanded an audience, which, on account of his commanding presence, was instantly granted. The Sultan was incredulous and very angry when El Khudr proclaimed the identity of his companion, while the woman declared that the old fright had never been her husband. The saint offered to settle the question, and commanded that the woman should resume her shroud and be taken back to the graveyard. The Sultan, in awe of El Khudr, was bound to submit, and the woman was brought to the brink of her former grave. She suddenly fell into it a lifeless corpse; some say in consequence of a withering look from El Khudr, and others as the result of a blow from the beak of a great eagle which suddenly swooped down out of heaven.

El Khudr then closed the grave with a stroke of his rod; and by the command of Allah her husband regained the seven years which he had lost. He was thus enabled to marry again and live long and happily with another wife, whom, having lost his illusions, he was wise enough to keep in her place.

Two good friends, who were merchants, went into partnership. The one, a fat man, had a wife who loved him; the other, a lean one, was tethered to a shrew who made life wretched for him. When the fat man asked his partner to go home with him and spend the evening, his wife, though

not a party to the invitation, made them heartily welcome;
but when the lean man ventured to return the hospitality,
he was met with abuse and driven forth with his guest.
The fat man simply laughed and carried off the henpecked
husband to his own house, saying: "Now I know the cause
of your thinness and your sad looks; and I think I know a
remedy. Take my advice, and travel with our merchandise
for, say, six months, then send me a report that you are dead.
Your wife will then realise the good fortune she has lost and
repent of her ill-treatment of you. When I and my wife
perceive that she is really humbled, I will let you know, and
you can return." The lean man approved of the plan, and
in due time started on his travels. Six months later his
partner received the letter announcing his death. The fat
man then informed the widow that the shop and all the
merchandise were his alone. He further seized all her
belongings under pretext of some debt or other, leaving her
destitute. As a well-known virago she could find no employment, and was at last compelled to ask the fat man's
help. He reminded her coldly of the rudeness she had
formerly shown him, and reprehended her ill-treatment of
his friend, her late husband. It was purely out of respect
for that dead husband's memory that he finally prevailed
upon his wife to employ her as a servant. The excellent
couple contrived to make her life with them so wretched
that she thought of her former life as paradise, of her husband
as an angel of light. When, therefore, the lean man reappeared she fell at his feet, and thenceforth to the end of her
life was submissive.

There was once a merchant who knew the language of
beasts. But this knowledge had been granted him only
upon condition that, if he told the secrets learnt by its means,
he should instantly die. No one, not even his wife, was
aware that he was gifted beyond the common.

One evening, standing near his stables, he heard an ox,
which had just returned from ploughing, complaining bitterly
of his hard labour, and asking the ass on which the merchant
rode to business how he might lighten it. The ass advised
him to be very ill, to leave his food untouched and roll on
the ground in pain when the ploughman came to take him
to the field. The ox took this advice, and next day his
master was told he was too ill to work. The merchant
prescribed rest and extra food for the ox, and ordered that

the donkey, which was strong and fat, should be yoked to the plough in his place.

That evening the merchant stood again by the stable, listening. When the ass came in from ploughing, the ox thanked him for his advice, and expressed his intention to act upon it again next morning. "I don't advise you to do that," said the ass, "if you value your life. To-day, while I was ploughing, your master came and told the ploughman to take you to the butcher's to-morrow, as you seemed ailing, and have you killed to save your life; for should you sicken and die, he would lose the value of your carcase." "What shall I do?" cried the ox in terror. "Be well and strong to-morrow morning," said the ass. At that the merchant, unaware that his wife stood near him, laughed aloud, and excited her curiosity. His evasive answers only made her more inquisitive; and when he absolutely refused to satisfy her, she lost her temper, and went to complain of him to her relations, who soon threatened him with a divorce. The poor man, who really loved his wife, in despair resolved to tell her all and die; so he put his affairs in order, made his will, and promised to content her on the morrow.

Next morning, at a window overlooking the stable yard, where the cock was gallanting with a number of hens, he heard his watch-dog reprove the bird for such light conduct on a day of grief. "Why! what is the matter?" inquired the cock. The dog told the story of their master's trouble, when the cock exclaimed: "Our master is a fool. He cannot keep one wife in order while I have no trouble with twenty. He has only to take a stick and give his mistress a sound thrashing to make her amiable." These words came as light to the merchant's gloom. Forthwith he called his wife into an inner room, and there chastised her within an inch of her life. And from that hour she gave him no more trouble.*

"You see from these true stories," concluded the hoopoe, "what silly, vain and tiresome creatures women are, and how wrong it was of Suleymân to ask us to do homage to one of them. When you find a good woman, like the fat man's

* [This will be recognised as the identical story in which the wazìr, her father, delicately conveyed a threat to Scheherezade when she persisted in asking him to give her to the murderous Shariar (v. *Arabian Nights*).—M. P.]

wife, you may be sure that her virtues are the fruit of the stick."

The assembled birds acquiesced in the soundness of the hoopoe's remarks. They considered that, if these valuable facts were known to Suleymân, he would mend his ways with the sex and perhaps reward the hoopoe for having dared, from such humane motives, to disobey him. They all returned to the king, who, when he had listened to the hoopoe's three stories, took the crown off his head and placed it on that of the bird, whose descendants wear it to this day.*

* For this reason the hoopoe is called by the fellahîn " the wise man's bird," or " the bird of Suleymân el Hakim."

X

ABOUT ANIMALS

The dog and the cat were not always the enemies we now see them. There was once a strong friendship between them. Their hostility arose from the following incident:—

Ages ago when the different kinds of animals in the world had their various offices and duties assigned to them, the dog and the cat, though classed amongst the domestic animals, were exempted from drudgery, the former for his fidelity, the latter for her cleanliness. At their special request they received the written document attesting and confirming this privilege. It was handed to the dog for safe-keeping, and he buried it where he kept his bones. Filled with envy, the horse, ass and ox purchased the services of the rat, who, burrowing, found and destroyed the charter. Ever since that time the dog has been liable, on account of his carelessness, to be tied or chained up by his master; and, besides that, the cat has never forgiven him. Both the cat and the dog hate rats and kill them when they can. The horse, ass and ox, on the other hand, permit the rats to share their provender.

There are, however, some who say that the dogs were once classed amongst wild beasts, and lived in the fields, while the jackals had the duty and privilege of being the friends and guardians of mankind. The reason why their positions are now reversed is given as follows:—
The dogs, being envious of the jackals, plotted to oust their rivals from the towns and villages. One day the sheykh of the dogs being ill, they asked the jackals to be so kind as to exchange duties with them for a while that their chief and other sick persons among them might have the benefit of medical treatment, and they themselves might acquire some civilisation. The jackals good-naturedly agreed, but the dogs, being the more numerous, the stronger

and much the cleverer, having once obtained the position they coveted, altogether declined to give it up again. To this day people who know Arabic and live in the country can distinctly hear at night the distant jackals' howl of inquiry "Kayf-hoo, Kayf-hoo?" meaning "How is he? How is he?" and the dogs barking in reply, "Ba'ad-oh, Ba'ad-oh," "Still the same, still the same."

The cat is a clean beast, and has the blessing and seal of Solomon set upon it. Therefore, if a cat drinks out of a can containing milk or drinking-water, what remains after she has quenched her thirst is not unclean, and may be used by human beings. So, at least, I was assured by a fellâh of Bethlehem. The dog, however, is unclean, and a vessel from which he has drunk is polluted. Indeed the dog is considered so foul an animal by the stricter Moslems, more especially members of the Shafe'i sect, that if, while they are at prayers, a dog that has got a wetting shake himself at a distance of forty steps from them, they at once arise, perform the preliminary ablutions, and start afresh from the very beginning. On the other hand, there are always to be found people who are fond of dogs. A story is told of a Moslem who owned a handsome " Slugi " * to which he was very much attached. When it died he buried it in his garden reverently, with his own hands. His enemies thereupon went to the Kadi and accused him of having buried an unclean beast with the respect and ceremonies due only to a believer. The man would have been severely dealt with had he not told the Kadi that the animal had proved his sagacity by leaving a will, in which a large sum of money was mentioned as a legacy to his worship. On hearing this the Kadi decided that a dog of such rare wisdom and discernment had indeed earned a right to decent burial.[1]

It is also related of Ibrahìm El Khalìl, on whom be peace, that he was kind and hospitable, not only to men, but to

* [Properly Selûki (from the town of Selûk), a kind of greyhound.— M. P.]

[1] See p. 267.

dogs as well. His flocks were so numerous that 4000 dogs were needed to guard them, and were fed daily by the Patriarch's bounty. It is also said that in ancient times if one killed his neighbour's dog he was liable to pay blood-money for the creature just as for a human being. The amount of compensation is said to have been calculated in the following manner. The dead creature was hung up by the tail with its nose touching the ground. A stake was then fixed in the ground, of a height the same as that of the suspended animal. Wheat—or, according to another statement, flour—was then heaped round the stake till the top was quite hidden, and as high as the tip of the dog's tail would have been had its carcase been left hanging there. The value of the grain or meal heaped up was then estimated, and the slayer of the dog had to pay the equivalent.

Just at the point where the road from Herod's Gate in the northern wall of Jerusalem joins the great road to Nablus, and close to the Tombs of the Kings, there was till recently a cistern concerning which the late guardian of the adjacent Moslem shrine of Sheykh Jerrâh told me the following legend:—

Many years ago a man was murdered, and his dog would not leave the place, but attacked all passers-by. The animal was therefore killed; but that was of no use, for his ghost now appeared in the company of that of his master, and frightened wayfarers. In order to lay the ghosts the brother of the murdered man had the cistern and drinking-fountain constructed on the fatal spot for the free use of men and beasts. Since then the spectres have no longer been seen, but the cistern, formerly called " Bìr el Kelb," [2] the dog's well, has now been filled up. Another version of the story is, that the dog discovered the body of his murdered master, which had been thrown into the well.*

Here are three of the commonest proverbs concerning dogs: " It is better to feed a dog than to feed a man," meaning that the canine will not forget the kindness, while

---

* Since the British Occupation this cistern, being in the way of traffic, has been filled up and the fountain destroyed.

[2] See p. 267.

the human animal may. " For want of horses and men, saddle dogs." " It is the sheykh's dog that is sheykh."

The cat is liked by the Moslems, it is said, for the following reason. When the Prophet was a camel-driver, he was asleep one day in the shade of some bushes in the desert. A serpent came out of a hole and would have killed him had not a cat that happened to be prowling about pounced upon it and destroyed it. When the Prophet awoke he saw what had happened, and, calling the cat to him, fondled and blessed it. From thenceforth he was very fond of cats. It is said that one day he cut off the long sleeve of his robe, upon which his pet cat was asleep, rather than disturb her slumbers. But while the cat is a blessed animal, strange cats that come to houses, and especially black cats, should be avoided, as they may be demons in disguise.

A great Mohammedan sheykh in Egypt had a pet black cat of which he was very fond, and which used to sleep near him at night. One night the sheykh was ill and could not sleep. As he lay awake he heard a cat mewing in the street near his window. His favourite at once arose and went to the window. The cat outside the house called her distinctly by name and asked her, in Arabic, whether there were any food in the house. She answered, also in Arabic, that there was plenty, but that neither she nor the other could get it because " the Name " was always pronounced over the stores of provisions there, and so the would-be guest must go elsewhere.

The female demon " Lilith," the first wife of Adam,* sometimes disguises herself as an owl, but more frequently as a cat. The following story related by a Spanish Jewess illustrates this belief. " It is quite true that La-Brûsha " (that is, Lilith) " often takes the form of a cat. This is what my mother told me happened when she was born. It was told her by her mother, my grandmother. Both were very truthful women. For nine days after a child has been born the mother ought never to be left alone in the room. What happened when my mother was born was this. My

* See Section I, " Our Father Adam."

great-grandmother, who was nursing my grandmother, had gone out of the room, leaving the latter and the infant (who was afterwards my mother) dozing. When she came back the patient told her that she had had a strange dream during her absence. She had seen a great black cat come into the room as soon as her mother's back was turned. It walked into a corner of the chamber and turned itself into a jar. A cat was then heard mewing in the street, and the jar thereupon became a cat again. It came up to the bed (my grandmother being paralysed with fear and helpless), took up the baby, and went with it to the window and called out 'Shall I throw?' 'Throw,' was the answer given by the cat outside. Thrice the cat in the sick-room asked the same question and got the same answer. She then threw the infant (my mother) out of the window. Just at that moment my great-grandmother returned and the cat suddenly vanished. My great-grandmother, noticing that the child was neither in its cradle nor in its mother's bed, with great presence of mind hid her alarm and said to my grandmother, 'Of course you were only dreaming. It was I who came and took the little one in order to change its clothes whilst you were fast asleep, and I shall bring it back again in a moment.' So saying, she left the room quietly, but as soon as she got outside and had closed the door behind her, she rushed out of the house and beheld a huge cat crossing a field with the child in its mouth. Love lent her speed. She soon overtook the creature, and being a wise woman who knew exactly what to do in such an emergency, she uttered a form of adjuration which forced the demon not only to drop its prey but also to swear that for eleven generations to come it would not molest her family or its descendants. My great-grandmother then brought the infant back, but it was not till long after its mother was was well and strong again that she told her that her supposed dream had been a frightful reality."

To kill a cat is considered by many of the fellahîn to be a great sin which will surely bring misfortune upon the perpetrator. When a fellâh of Artass lost his eyesight, he and others attributed the misfortune to divine retribution, seeing he had in his youth been a killer of cats. Though generally respected, the cat is sometimes considered as the personification of craft and hypocrisy.

A town cat, having destroyed almost all the mice and rats in the place, found itself forced, for lack of prey, to go into the fields and hunt for birds, mice, rats and lizards. In this time of need it thought of the following ruse. It stayed away for some weeks from its usual haunts, and, returning, lay down in front of a mouse and rat warren, with a rosary round its neck; then, with its eyes closed, fell to purring loudly. Soon a mouse peeped out of a hole, but, seeing the cat, hastily returned. " Why do you flee? " said pussy gently. " Instead of showing pleasure at the return of an old neighbour from the pilgrimage you run away as soon as you see him. Come and visit me, fear nothing." Surprised at hearing itself thus addressed, the mouse again ventured to the door of its hole and said, " How can you expect me to visit you? Are you not the enemy of my race? Should I accept your invitation you would surely seize and devour me as you did my parents and so many others of my kindred."

" Alas! " sighed the cat, " your reproaches are just; I have been a great sinner, and have earned abuse and enmity. But I am truly penitent. As you see from this rosary round my neck, I now devote myself to prayer, meditation and the recital of holy books, the whole of which I have learnt by heart, and was just beginning to repeat when you happened to look out of your hole. Besides this, I have visited the Holy Places, so am a Hajji * as well as a Hâfiz.† Go, my injured but nevertheless generous and forgiving friend, make my change of life and sentiments known to the rest of your people and bid them no longer shun my society, seeing that I am become a recluse. Whilst you are absent I shall resume my recitations. Purr, purr, purr."

Much surprised at the news he had just heard, the mouse made it known to the rest of the tribe. They were at first

* Pilgrim.
† One who has the whole Koran by heart.

incredulous; but at last, after one and another had ventured
to peep from the mouth of its hole and had beheld the
whiskered ascetic with the rosary round his neck apparently
oblivious of earthly things, and steadily repeating his purr,
purr, purr, which they supposed to be the contents of holy
books, they thought that there might be some truth in the
matter and they convened a meeting of mice and rats to
discuss it. After much debate it was judged right to test
the reality of the cat's conversion, but to be prudent at the
same time; and so a large and experienced rat was sent
out to reconnoitre. Being a wary veteran, he kept well out
of the cat's reach, though he saluted him respectfully from
a distance. The cat allowed the rat to prowl about unmolested for a long time in the hope that other rats and
mice would come out, when his prey would be easy to
catch and plentiful. But no others came, and at last the
pangs of hunger made him resolve to wait no longer. The
rat, however, was on the alert and darted off the instant he
noticed, from a slight movement of the cat's muscles, that
the pretended saint was about to kill him. " Why do you
go away so abruptly? " mewed the cat; " are you tired of
hearing me repeat scripture, or do you doubt the correctness
of my recitation? " " Neither," answered the rat as he
peeped from the hole in which he had taken refuge. " I
am convinced that you have indeed committed the holy
books perfectly to memory, but at the same time I am
convinced that, however much you may have learnt by rote,
you have neither unlearnt nor eschewed your habits of
pouncing upon us."

The ass is a very useful, stolid, much-enduring animal.
He does good work, but takes his time to do it. He hates
hurry, and his hoofs bear the inscription " Haste is of
Satan, but patience comes from the Most Merciful."
He is, however, by no means stupid, and when on a
certain occasion the invitation to a wedding reached
him, he is reported to have made the shrewd remark, " It
is only because I am wanted to carry either wood or
water."

Though very valuable and useful the camel is an ungainly, ill-tempered and evil-smelling beast. He has inherited his split (hare) lips from an ancestor who was thus punished because he laughed immoderately at other camels' humps whilst forgetting his own. However, a well-authenticated incident that happened a few years ago, goes to show that he is not altogether devoid of gratitude and bravery. A peasant who lived with his wife, child and camel in a lonely hut on the outskirts of a village in the Hebron district was one day obliged to leave them because business called him to a distant village where he had to spend the night. The thought that danger might threaten his loved ones during his absence came suddenly upon him during the night, and forced him to return home as soon as possible. He found that his forebodings were well-founded. An evil-minded neighbour who had a grudge had taken advantage of his absence in order, during the hours of darkness, to break into his dwelling, intending to injure his family, and, being armed, might have succeeded, had not the camel bravely fought and driven the assailant off. When the animal's owner got home he found the faithful beast dying from numerous dagger-stabs. It expired shortly after his arrival. Under ordinary circumstances the hide would have been sold to a tanner and the flesh for food; but the fellâh was so touched by the creature's fidelity to its mistress and her child, that he actually purchased a shroud for the carcase and gave it honourable burial.

That, on the other hand, the camel is vindictive and will cherish a grudge against its owner for a long time until it finds an opportunity for revenge is well known.

The horse, as might be expected, figures prominently in Eastern folk-lore. There are five noble strains or races, to one or the other of which the horse with a pedigree belongs. These are the Siklawi-Jedrani, the Umm Arkub-Shoovay, the Shuweineh-Sabbah, the Kuheile el Ajuss, and the 'Ubbeyeh-Sharrak. Whilst the first compound of each respective name commemorates the breed, the latter reminds one of the name of the man who first captured the equine ancestor of the strain. According to the ancient Arab legend, horses and other creatures found safety from the Deluge by fleeing to the highlands of Nejd. Five hunters, namely Jedran, Shooway, Sabbah, El Ajuss and Sharrak succeeded in capturing the first horse of each special pedigree. They noticed the only fountain in the wilds to which the horses came to drink, and by preventing their escape managed to tame by starving them. Having at last caught them, they each mounted his steed and set off to return to their own home, which was several days' journey distant. Their own provisions having failed, they decided to ride races and sacrifice the slowest for food. Its owner, however, objected and asked for another trial. This was agreed to, and as his horse won the race, other trials had in all fairness to be made, and thus all five horses were found to be equally swift. Not long afterwards their riders saw a herd of gazelles which they successfully chased, each man capturing one. Thus their food-store was replenished and the necessity of killing a horse obviated. The Siklawi steed derived its name from its shining soft white hair; the Umm Arkub had high flanks; the Shuweineh was spotted; the Kuheile was remarkable for its dark eyes, which looked as if treated with kohl or antimony; and the 'Ubbeyeh (diminutive of *'aba*, goat's-hair cloak) received its name from the circumstance that whilst racing, its captor's *'aba* fell off his shoulders, but was saved from being lost because the horse, noticing this, stuck up its tail and prevented the cloak from falling to the ground and being lost.

There are several Arabic proverbs about the horse, such as:—" There can be no happiness in the house which has no horse; " " Let him who has no horse keep the skull of one; " " Fortune is attached to the horses' manes," etc. The Orientals are also very superstitious with regard to horses and therefore very careful when buying one. For a horse to have two white forefeet is a bad omen, which denotes that Misfortune will chase away all good from the house possessing such a horse. Another bad sign for a horse is that it has two curiously curled locks growing apart upon its forehead—it means an open grave. One white fore-foot denotes " a shroud " for the creature's owner. Curling hair on the side of the neck below the mane, and running in the direction of the beast's body, means, " The foeman's sword in the rider's heart "; whilst, on the other hand, curling hair underneath the mane, but in the direction of the horse's head, means that " the rider's sword will pierce the foeman's heart." All a horse's feet white except the right fore-foot signifies that the rider will have " a free hand," that is, he will be victorious in fight.

The hyæna is an evil and accursed beast. Whenever an owl is heard to hoot at night, it is because she, who is herself a metamorphosed woman, or Lilith in owl-form, sees either a human thief or a hyæna. Among the Jews there is a belief that the hyæna is formed out of a white germ, and that it has as many different colours as there are days in the solar year. When a male hyæna is seven years old it becomes either a female of the same species or else a bat.[3] The natives of Palestine generally believe that the hyæna, not content with digging up and devouring dead bodies, often bewitches the living and lures them to his den. He is wont to come up at night to the solitary wayfarer, rub against him endearingly and then run on ahead. The man against whom he has rubbed himself is instantly bewitched, and with the cry, " O my uncle, stop, and wait for me," he follows the hyæna as fast as he can till he gets into the beast's den and is devoured. It sometimes happens that the entrance to the den is very low, and that, when he tries to enter, the human victim hits his head against a projection of the rock. If that happens, he at once recovers his senses and saves himself by flight, for the hyæna is a great coward, and never attacks a man unless the latter be asleep, or disabled, or has been bewitched by him. Sometimes the frightful creature hides itself behind stones or bushes near the roadside; and when, after nightfall, a single person passes without a lantern, the hyæna sets up a groaning like that of somebody in great pain. If the wayfarer turns aside to see what is the matter the wild beast

[3] See p. 267.

will leap upon him and so startle him that he will be at once bewitched and follow it.

The following story is often told of a fellâh who caught a hyæna in a very clever way. The fellâh was on a journey and had with him a donkey bearing a heavy sack of grain. About sunset the man reached a wayside khan. As it was a hot night, he put up his donkey in the stable but left the sack outside, and, wrapping his *'abba* around him, lay down upon the sack and went to sleep. About midnight he was disturbed by something scratching up the ground near him. Opening his eyes, he saw a large hyæna digging a grave alongside of him, evidently intending to kill and bury him, and later on to exhume and devour him at his leisure. The fellâh let the hyæna dig on till the ridge of its back was below the level of the ground. Then, starting up, he rolled the sack of corn on to the animal, and thus kept him down in the grave till morning, when it was an easy task to secure him, for, though a lion at night,* the hyæna is but a cur in the day-time. However, even at night he fears fire, and a simple way to drive him off is to burn matches or to strike sparks with flint and steel.

In spite of the evil qualities popularly ascribed to the hyæna, this animal is credited with one good trait, that of gratitude to those who treat him well.

A Bedawi having been found murdered, suspicion pointed to a young man in a certain village as the murderer, and though innocent, he had to flee from his home to escape the vengeance of the dead man's relatives. Flying north-wards he encountered a sheykh of his acquaintance who asked him whither he was going, and dissuaded him from going further in that direction, because the avengers of blood lay in ambush ahead of him. The young man then turned westwards, but had not gone far before he met another friend who turned him back, saying that the kinsfolk of the dead Bedawi were waiting for him a little further on. He then went eastward, only to meet a third friend, who warned him that in that direction also a party of his enemies

* Ed-dab' bil-leyl sab'. Arabic proverb.

were on the look-out for him. In this trouble he cried out, " O Allah, Thou knowest that I am innocent, and yet, whichever way I turn, I shall meet with those who seek my life." He then left the beaten track and went down a hillside which was covered with thicket and brushwood, towards a valley where he knew of some caves, one of which he entered. As soon as he got used to the gloom of his hiding-place he perceived to his horror that he was in the den of a female hyæna which, leaving a litter of cubs asleep, had gone abroad in search of prey. He was going to fly the place when he heard human steps approaching. Fearing that his enemies had found him out, he drew back into the darkest recess of the cavern. He saw a man crawl in, take up one hyæna cub after the other and put it into his 'abba to carry them off for sale. The fugitive recognised the man, and coming forward, begged him to spare the cubs, saying that he himself now knew the bitterness of being hunted. Were his friend to spare the young hyænas, perhaps Allah would one day save them both from evil. The man was moved, and, putting down the cubs, left the cave, promising not to betray the fugitive, but let him know when it was safe for him to return home. He had just gone when the hyæna returned and, seeing a man in her den, was going to attack him, when the cubs rushed up, and by their yelping attracted her attention. After much hyæna talk between her and her children, she seemed to understand that the man had been their protector, and showed her gratitude by bringing him food; not carrion such as hyænas love, but hares, partridges and kids, which she caught alive. Thus the youth abode as the hyæna's guest till his friend came and told him that the real murderer had been found and punished.[4]

The fox is the most crafty and cunning of beasts. His tricks and wiles are innumerable. If there are partridges about, he notices the direction in which they will be likely to run, and then he runs ahead of them and lies down as if dead, foaming at the mouth. When the birds come to the

[4] See p. 267.

spot they think him dead, and peck at him. They dip their bills in the saliva running from his mouth, and then he snaps at and catches them. He one day played a similar trick on a peasant woman who was carrying a basketful of live fowls to market. Seeing the way she was going, he ran ahead and lay down as above described. When passing the spot she saw him, but did not think it worth her while to stop and skin him. As soon as she was out of sight the fox jumped up and, making a detour, again ran ahead of her and lay down a second time in the road at a point she would have to pass. She was surprised to see him, and said to herself, " Has a pestilence broken out amongst foxes? Had I skinned the first I saw lying by the roadside it would have been worth my while to stop for this one, but as I did not do so then, I shall not do so now." She went on her way, and her surprise was unbounded when, after a while, she noticed what she believed to be a third fox dead on the roadside. " Verily I have done wrong," thought she, " to neglect the good things Allah has placed in my way. I shall leave my fowls here and secure the pelts of the first two before the others take them." No sooner said than done; but before she had time to return wondering, but emptyhanded, the cunning fox had secured his prey and departed.

The fox is fond of playing practical jokes on other animals; he sometimes, however, gets practical jokes played on him.

Meeting the eagle one day, he inquired how large the world looked when seen from the highest point to which he had ever soared. " Why," answered the king of birds, " it is so small as to be almost invisible." The fox looked incredulous, so the eagle invited him to mount on his shoulders while he soared, so that he might judge for himself. " How big does the earth look now? " he asked, when they had risen a great way. " As large ·as a straw basket made at Lydda," answered Abu Hassan.* They still went up and up, and the eagle repeated his question. " No bigger than an onion," said the fox. Higher they went and still higher, and at last, when questioned, the fox acknowledged that the world was out of sight. " How far

* Ar. for Reynard.

do you suppose it to be?" asked the eagle maliciously. The fox, who by this time was frightened out of his wits, replied that he did not know. "In that case you had better find out," said the great bird, turning over suddenly. Down went the fox, and would, of course, have been killed had he not had the good fortune to fall on soft ploughed ground and to have come down on to the soft sheepskin jacket which a ploughman, at work close by, had left lying there. Giving thanks for his narrow escape, the fox slipped under the jacket and ran off with it on his back. He was out of sight before the ploughman realised what had happened. As he ran he came suddenly face to face with a leopard, who asked from whence he had obtained his new dress. Abu Suleymân * promptly replied that he had become a furrier and dealt in sheepskin jackets, and advised the leopard to order one for himself, warning him however that he would have to provide six lambskins, two for the front, two for the back, and two for the sleeves. The leopard agreed to this, and having taken the fox's address, promised to send him six lambs, whose flesh the fox would take as payment for his work. Next day the lambs were brought to the door of the fox's den. Abu Hassan, with his wife and seven cubs, lived in luxury, and thought no more about the jacket till the leopard called to ask whether his garment were ready, when the fox said that he had made a mistake in his estimate, and that he had used all six lambs for the body of the coat. Two and a half lambskins were required for the sleeves. "You shall have three," said the liberal-minded customer; and sure enough, he next day brought three lambs to the fox's door, and was promised his jacket for the following week. At the appointed time he came and asked for it, but was put off with another excuse and told to come the next day. Whenever he appeared the fox had some new story to account for the non-appearance of the jacket. At last the leopard refused to wait any longer, and losing patience, struck at the fox and managed to catch hold of his tail just as he was slipping into his den. The tail gave way and

* Another name for the fox.

the fox escaped with his life, as his hole was too small for the leopard to enter.

"The rogue has lost his tail," said the leopard to himself; "so I shall know him again when we meet; but in the meanwhile I will ensure his receiving severe punishment whenever he attempts to leave his den." He waited till nightfall, when hornets are asleep, and then dug up a nest of them and placed it just above the fox's doorway. When the fox awoke next morning and wanted to leave his den he heard the humming of the hornets outside, and thought it was the leopard purring. Instead of going out, he slunk back into the innermost recess of his dwelling. For many days he dared not venture forth, as the noise continued. He was compelled by famine to devour his own cubs, one at a time; and at last persuaded his wife to wrestle with him, on the understanding that the winner should devour the other. Though worsted in the trial of strength, he each time persuaded his mate to spare his life and give him one more trial, when he instantly killed and devoured her. After that he starved for several days, till at last, as the humming at his door still continued, he decided to stake his life on a bold and sudden dash for liberty. He slunk cautiously to the door of his cave, and then rushed out, only to find that the humming which had frightened him into the destruction of his family was caused by nothing worse than hornets. However, it was useless to grieve, and he had still to secure himself from the vengeance of the leopard, who would know him anywhere, tailless as he now was. He invited all the foxes to a feast on grapes in a certain fruitful vineyard. When they arrived he led each guest to a different vine; and explaining that, should they be allowed to roam at liberty and eat from any vine they chose, quarrels might arise and the noise of strife endanger all, he tied each one firmly by the tail to his special vine. When all were tied up and gorging silently, he slipped away, unperceived, to the top of a hillock and shouted out, "Assemble yourselves, O sons of Adam, assemble and see how your vineyard is being plundered." On hearing this alarm, the foxes, in their desperate efforts to escape, tugged and pulled till they left their tails behind them. As all were tailless, the leopard, when meeting our hero, was unable to prove that he was the identical fox who had cheated him over that lambskin jacket.[5]

A poor old widow, whose relations were all dead, lived alone in a little mud-roofed hut far from any village. It was a dark and stormy night, and the water came dripping through the roof on to her wretched bed. She rose and dragged her straw mat and old mattress that lay thereon into another corner of the hovel; but in vain, for the water came through there as well, making, as it fell, the noise " Dib, dib, dib, dib." Again she rose and dragged her bed into another corner, but here also the water dripped, dib, dib, dib, dib, till, worn out and in despair, she moaned: " O my Lord! O Allah! save me from this dreadful dib, dib, dib, dib. See how it torments me, robbing me of my sleep, and to-morrow it will have made all my bones to ache with intolerable pain. I fear and hate nothing so much as I do this dib, dib. I fear no wild beasts, whether lion, leopard, or wolf, or bear, or hyæna, as much as I fear this horrible dib, dib, dib, that will not let me sleep now, and will be sure to torment me to-morrow."

Now, crouching outside the door of her hut lay a wild beast waiting for the old woman to go to sleep that he might break in and devour her. Hearing her cry out thus, he began to wonder what sort of creature the " dib, dib, dib, dib " could be, and came to the conclusion that it would be prudent not to interfere in a case which even at that moment the " dib, dib " was attending, and which it " would be sure to torment to-morrow." One thing seemed certain to the crouching wild beast, and that was that the " dib, dib " must be a very frightful monster, with whom he had better not contend. " I know what the dûb * is," said the wild beast, " and I know what the dib † is, but I have never before heard of the ' dib, dib,' and as I do not care to run unnecessary risk, I think I will leave the old woman alone.

* Bear. † Wolf.
[5] See p. 268.

She has not much flesh on her as it is, and if the ' dib, dib '
finds her a toothsome morsel, well, let him have her; I shall
sup elsewhere. But hark! what is that approaching? I
should not wonder if it were the ' dib, dib ' himself come to
get the old woman. I had better lie quite still till he is
gone, lest he find me too and torment me."

Now the creature approaching was a man, a water-seller
from the nearest village, whose donkey had run away that
evening. It was a very tiresome donkey, that was always
running away, and it had lost both its ears or the greater
part of both, having been repeatedly caught trespassing in
corn-fields not belonging to its owner. It was, in short, an
ass of bad character, whose owner had been out for several
hours searching for it that stormy night. He was in a very
bad temper, and when he came up to the spot on which the
wild beast was lying trembling in every limb for fear of the
" dib, dib," he caught sight of an animal with short ears and
about the same size as his donkey. So he swore a great oath
that he would break every bone in its body, and he cursed
its father and all its forefathers and the religion of its owner,
and of his ancestors; and, without stopping to ascertain its
identity, he began to rain heavy blows upon the panic-
stricken wild beast with a great stick which he had in his
hand. The wild beast, now quite sure that it had fallen
into the power of the " dib, dib," was so frightened that it
lay quietly crouching without making the least resistance
to this furious onslaught, and when the man, still cursing
furiously, made it get up, and mounted its back, it bore the
indignity with the greatest meekness, and carried him in the
direction that he wanted to go. When the man had got
over his passion and was fairly on his way, he began to
realise that the seat on which he sat was different from that
which he was used to, and also that the animal he was now
riding had a noiseless tread quite different from that of any
donkey; and he saw that in his haste he had put himself
into the power of some wild creature. But so long as he was
on its back, he considered it would not be able to kill him;
and, as it seemed afraid of him, he determined to keep it in
that condition till he should be able to find out what it was

and a way of escape from it. So, whenever the pace slackened, he thrashed the beast well, and kept up a storm of cursing. When daylight broke he found himself riding an enormous leopard, and wondered how he could ever get off its back without the certainty of being torn to death. The leopard, on the other hand, did not discover that it was a man ill-treating him, but still thought that it was the " dib, dib." As they were passing under some trees with low branches, the man, with quick resolve, seized hold of one of them, and loosening his legs let the beast slip through between them while he swung himself into the branches. The leopard thus unexpectedly set free did not stop to look at his tormentor, but rushed off as fast as his legs would carry him. He suddenly encountered a fox, who, surprised to see a leopard in terror, very civilly inquired of the matter. Finding himself in safety, the leopard stopped and related all that he had suffered at the hands of the " dib, dib." " Well," said the fox politely, " I am acquainted with all sorts of animals, but I never heard of such a creature as the ' dib, dib ' "; and he suggested that it might possibly have been a man. " Come back with me to the tree where you left him, and see whether I am right or not. In case I am wrong, we can run away before he gets near enough to hurt us, and if he is a man, you can easily kill him and be avenged for all the trouble he has caused you." " How do I know you are sincere? " replied the leopard. " Everyone speaks of you as a swindler and a tricky rogue; and what proof have I that you may not have been employed by the ' dib, dib ' himself, in order to lure me to my ruin? " " Tie your tail to mine," answered the fox, " and then, if I play you false, you will have me at hand and can kill me." The leopard accepted this handsome offer. Having tied his tail to that of the fox, and made an extra knot, they went towards the place where the water-seller had been left. The latter was still in the tree, for, though it was now broad daylight, he feared to descend before all the world was astir lest he should be ambushed by the leopard. So, although it was the kind of day on which the sheykh of the Haradìn * gives his

* Haradìn, plural of Hardûn = a kind of lizard (*Stellio vulgaris*).

daughter in marriage, the poor drenched fellow stayed shivering in his tree. At last he made up his mind, and was on the point to climb down when he saw the leopard, accompanied by the fox, emerge from a thicket and come towards him. At first he could not understand why the two animals should have tied their tails together, but being a man of ready wit, the true cause flashed upon him; and while the pair were still a good way off, he cried: " O Abu Suleymân, why have you kept me so long waiting? Hurry up with the old marauder that I may break his bones." On hearing those terrible words the leopard turned fiercely on the fox, saying, " Did I not tell you you were a treacherous villain, and would play me false?" Then he turned tail and ran for his life, dragging after him the hapless fox, who was soon bumped to death against the stones and tree-trunks which the leopard passed in his headlong flight. The water-seller came down from the tree and returned home. Thus Allah, to Whom be praise, punished the fox for his former crimes and the leopard for his wicked intentions, whilst at the same time He protected the poor old woman and taught the water-seller to be more careful.[6]

As might be expected, the serpent figures largely in the animal folk-lore of Palestine. According to Jewish notions, " the spinal cord of a man who does not bend his knees at the repetition of the benediction,[7] which commences with the word ' Modim,' after seven years becomes a serpent; when it has attained the age of one thousand years it finds its way to the sea and becomes a whale." [8] According to the Talmud, " Seventy years must elapse before a viper can reproduce its own species, and a similar period is required for the carob tree, while the wicked serpent requires seven years." [9] The following is a characteristic serpent story.

The serpent is the most accursed of all created things, and very treacherous. It is at the root of all the evil in the

---

The phrase is a proverbial expression for a day of heavy showers alternating with sickly gleams of sunshine.

  [6] See p. 268.   [7] See p. 268.
  [8] See p. 268.   [9] See p. 268.

world. Who does not know that when Iblìs was refused admission into Paradise he went sneaking round the hedges and trying in vain to persuade the different animals to let him in? At last, however, the serpent, bribed by a promise of the sweetest food in the world, which the Evil One told him was human flesh, introduced the devil into the garden, concealed in the hollow of his fangs. From this hiding-place Iblìs conversed with Eve, who supposed it was the serpent speaking to her. The mischief that resulted is well known. However, the serpent did not get his reward; for when, after the Fall, an angel was appointed to assign to every creature its special food and country, the serpent—who even before the devil tempted him had felt jealous of Adam reclining in Paradise while angels served him with roast meat and wine—shamelessly demanded that he should have human flesh for sustenance in accordance with the promise given him. Our father Adam, however, protested, and pointed out that, as nobody had ever tasted human flesh or blood, it was impossible to maintain that it was the most luscious of food. Thus he gained a year's respite for himself and his race; and, in the interval, the mosquito was sent round the world with instructions to taste and report upon the blood of every living creature. At the end of twelve months it was to proclaim in open court the result of its researches. Now Adam had a friend in that sacred bird the swallow, which annually makes its pilgrimage to Mecca and all Holy Places. This bird, unseen of the mosquito, shadowed it all the twelve months till the great day of decision came. Then, as the insect was on its way to the court, the swallow met it openly and asked what flesh and blood it had found the sweetest. " Man's," replied the mosquito. " What? " said the swallow. " Please say it again distinctly, for I am rather deaf." On this the mosquito opened its mouth wide to shout the answer, when the bird, with incredible swiftness, darted in his bill and plucked out the dangerous insect's tongue. They then proceeded on their way to the place where, by appointment, all living creatures were assembled to hear the final decision. On being asked the outcome of his investigations, the mosquito, who could now only buzz, was unable to make himself understood, and the swallow, pretending to be his spokesman, declared that the insect had told him that he had found the blood of the frog most delicious. In corroboration of this statement, he said that he had accompanied the

mosquito on his travels; and many of the animals present,
who had come from different remote regions, testified to
having seen both the mosquito and the swallow at the same
time in their special countries. Sentence was therefore
given that frogs, and not men, should be the serpent's food.
In its rage and disappointment the serpent darted forward
to destroy the swallow; but the latter was too quick, and
the serpent only succeeded in biting some feathers out of the
middle of its tail, which is why all swallows have the tail
forked. Baffled in this manner, the serpent—which was
then a quadruped, and could in one hour travel as far as a
man could walk in seven days—though he might neither
devour men nor suck their blood, yet sought every opportunity for stinging and slaying them, and did no end of harm
till the time of Solomon, the king and sage, who cursed
him so effectually that his legs fell off and he became a
reptile. He indeed begged hard to be spared the punishment, but the king, who knew what his promises were
worth, remained inexorable. Once, when Solomon was at
Damascus, the serpent and the mole came to him, the former
asking that its legs might be restored, and the latter to be
provided with eyes. The king replied that he was at
Damascus on special business, and could only hear petitions
at Jerusalem, where he would be in one week's time. On
his return to El-Kûds, the first petitioners announced to him
were the serpent and the mole. In reply to their requests
he said that, as they had both been able to travel from
Damascus to the Holy City in as short a time as he had done
with chariot and horses, it was clear that the serpent did
not need legs nor the mole eyes.

Next to life and good health, 'Aish, i.e. bread, the staff of
life, is the most precious of Allah's good gifts to men—
Orientals treat it with great reverence. A morsel noticed
lying on the floor or ground is at once picked up, kissed as
something sacred, and then placed somewhere where it will
not be trampled on, but may be reached by birds, mice or
insects. The following is related to teach the sinfulness of
misusing bread.

A woman carrying her infant in a small hammock hanging
at her back and bearing a batié, or circular wooden trough,
full of hot loaves covered with a tabak, or round straw tray,

upon her head, was walking in a peasant wedding procession on its way to Malha, a village S.W. of Jerusalem.
The babe began to cry, and the mother realised that it
needed cleaning.   Having nothing else handy, the wicked
woman took a loaf for the purpose.   Instantly the sky
clouded over, a terrific storm arose, the other people in the
procession were turned into a line of rugged rocks which
are to this day pointed out, and the woman, being blown off
her feet and lying on her face, found the overturned *batié*
grown on to her back, and the *tabak* lying under her and grown
into union with the *batié*, thus forming the carapace or shell
to her person which had, as a Divine punishment, become a
tortoise, the ancestress of all tortoises; whilst her child had
been changed into a monkey, the ancestor of all monkeys. [10]

[10] See p. 269.

XI

ABOUT PLANTS

THE Kharrûb,* among other trees and shrubs, such as the fig, the sycamore and the caper-bush, is a perch for demons of various kinds and so classed among the unholy plants; while the olive tree, among others, is sacred, not only because of its great value in furnishing oil and food, but also on account of the following legend:

At the death of Mohammed the trees, with a few exceptions—such as the oak, the pine, the orange and the citron—went into mourning by shedding their leaves as they do in winter. When the others were asked why they did not do the same, the olive, as their elder and spokesman, replied, "You show your sorrow by external signs, but our grief, who care not for the opinion of others, but only that Allah, who reads the secrets of the heart, should approve of our motives, is no less sincere, though inward. Should you cleave my trunk open, for instance, you will find that at its core it has become black with grief."

The Abhar † is another sacred tree, because its nut is used in the manufacture of rosaries,‡ and because, when he fled from Pharaoh, Moses, tired in the shadeless desert, planted his staff of storax in the soil and lay down in its scanty shade, which was instantly increased, Allah causing the staff to sprout and put forth branches bearing leaves and blossoms. In like manner the Miriamiyeh or sage § is much esteemed; not only for its medicinal properties, which cause its dried leaves to be burned in fumigation in cases of cholera, small-pox, measles and other contagious and

* *Ceratonia siliqua.*
† *Storax officinalis.*
‡ Called in Arabic Massâbin (praising instrument), and used by Moslems and Christians at their devotions.
§ *Salvia ceratophyx vel controversa.*

epidemic diseases, while an infusion of its leaves is a specific for various maladies; but also because the Virgin Mary, being overcome with fatigue during her flight into Egypt, rested under a sage bush, and, breaking off a bunch of its leaves, wiped her brow with them; and when she rose refreshed, blessed the plant and bestowed upon it the virtues it now possesses.

The Nubk of Lotus * is also a sacred plant. It often marks the boundaries between the lands of different villages, and some believe that the hedge surrounding Paradise is formed of it. When a lotus tree has attained the age of forty years it often becomes the abode of some departed saint. It is therefore a dangerous thing to cut down a lotus tree that is above that age, as the saint might resent the deed. In travelling through Palestine one usually meets with clumps of sacred trees, not necessarily always lotus, which are thus haunted by the spirits of holy men; and on Thursday evening especially, one sometimes sees these trees lighted up, and can hear snatches of sacred instrumental music proceeding therefrom, while lights appear to be darting from tree to tree. It is a sign that the saints are keeping festival and exchanging visits. A sacred tree much affected by such spirits is the Tamarisk.† If, when passing these trees on windy nights, you listen attentively, you may sometimes hear the holy name of " Allah " soughing through the branches.

It is not generally known that one of the proofs that the time when the Orthodox Greek Christians celebrate Christmas is the right one, and that the Latins and other Westerns are wrong in the time of their celebration, is that on the Greek Christmas Eve all trees and plants, but especially those on the banks of the Jordan, worship the Saviour. This important fact was discovered in the following manner:—A certain man rode into Lydda shortly before midnight on the Greek Christmas Eve. On reaching his quarters he tied up his donkey to the trunk of a palm tree which, as it lay prostrate in the yard, he naturally supposed had been blown down by a recent storm. Next morning, however,

Zizyphus spina Christi. †*Tamaria Syriaca.*

when he arose and went to look after his donkey, his astonishment was great to find the tree erect and the ass hanging beside and from the palm trunk. As the animal was quite dead, the fact was proved beyond dispute.

Another remarkable plant, much talked about, is the " 'Ushbet el Kurkaa " or " Tortoise-herb." [1] He who finds this plant has made his fortune in more senses than one. In the first place, its leaves are of pure gold. Further, if one is so fortunate as to find and gather it, he has the marvellous power of unconsciously gaining the good-will of everybody, and can, if he choose, fascinate both men and women and make them his willing slaves. Even should he unconsciously tread upon this plant, without picking it, he is able, without himself being conscious of the fact, or others being able to explain it, to win the love and esteem of all whom he meets. Even goats which browse upon it have their teeth turned to gold. Unfortunately this plant is extremely rare. Some years ago there was a fellâh living in a village in Judea who knew all about it, where it grew, at what season it might be found, its appearance, and so forth. He was offered a large sum of money by a rich Bethlehemite for these secrets, but, being a man of high principles, he refused the offer rather than betray the honour of the countryside by putting a Christian in possession of such powers. He is dead now, and his knowledge perished with him.

[1] See p. 269.

XII

ABOUT COFFEE

THE origin of coffee-drinking is connected with various legends and superstitious ideas. The shrub on which the coffee-berry grows is said to be indigenous in Abyssinia, and the story runs that the virtues of the plant were discovered by accident. Fleeing from persecution, towards the end of the third century, a party of monks from Egypt found refuge in the Abyssinian highlands, where they settled and supported themselves by agriculture and the care of flocks, which were entrusted in turn to the pastoral care of different brethren. One of these came to the prior one night with the strange tale that the sheep and goats would not go to rest in their fold, but were frisking and lively to such a degree that he feared that they had been bewitched. This state of things continued, in spite of prayers and exorcisms, for several days, till at last the prior resolved himself to herd the animals. Leading them out to pasture, he observed what plants they browsed on, and thus discovered that their sleeplessness was the effect of the leaves of a certain shrub. Experimenting on himself by chewing some buds of the same plant, he found that he was easily able to keep awake during the long night services which his form of religion prescribed. Thus was coffee discovered.

It was not at first used as a beverage, but eaten in the form of a paste, something like chocolate. It was introduced into Arabia in pre-Islamic times, probably not later than the time of the famous Crusade undertaken by Elesbaan, or Caleb Negus, the Nagash of Arab authors, in order to punish the Himyaritic Jewish ruler, Yûsif Yarûsh, surnamed " Dhu Nowâs," who had been persecuting the Christians. When Mohammedans were prohibited the use of wine, its place was taken by decoctions of coffee-berries. The name

" coffee " is derived from the Arabic *Kahweh* (pronounced *Kahveh* by the Turks), and, in its primary sense, denoted wine or other intoxicating liquors. " The city of Aden," says Crichton, " is the first on record that set the example of drinking it as a common refreshment, about the middle of the fifteenth century. A drowsy mufti, called Jemaleddìn, had discovered that it disposed him to keep awake, as well as to a more lively exercise of his spiritual duties." This is clearly a version of the story of the Abyssinian monks above given. Jemâl-ed-dìn, according to Crichton, died A.D. 1470, " and such was the reputation which his experience had given to the virtues of coffee, that in a short time it was introduced by Fakreddin at Mecca and Medina. It seems, however, that it was not till the commencement of the sixteenth century that it was introduced to Cairo.

Its introduction caused a bitter theological controversy among the Moslems. In A.D. 1511 it was publicly condemned at Mecca by a conclave of the 'ulema, who declared its use contrary to Islâm and hurtful both to body and soul. This decision of the learned was echoed at Cairo. All the warehouses where the " seditious berry " (*bunn*) was stored were purposely burnt down, the coffee-houses closed, and their keepers pelted with the sherds of their pots and cups. This was in 1524, but by an order of Selem I, the decrees of the learned were reversed, the disturbances in Egypt quieted, the drinking of coffee declared perfectly orthodox; and when two Persian doctors, who had asserted it to be injurious to health, had been hanged by the Sultan's orders, the coffee-cup began its undisturbed reign. It now rules supreme in the East. If you want anyone, to whom it would be an insult to offer bakshìsh, to do you a favour, you find that " a cup of coffee " renders him gracious and open to persuasion; and in the same way, if you want to get rid of an enemy, all you have to do is to get someone to administer " a cup of coffee " to him. This double usefulness of " a cup of coffee " is proverbial. Coffee-making and drinking among the desert Arabs are associated with observances which make it a quasi-religious ceremony. Only a man is allowed to prepare the beverage, and he must do it with the greatest care. The berries are roasted in a shallow ladle or pan (*mahmaseh*), and when half-roasted they are pounded in a stone or wooden mortar with a great pestle (*mahbash*), the pounding being carried on rhythmically thus. Whilst the pounding is proceeding a coffee-pot (*búkraj*) is placed on the fire. When the water boils the pot is taken off the fire and the coffee-meal is put into the hot water. It is then placed on the fire again, and when it has boiled up, the pot is again taken off, and then allowed to boil a second and a third time. The coffee-maker, holding in his left hand a row of small cups placed one inside the other, then pours a little coffee into the topmost and rinses it with the liquid, which he then pours into the second and others in turn, rinsing them all in turn with the coffee he poured into the first cup. When he has rinsed the last cup he pours its contents into the fire as a libation to the Sheykh esh Shadhilly, the patron of coffee-drinkers. Half a cupful is now handed to the eldest and most honoured guest, and then a second cup, and so on to all others in turn. To offer a full cup is considered a studied insult, and so also is the offer of a third cup. The saying is, " The first cup for the guest, the second for enjoyment, and the third for the sword." *

Wherever a party of coffee-drinkers assemble, there the spirit of esh Shadhilly is present to keep them from harm; and in like manner when a bride is leaving her parents' house in order to be taken to that of her bridegroom, the keeper of a neighbouring coffee-house will show his good-will by rushing out of his place of business and pouring a cup of coffee on the ground on the pathway at her feet in order to propitiate his patron saint and dispose him in her favour.

A large number of people were assembled in a village guest-house. Coffee was being prepared for them. Beside the fire stood a very large stock-pot, out of which the person who made the coffee replenished a smaller pot in which he boiled the liquor after adding fresh coffee-meal. He then, after the libation above described, handed a cup of coffee

* Who the mysterious Sheykh esh Shadhilly is I cannot tell, but must refer the reader to page 121 of the *Palestine Exploration Quarterly* for April 1905.

to the man nearest him, who out of politeness handed it to the one next to him, and who in his turn gave it to the next, and so on, till it had passed all round the company untasted. The coffee-maker was surprised when the cup was returned to him untasted. Somebody suggested that esh Shadhilly must have had some hand in the matter, and had purposely prevented those present from tasting the coffee. Hereupon the coffee-pots were emptied out, when, to the horror of all beholders, the dead body of a venomous serpent (according to one version of this story, of a toad) fell out of the stockpot. How it got in no one ever knew, but it was seen how esh-Sheykh esh Shadhilly had protected his votaries.

Besides the large stock-pot it is no uncommon thing to have little brass or tinned copper pots standing near the fire ready to be filled from the larger vessel and set to boil. It is not always safe to partake of coffee made in such vessels, as they are not always kept clean and freshly tinned, and sad cases of copper oxide poisoning have happened through their use.

The proverbial saying above quoted concerning the third up is illustrated by the following story :—

During a famine in the early part of last century a Bedawi sheykh left his encampment somewhere in the Gaza district and went down to Egypt with men and camels to buy corn. Night came on after he had crossed the frontier, and about midnight, seeing a light in the distance, the sheykh, who had never before visited that part of the country, thought that some village must be near by. He left his men and camels where they were and went to reconnoitre. The light proceeded from a house the door of which was ajar. As he smelt coffee-berries roasting, he concluded it was a guest-house, and boldly entered. But he was mistaken. The only persons in the lighted chamber were an unveiled woman and a Memlûk, her husband. The woman screamed and hid her face at sight of a man in the doorway, but her husband rebuked her fears and asked the stranger what he wanted. The sheykh replied that he had thought the place was a guest-house but, since he was mistaken, would go away again. The Memlûk, however, insisted on his remaining, and gave him a cup of coffee. When he had drunk this his host offered him a second cup, which he accepted. A third cup he declined, although pressed to take it. Finding his solicitations useless, the Memlûk drew his sword and threatened to kill the Bedawi unless he took a third cup. The man still refused, saying that he preferred being killed. " Why? " asked his grim host. " Because," answered the sheykh, " the first cup is for the guest, the second for enjoyment, and the third for the sword. Though, indeed, I am a warrior, even as thou art, yet at present I am unarmed, seeing that I am here on business connected with peace and not with war." " Well," answered the Memlûk, sheathing his weapon, " thy answer shows thee to be a true man. I took thee to be a skulking thief, but I see that I was mistaken. Remain under my roof as my guest." The sheykh accepted the invitation, and when he told his host the purpose of his visit to Egypt, the latter, who had a great deal of corn for sale, transacted business with him, and for several years in succession supplied him and his tribe with grain. In the year 1811, however, the massacre of the Memlûks, by the orders of Mohammad Ali, took place, and it so happened that the only person to escape was the one who figures in this story. He, it is said, managed to make his escape to the tents of his Bedawi friend and was protected and harboured by him till the time came when he could return home without fear.

Tourists visiting the citadel at Cairo are, indeed, shown the place where, according to legend, Emin Bey made his horse leap from the battlements; but many of the native Cairenes assert that he was not there at all, having received warning of the Pasha's plot through someone connected with the harîm. What the truth is Allah knows !*

* The greater part of the foregoing paper was originally contributed by the writer to the Palestine Exploration Fund's Quarterly Statement as well as several of the animal stories in Section III; and they are reproduced with additional remarks by permission of the P.E.F. Committee.

XIII

SOME MAGIC CURES

THE Hebrew part of A. M. Luncz's interesting *Jerusalem Year-Book* for 1881 contains on pages 20–28, and under the title " Vain Belief," an account of some abject and degrading superstitions connected not only with quack nostrums but even with demon-worship. From this account as well as from my personal investigation the following notes are compiled, as I have ascertained that the said superstitions are still common among all creeds in Palestine.

Of all popular quack remedies the chief is *múmmia* or mummy. The drug is sold at a high price, about five piastres, or tenpence, a dram, by the native apothecaries, and is supposed to consist not only of fragments of human bodies, bones, etc., embalmed in Egypt centuries ago, but also of human remains found among the sand-hills on the Hâj route to Mecca and Medìna. It is said to be specially efficacious against the " evil eye," sudden frights and nervous complaints; and is generally used in the following manner.

A small piece of *múmmia* is pounded very fine in a mortar, and sometimes mixed with sugar or spice. A handful of this powder is then placed over-night on the house-top in order to be wet with the dew, or it is mixed with a cup of coffee and administered to the patient on nine successive nights. On the fifth and the ninth night the patient is bathed from head to foot before the drug is administered to him, or her; and somebody must sit beside the sick person the whole night through, to see if the remedy takes effect, which it is supposed it ought to do on one of these two nights. The patient is generally restricted to a diet of bread and milk; though I know of the case of a girl nine or ten years old who had sustained a severe injury to her neck by a fall from a mule (or, as the natives asserted, " had received a slap on the face from an angel "), being kept for six weeks on a diet of honey and almonds only. Throughout the period of treatment the patient must be prevented from smelling any strong or offensive smells, such as onions or fish; and women who are at all unwell or pregnant must not approach the dwelling lest either they themselves or the patient receive an injury. Whilst the *múmmia* cure is being carried on, such of the neighbours as live in the same building or courtyard and have faith in the nostrum forsake their dwellings for fear of contagion or other evil effects, which are, however, supposed to be neutralised by drawing the picture of a hand over the door of the dwelling.

More remarkable than the *múmmia* is the " Indúlko " cure which is practised by the Sephardim, who believe it to be a remedy for nervous complaints, fits caused by sudden fright, barrenness, proneness to miscarriage, etc., etc. It is divided into two categories, that of the " lesser " and the " greater " Indúlko (possibly the original name was " indulgo "), and is connected with an actual ritual of demon-worship conducted by a witch priestess, or " knowing woman." The details of the ceremony may vary in unimportant points, but its general features are as follows:

All members of the family and all neighbours living in the same building or court are obliged to quit the dwelling for some days, during which time the patient lives alone attended by no one but the female who is to perform the ceremony. The house is carefully cleared of all books, papers, etc., on which the name of God or any words of Scripture are written, and even the *Mezuzahs* are removed from the doorposts. The patient is instructed that he must carefully abstain from offering up any prayer to the Almighty, quoting words of Scripture, or mentioning any of the names, attributes, etc., of the Most High, during the nights on which the invocation of the demons is to take place. The " wise woman " brings with her a small quantity of wheat, barley, water, salt, honey, four to six eggs, some milk and two kinds of sweetmeats or sugar. At midnight she takes these eatables, the eggs excepted, and having mixed them up she sprinkles them round the patient's bed, at the threshold of the chamber, and in its four corners. Whilst doing this she utters the following petition:—

" We beseech you, O our lords, that you would have mercy and pity upon the soul of your sick servant So-and-So, the son of your handmaiden So-and-So, and that you will cause his iniquity to pass away, and in case he have sinned against or injured you, that ye would pardon his sin and restore to him his soul, his strength and creation, *i.e.* perfect health." (Should the patient be a barren woman desiring offspring, the sorceress says: " And that ye would open her womb, restore the fruit of her belly, and loose her fetters." For a female liable to miscarriage the petition runs thus: " And that ye would quicken for her the lives of her sons and daughters." The prayer continues thus: " And lo, here is honey " (or sugar), " which is in order to sweeten your mouths or jaws; and corn and barley as food for your kine and lesser cattle; and the water and salt are to establish love, brotherliness, peace and friendship as by an everlasting covenant of salt between us and you." The woman then breaks the eggs into the latrines, etc., prostrates herself on the floor in the attitude of worship, and after kissing the pavement several times continues the invocation as follows:—
" Lo this shall be to you the sacrifice of a soul in substitution for a soul,* in order that ye may restore to us the soul of this sick person and grant his desire." This invocation is several times repeated, and during three successive nights. It may be done, should the three nights not prove effectual for a cure, seven or even nine nights in succession. We must remark that the latter part of these ceremonies is performed in latrines, wash-houses, subterranean chambers, cellars, and round about cisterns, etc.; and that the sick person is sometimes kept all night in such quarters.

However, if the patient be poor and unable to afford the expense of the ceremony above described, or in case the neighbours refuse to vacate their dwellings, then the person who officiates goes to the cistern, cr the wash-house, latrines,

* As an egg contains the germ of a life, it is supposed to be a fit substitute for a human life.

etc., and pours out a little salt water and utters the aforesaid prayer, shortening it thus:—" Behold, here is salt and water, let there speedily be peace between us and you." On account of its being cheap this form of adjuration is very often used. In the case of a poor man being discouraged because his business does not prosper, salt water is in like manner sprinkled at the entrance of his shop, etc., whilst the shortened formula is uttered. Should a man or woman meet with an accident, such as a fall which has resulted in a broken leg or arm, a sprained ankle, etc., etc., the exact spot where the misfortune occurred is ascertained and sprinkled with water, whilst the short formula is repeated. In some cases, however (as the present writer has ascertained by personal inquiry), should the injury received be a very severe one, the ceremony is varied in the following manner:— At midnight, the knowing woman, after having sprinkled the exact spot where the accident happened with salt water, and then strewed sugar over it, adds to her petition the following clause: " Forgive, we pray you, So-and-So, son or daughter of your handmaiden So-and-So, for having unconsciously, and without intending it, disturbed and perhaps hurt one of you, and restore him or her to health, etc., etc." The dust of the spot is then carefully gathered up and mixed with water. Doses of this precious mixture are then administered to the patient from time to time. " The greater Indûlko " differs from " the lesser " above described in being more expensive, and continued for a greater length of time, sometimes for forty or even fifty days. The sick-room is luxuriously furnished, the patient arrayed in " costly white garments," whilst the room is brilliantly lighted up with candles, and a table spread not only with the edibles above mentioned, but with other sweetmeats and delicacies as well as with flowers, perfumes, etc., in abundance. The form of adjuration, or prayer to the demons, is the same as that above described.

" Freskûra " is the name of another superstitious remedy used by Sephardim women for the benefit of their children, if the latter happen to suffer from fits, fever, etc. The nostrum is prepared in the following manner:—

Vegetable-marrows or cucumbers (those grown at Ain Kârim are said, for reasons not ascertained, to be best suited for the purpose) have their insides carefully scooped out. They are then soaked in a solution of indigo and exposed on the roof over-night in order to be wetted with dew. On the eve of the ninth day of Ab, the anniversary of the destruction of the Jewish Temples, no other day or night of the year being appropriate, they are taken to the Synagogue, and when the service has reached a certain point at which the ceremony of extinguishing lights takes place, the vegetables are stuffed with a mixture of pine-seeds (*snobar*) and yellow clay, moistened with the juice of unripe grapes. The vegetables thus stuffed are then left to dry in the sun for several weeks till their insides have been baked hard. If the child happens to be ill with fever, a fragment of one of these marrows is put into his mouth and rubbed by the " knowing woman " against his palate. Whilst she does this she says, " Depart heat, enter coolness (*freskûra*); enter coolness (*freskûra*), depart heat." Pieces of the dried vegetable and its contents are then rubbed over the sufferer's body and limbs. The nostrum is said to be efficacious, if worn as an amulet, to keep off danger from " the evil eye," etc.

The superstition concerning " the evil eye " has been so often written about by others, that it is unnecessary to describe it here. Among the notes to this section is the translation of a typical written Jewish charm or amulet which bears on the subject.[1]

[1] See p. 269.

XIV

SUNDAY.—Is a specially favourable day for planting and building. A child born on a Sunday is blessed. It is not good to pare one's nails on a Sunday; but cupping is permitted.

MONDAY.—Is a good day on which to start a journey, and to take precautions about obtaining food. Roman Catholic and also Protestant natives are generally of the opinion that a child born on a Monday has a chubby round face. The Jews fast on Monday in memory of Moses' descent from Sinai and breaking the first tables of the Law on that day. Go into debt for your food, but do not work on a Monday. Do not visit an infirm person on a Monday, for your doing so will augment his sufferings. If you spend any of your money on Monday morning you will be a loser the whole week through. Maidens fast on Mondays in order that they may soon be married; and old women in order that St. Michael may be with them when they die.

TUESDAY.—According to the Hadith, or written Mohammedan tradition, it is good to pare one's nails on a Tuesday. This is the day for fighting and bloodshed. Mars' day.

WEDNESDAY.—Is the day for misfortune. Every Wednesday has at least one unlucky hour. It is the day for cleansing. The child born on a Wednesday is amiable and cheerful.

THURSDAY.—Is the proper day for bleeding and cupping. The child born on this day is inclined to theft. The Jews fast in memory of Moses' ascending Sinai in order to fetch the tables of the Law. This is the day on which widows are married, maidens on Wednesdays.

FRIDAY.—The day for betrothals and weddings. The Hadith prescribes, " Anoint yourselves with precious ointments on Fridays." Whoever falls sick on a Friday will die. If a person is born on a Friday he will either die himself or else his father or mother will. If a mother strike her son on the eye on a Friday, whilst standing on the doorstep when the muezzin calls to prayer, she causes the Jân to ride the child and drive him mad. The great underground river which runs past the Damascus gate stops running in order to worship on Fridays. Do not crave water from a well on Fridays at the time of the muezzin's call to prayer. Should you do so the Jân in the well will snatch away your intellect.

SATURDAY.—It is a meritorious act to visit (the graves of) the dead on Saturdays. It is injurious to a sick person to be visited on Saturday. A child born on Saturday will be poor and hardly ever become strong and healthy.

The first four days of every month, and also the four days immediately following the tenth, are "full" or lucky days, and should therefore be chosen for sowing, planting, or starting a new enterprise.

The five days after the fourth, and the fifteenth, are "empty" or unlucky.

KANÛN EL AWWAL = DECEMBER.

On St. Barbara's Day (Dec. 4), water gushes out at the mouse-hole. Maidens put kohl to their eyes; and in every family corn is boiled. A plate of this boiled grain is set apart for each member of the household, relatives, friends, etc., respectively, and, with sugar and pomegranate seeds sprinkled over it, is put away for the night in order that Mar Saba, whose day is that immediately after St. Barbara's, may trample upon it and bless the household and the household stores.

The local form of the legend of St. Barbara is curious and runs thus:—

Barbara's father was a great Roman officer, a Pagan, who lived in the Kula'a or Citadel at Jerusalem, where, it is said, his dwelling still exists. The daughter was converted to

Christianity, and as she refused to recant, her father and brother were so angry that they shut her up for four days in a hot oven. When, at the end of the time, they opened the oven, the maiden, to their great surprise, came forth alive and well. As she still refused to deny Christ it was resolved to boil her to death. A great cauldron full of water was therefore put on the fire; but when it began to boil and the heathen were about to put Barbara in, it was found to be so full of wheat that there was no room for the saint. Her father and brother then took their swords and between them slew her, but were themselves struck by lightning immediately afterwards. St. Barbara's Day is kept by Latins, Greeks and Armenians.

Kanûn eth Thâni = January.

This month is dumb (*i.e.* damp and miserable), and so cold that the hens lay blood-stained eggs. On New Year's Day the table is left as it is, with the dishes and food upon it, after meals, in order that the mighty ones amongst the Jân (El furrâs el Janìyen) may deposit bags of gold upon it. On other days of the year, however, the table is not left in this condition. If it were, it would be carried off by angels.

At the Feast of the Epiphany the dough rises without being leavened, and leaven made from this dough must on no account be lent to anyone. Special graces are showered down at the Epiphany, and it is said that the trees on the banks of the Jordan adore the Saviour on this festival. (See "Animal and Plant-lore" chapter.) Whoever eats lentils during the twelve days following the Feast of the Nativity is sure to be smitten with the mange.

Shebât = February.

A smiter, a plunger, a wallower, and nevertheless with a summer-scent about him. No reliance can be placed on February. This is the month for cats to kitten. The sunshine of February sets the head throbbing, *i.e.* causes violent headaches.

Adâr = March.

Adâr is the father of earthquakes and showers. Save up your largest pieces of charcoal for your uncle Adâr. He will satisfy you with seven great snowfalls, not reckoning small ones. And yet, during Adâr, the shepherd can dry his drenched clothing without a fire. It is said that the sunshine of Adâr causes clothes hung out to dry to become exceedingly white. For this reason it is a favourite time for women to do their washing, and more especially to wash their *azars*, i.e. the white sheets in which they envelop themselves when they go abroad.* The sunshine of Adâr also makes the complexion fair. Therefore old women say, " The sunshine of Shebât for my daughter-in-law (because it causes headache); that of Adâr for my daughter (because it beautifies the complexion); and of Nisân (April) for my senility (because it brings fresh life and vigour)." On the Festival of the Forty Martyrs it is customary to light forty wicks, placed in oil, in honour of those saints " who were Christians of the days of Nero. In order to force them to recant they were exposed naked the whole of a snowy night in Adâr, with revelry and festivity going on before their eyes in a palace in front them; and they were informed that if, during the night, any of them desired to deny Christ, all he had to do was to enter the palace and join in the festivities. At midnight one of them did so; but his place was immediately taken by one of the Roman sentries, who thus proved his sincerity in confessing the Saviour. Next morning the whole party, whose number had thus been preserved intact, were found frozen to death." The three first days of Adâr were called " El Mustakridât," a name which means " Lent-out ones," and is generally explained by the following legend:—

An aged Bedawi shepherdess, keeping her flocks in one of the wadies trending downwards to the Dead Sea, was heard by Shebât, who is thought of as a personality, mocking him because he had failed to send rain. Furious at being thus derided, Shebât said to Adâr, " O my brother Adâr, I have only three days left me, and they are not sufficient to enable me to be revenged on the old woman who has derided me. Lend me, therefore, three days of thine." Adâr willingly

* The custom of wearing an *azar*, which was universal during the early part of the nineteenth century, has become obsolete. One very rarely sees a woman thus dressed nowadays.

granted his brother's request. Six days of heavy rain were
the result, and the *seyls*, or winter torrents from the hills,
swept the old woman and her flock into the sea.   If the year
is to be good it depends upon Adâr.   The Moslems say,
" The meat and *leben* of Adâr are forbidden to the infidels,"
meaning that they are so good that the Christians must not
taste them—a chuckle at the strict Fast of Lent.

NISÂN = APRIL.

Nisân is the life of mankind, *i.e.* it revives and invigorates.
During the rain-showers of Nisân the bivalves (oysters)
living at the bottom of the sea rise to the surface and open
their shells.   As soon as a drain-drop falls into one of these
open oysters, the shell closes and the creature sinks to the
bottom.   The rain-drop inside it becomes a pearl.

It is customary for people to picnic out during Nisân and
drink milk at such picnics.

IY-YÂR = MAY.

Iy-yâr ripens the apricots and cucumbers.   Serpents and
partridges become white.   (I suppose that this means that
during this month snakes change their skins and partridges
moult.)

HEZERAN AND TAMMÛZ = JUNE AND JULY.

Boil the water in the cruse, *i.e.* these are hot months.

AB = AUGUST.

The dreaded month.   However, pluck the cluster (of
grapes) and fear nought, *i.e.* the grapes are ripe, and may be
eaten with impunity.   Beware of holding a knife on Ab 29,
the Day of the beheading of St. John the Baptist.

EYLÛL = SEPTEMBER.

On the Eve of the Festival of the Cross (Holy Cross Day,
Sept. 14) it is customary to expose on the house-top during the
night seven small heaps of salt, which respectively represent
the seven months following Eylûl.   By noticing next morning
which of these heaps of salt is dampest it is possible to know
in which months there will be heavy rain.

TASHRIN EL AW-AL AND TASHRIN ETH-THÂNI = OCTOBER
AND NOVEMBER.

People born during these two months are swift to be
angry.

In case of a death in the house, it is not permitted to sweep
it for three days, lest other members of the household should
die in consequence.

Be careful never to spill water without " naming," otherwise the Jân may molest and stick to you. Beware never to
step over a boy's head lest he either get a scabby head or die
in consequence.

During the period between the Carnival and Palm
Sunday, the souls (ghosts) of the departed have permission
to visit their living friends.

Every odd number, and especially the number eleven, is
unlucky.

It is better to meet a demon (kird) the first thing in the
morning than to meet a man who has naturally a hairless
face.

A one-eyed man is very difficult to get on with, and a
man with a kûsa or pointed goat's beard is more cunning
than Iblîs himself.

Boils are the consequence of the sufferer's having attempted
to count the stars. He who spills salt will suffer from tumours.

It is a sin to kill a turtle-dove because this bird was tinged
with drops of the Saviour's blood at the Crucifixion.

If a quarrel is proceeding, and a person present turns a
shoe upside down, the stife will become more violent.

Tall people are simpletons.

If a dog howls at night under the window of a house, it is a
sign that someone in that house will die.

Should you hear a dog howling at night, turn a shoe upside
down and he will be sure to stop.*

* The overturning of a shoe has been explained to me as an act of
respect towards the Jân. When Allah is worshipped the face is directed
towards Him and the soles of the feet are furthest away. By turning
the sole of the shoe, therefore, furthest away from the Jân, one implies
a respect bordering on worship. The demons accept the compliment
and are mollified, and Allah, Who is good, and knows that no insult
is intended to Him, does not resent the act.

NOTES

NOTES

SECTION I

I

[1] The contents of this chapter are practically identical with Mejr-ed-din, Vol. I, though it is here derived from the lips of an Arab Khatib.

[2] (P. 4.) The idea of the great serpent is analogous to that of the great Midgard-snake in Scandinavian myths.

[3] (P. 5.) *The great Kàf range*, or the Caucasus.—Washington Irving's book *The Successors of Mahomet* contains in Chapter XXXII the following information:

"According to Moslem belief, a great irruption of Gog and Magog is to be one of the signs of the latter days, fore-running the resurrection and final judgment. They are to come from the north in a mighty host, covering the land as a cloud; so that when subdued, their shields and bucklers, their bows and arrows and quivers, and the staves of their spears, shall furnish the Faithful with fuel for seven years. All which is evidently derived from the book of the prophet Ezekiel, with which Mahomet had been made acquainted by his Jewish instructors.

"The Koran makes mention of a wall built as a protection against these fearful people of the north by Dhu'lkarneym, or the Two Horned; by whom some suppose is meant Alexander the Great, others a Persian king of the first race, contemporary with Abraham.

"And they said, O Dhu'lkarneym, verily, Gog and Magog waste the land. . . . He answered, I will set a strong wall between you and them. Bring me iron in large pieces, until it fill up the space between the two sides of these mountains. And he said to the workmen, Blow with your bellows until it make the iron red hot; and bring me molten brass, that I may pour upon it. Wherefore, when this wall was finished,

Gog and Magog could not scale it, neither could they dig through it.—Sale's *Koran*, chap. 18.''

The Czar Peter the Great, in his expedition against the Persians, saw in the neighbourhood of the city of Derbend, which was then besieged, the ruins of a wall which went up hill and down dale, along the Caucasus, and was said to extend from the Euxine to the Caspian. It was fortified from place to place, by towers or castles. It was eighteen Russian stades in height; built of stones laid up dry; some of them three ells long and very wide. The colour of the stones, and the traditions of the country, showed it to be of very great antiquity. The Arabs and Persians said that it was built against the invasions of Gog and Magog.—See *Travels in the East*, by Sir William Ousley.

In one of the stories told by Shahr-Zad the reader will perceive the germ of one of the Arabian tales of Sindbad the Sailor. It is recorded to the following purport by Tabari the Persian historian:—" One day as Abda'lrahman was seated by Shahr-Zad, conversing with him, he perceived upon his finger a ring decorated with a ruby, which burned like fire in the daytime, but at night was of dazzling brilliancy. ' It came,' said Shahr-Zad, ' from the wall of Yajuj and Majuj; from a king whose dominions between the mountains is traversed by the wall. I sent him many presents, and asked but one ruby in return.' Seeing the curiosity of Abda'lrahman aroused, he sent for the man who had brought the ring, and commanded him to relate the circumstances of his errand.

" ' When I delivered the presents and the letter of Shahr-Zad to that king,' said the man, ' he called his chief falconer, and ordered him to procure the jewel required. The falconer kept an eagle for three days without food, until he was nearly starved; he then took him up into the mountains near the wall, and I accompanied him. From the summit of one of these mountains we looked down into a deep dark chasm like an abyss. The falconer now produced a piece of tainted meat, threw it into the ravine, and let loose the eagle. He swept down after it, pounced upon it as it reached the ground, and returning with it, perched upon the hand of the falconer. The ruby which now shines in that ring was found adhering to the meat.'

"Abda'lrahman asked an account of the wall. 'It is built,' replied the man, ' of stone, iron, and brass, and extends down one mountain and up another.' ' This,' said the devout and all-believing Abda'lrahman, ' must be the very wall of which the Almighty makes mention in the Koran.' "

⁴ (P. 5.) *Behemoth and the great whale.*—This is apparently drawn from Talmudic sources. Thus we read in *Bava Bathre*, fol. 74, col. 2, R. Judah said: " Everything that God created in the world He created male and female. And thus He did with Leviathan the piercing serpent and Leviathan the crooked serpent, He created them male and female. But if they had been united, they would have desolated the entire world. What, then, did the Holy One do? He took away the strength of the male Leviathan, and slew the female and salted her for the righteous for the time to come, for he said: ' And he shall slay the whale (or dragon) that is in the sea ' (Isaiah xxvii. 1). In like manner with regard to Behemoth upon a thousand mountains, He created them male and female, but if they had been united they would have desolated the world. What then did the Holy One do? He took away the strength of the male Behemoth, and made the female barren, and preserved her for the righteous for the time to come." The Moslems, in like manner, believe that the meat of a great bull and a great fish shall furnish forth the feast of the righteous on their entry into Paradise.

There are in the Rabbinical writings many similar allusions to the great ox and the great fish or sea dragon.

⁵ (P. 6.) *Eclipses of the moon.*—On the 6th of October 1903, we had the good fortune to bivouac within the walls of the palace of Meshetta in Moab. While the sun was setting the moon was eclipsed, and a more magnificent spectacle, in surroundings so beautiful and so solitary, could hardly be imagined. Even the impassive Arab servants, most of whom had been long in European service, were impressed, and crowded together with exclamations of surprise and, perhaps, fear. The lady of our party went to remonstrate with them because they had taken a cock from out of the

fowl-crate and were whipping him . . . they alleged " for making noise "; he also had been surprised by the phenomenon, and had crowed. One added, " The people at home, who know no better, will be killing cocks and beating drums . . . this," point to the rival pageants of sun and moon, " will frighten them." Professor Euting then recited the " Sûra of the Daybreak," cxiii., which seemed to meet the needs of the case; the men expressed their satisfaction, and the cock was restored to his family. (Dr. Spoer's " Notes on Bloody Sacrifices in Palestine," Vol. XXV. pp. 312 ff. of *Journal of the American Oriental Society*, 1906, and p. 104 of Vol. XXVII, 1906.)

II

[1] (P. 9.) *The mother of devils.*—For the Jewish notions on this subject see Bodenschatz, III, ch. x. pars. 5–7, pp. 169, 170.

[2] (P. 10.) *Origin of ghouls*, etc.—For Jewish notions (which are also current amongst other Orientals) on this subject, see Bodenschatz, III. ch. x. par. 3, and Wünsche, *Bibliotheca Rabbinica, Midrash Bereshit Rabba*, p. 94, and Edersheim, *Life and Times of Jesus the Messiah*, Appendix XIII. Section III. par. 1; also note 41 of *Tales told in Palestine*, by J. E. Hanauer, edited by H. G. Mitchell (Cincinnati: Jennings and Graham; New York: Eaton and Mains).

[3] (P. 11.) *Cain and Abel.*—Kabil and Habil, or Cain and Abel, with their two sisters, were the first children born to Adam and Eve. Adam, by Allah's direction, ordered Cain to marry Abel's twin sister, and that Abel should marry Cain's, for it being the common opinion that marriages ought not to take place with those very near akin, such as their own sisters, it seemed reasonable to suppose that they ought to take those of the remoter degree, but this Cain refused to agree to, because his sister was the handsomer. [Allah ordained that Hawa should produce children in pairs, a male with a female, in order that some restraint of decency might be imposed on mankind from the outset. It was forbidden for a son to marry his twin sister. Cain, enslaved by

the beauty of his twin sister Abdul Mughis, transgressed this commandment, and eventually murdered Abel, to whom she was promised. To prevent such havoc being wrought by woman's looks, it was from that time forth decreed that all females having reached a certain age should go veiled. [A popular variant of the above.—M. P.] Hereupon Adam told them to make their offerings to Allah, thereby referring the dispute to His determination. . . . Cain's offering was a sheaf of the very worst of his corn, but Abel's a fat lamb of the best of his flock. Allah having declared His acceptance of the latter in a visible manner, Cain said to his brother, "I will certainly kill thee." Abel was the stronger of the two, and would easily have prevailed against his brother, but he answered, " If thou stretchest forth thine hand against me, to slay me, I will not stretch forth my hand against thee to slay thee; for I fear Allah the Lord of all creatures." So Cain began to consider in what way he should effect the murder, and as he was doing so the devil appeared to him in human shape, and showed him how to do it, by crushing the head of a bird between two stones. Cain, having committed the fratricide, became exceedingly troubled in his mind, and carried the dead body on his shoulders for a considerable time, not knowing where to conceal it, till it stank horribly; and then Allah taught him to bury it by the example of a raven, who, having killed another raven in his presence, dug a pit with his claws and beak and buried him therein. Another tradition is that Cain was at last accidentally slain by Lamech with an arrow, when the latter was hunting at Tell el Kaimûn, near the Kishon, at the northern foot of Mount Carmel. (See Sale's *Koran*, p. 76, text and footnote. Chandos Classics.)

4 (P. 11.) *Burial of Adam.*—A Christian tradition to the effect that Adam was buried with his head resting at the foot of Calvary, and that he was reawakened to life by some drops of Christ's blood trickling on to his skull at the Crucifixion, may be traced back to the time of Origen in the second century.

III

[1] (P. 13.) *The nâkûs.*—The *nâkûs* is a plank or plate of metal which is struck with a mallet to announce the time of service. When the Moslems under Omar Ibn el Khattab first took Jerusalem (A.D. 637), the use of church bells was prohibited, but the *nâkûs* was allowed because Noah, by Allah's command, used one thrice a day to call the workmen employed on the ark, and to attract people to hear his warnings of an approaching judgment. When the Crusaders took Jerusalem in A.D. 1099, bells were reinstalled in the churches. One of the complaints made by the Latin Patriarch against the Knights of St. John, was that they disturbed the services held in the Church of the Sepulchre by ringing the bells of their great church close by. The church bells throughout the Holy Land were silenced when the Crusaders were finally driven away in A.D. 1292, but they had ceased ringing in Jerusalem when the city fell into the hands of Saladin, October 2, 1187. In 1823, we are informed by a traveller of the period that the only bell in the city was a hand-bell in the Latin convent. Since the close of the Crimean War, many large church bells have been hung up and are in constant use in various Christian churches in Palestine, though the writer remembers the time when a great riot took place amongst the Moslems at Nablûs because a small bell had been put up in the Mission school in that place.

[2] (P. 15.) *The 'abâyeh,* or *'aba,* is the wide, coarse, outer garment worn by all classes in Palestine, and on occasion adaptable to other uses. See Deut. xxiv. 13; Amos ii. 8; P.E.F. Quarterly Statement, 1881, p. 298. The fables concerning Og are doubtless derived from Rabbinical sources; see article " Og " in Smith's *Bible Dictionary.*

[3] (P. 17.) " The ark informed Noah that here the Beyt el Makdas would be rebuilt." Cf. *Uns el Jelîl,* Cairo edition, Vol. I. pp. 19–22.

[4] (P. 17.) *Marriage of Noah's daughter.*—This story is a very common one. There is a version of it given by P. Baldensperger in one of the Quarterly Statments of the P.E.F. The tomb of one of Noah's daughters is shown as

'Ellar in Southern Palestine, and another, it is said, at or near Baalbec.

IV

1 (P. 18.) *Job*.—In the fourth Christian century many pilgrims used to visit the district east of Jordan in order to see and embrace the dunghill on which Job sat and scratched himself in his day, and even now there may be seen at the ancient santuary called " Esh Sheykh Sa'ad " in the Hauran, the famous " Rock of Job," which modern research has shown to be a monument commemorating the victories of the Egyptian monarch Rameses II. Besides this, there are in Western Palestine at least two " Wells of Job ": one on the western shore of the Sea of Galilee, the other, the well-known Bìr Ayûb, in the Kedron Valley just at the point where it is joined by the traditional Valley of Hinnom. This well is a hundred feet deep, and contains an unfailing supply of water, a great deal of which is carried in skins to supply the needs of Jerusalem. A few steps east of this well, under a ledge of rock, in which may still be seen the vats used by the fullers of antiquity, is a small opening. It is the entrance to a cave which, according to peasants of the neighbouring village of Siloam, was once the dwelling-place of the Patriarch. The existence of these vats so near the well is one of the reasons for believing, as many do, that Bìr Eyyùb is the En-Rogel of the Old Testament.

It is said that Ayûb was a Rûmi, a Greco-Roman descendant of Esau (*i.e.* an Arab subject of the Greco-Roman Empire), and that his wife's name was Rahmeh (Mercy). She, rather than her husband, is the bright example of human patience. A few years ago an Arab woman of the Orthodox Eastern Church disagreed with her husband and went for advice to a priest, who bade her take example from Job's wife.

2 (P. 19.) *El Hakìm Lokman*.—The greater part of the thirty-first sûra of the Koran is a record of wise sayings of Lokman. The following anecdote is related in the larger *Kâmûs* (Dictionary) of El Bistani: " A certain man asked Lokman, ' Did I not once see thee keeping sheep?' He

answered, ' Yes.' ' Then how didst thou attain this degree of greatness?' Lokman answered, ' By speaking the truth, restoring the pledge, and refraining from talk on matters which do not concern me.' "

³ (P. 20.) *Danger of sleeping in the fields where yellow melons grow.*—In order to prevent such accidents, in the occurrence of which they implicitly believe, the fellahìn who have to watch the melon-fields are said to eat a great deal of garlic, and to strew bits of that rank vegetable around their beds. The smell is said to be an effective protection, not only against snakes, but also the evil eye.

⁴ (P. 21.) *Benj* = bhang. Indian hemp, or hashish, figures in Eastern tales, and with effects more wonderful than those of chloroform. This story of Lokman is given in a different version in *Tales told in Palestine*, under the title of "El Hakìm Risto." Various editions and translations of the fables of Lokman have at different times appeared in Europe. The most recent that I know of is by A. Cherbonn (Paris: Hachette & Cie, 1884).

V

¹ (P. 31.) *The rite of circumcision.*—Sarah, in a fit of furious jealousy, is said to have sworn to imbrue her hands in the blood of Hagar. In order to save the life of the latter, and yet to enable his wife to keep her solemn though savage oath, Hagar, at Abraham's suggestion, allowed Sarah to perform upon her the rite of circumcision, to submit to which has, since then, become a *sunnah*, or traditional and religious custom amongst Mohammedan women. (See *Mejr-ed-din*, Vol. I. p. 46.)

² (P. 32.) *The patriarchs said to be not dead but living.*—The tomb of the patriarchs at Hebron is very jealously guarded against intruders who are not Moslems. Very few Christians have ever been admitted even into the courts of the *Haram*; the first in modern times who was allowed to enter being the Prince of Wales (later King Edward VII), who visited the Holy Land in 1862.

Even Mohammedans are forbidden to descend into the

cave below, which is generally supposed to be that of
Machpelah, lest they should disturb the patriarchs and their
harìm, who are conceived of as living in a state of sacred *keyf*
or *dolce far niente*. A couple of hundred years ago a Mohammedan had the temerity to enter the cavern. He suddenly
came upon a lady who was combing her hair. It is supposed
to have been Sarah herself. She threw her comb at the
audacious intruder and hit him in the eyes. He was, in
consequence, blind to his dying day.

It is also related that when Ibrahîm Pasha took Hebron
about a hundred years ago, he likewise attempted to
penetrate into the mausoleum of the patriarchs, and had an
opening made through the masonry enclosing it, but that,
just as he was going to enter, he was taken seriously ill and
had to be carried away unconscious.

VI

[1] (P. 35.) An old tradition, which has been traced back
to the time of Origen, in the second century, says that the
cross on which Christ suffered was, at the Crucifixion, planted
at the head of Adam's tomb, and that some drops of the
Saviour's blood, percolating through the soil and the fissure
made in the rock by the earthquake that then occurred,
touched Adam's skull and revived the progenitor of mankind
to life. He led the band of saints, who, as the Gospel
relates, rose from the dead after Christ's resurrection, and
entering Jerusalem, appeared unto many. The origin of
this legend seems to have been a misunderstanding of the
texts Eph. v. 14 and 21; 1 Cor. xv. 21, 22; 45, 47.

[A Maronite Christian once told me a story, beginning
with the burial of Adam and ending with the Crucifixion,
which lasted a whole summer afternoon. It included the
subject of this note and also that of the foregoing chapter,
yet seemed homogeneous. Melchizedek was, I remember, a
leading character. He buried Adam, carrying his body an
unheard-of distance to Jerusalem, and kept appearing and
disappearing mysteriously throughout the narrative. The
narrator assured me he had found it all in a great book in

the library of a certain convent in Mount Lebanon; but, as he could not read, I suspect the assurance was only to impress me, and I had been listening to a whole cycle of folk-tales.—M. P.]

VII

[1] (P. 37.) *Pilgrimage to Músa's grave.*—The writer was informed some years ago by a native Jew that he had been told by his late father that the latter had been informed by a Moslem sheykh that the annual Mohammedan pilgrimage to the traditional tomb of Moses had been instituted by the early Molsem conquerors of Palestine, in order that in case of disturbances in Jerusalem against the Christian pilgrims who come thither in order to celebrate Easter, a strong body of armed believers might be in reserve and within call in case of necessity. Whether this statement is correct I cannot tell; at any rate, the Neby Mùsa pilgrimage generally coincides in time with the Christian Easter festivities.

[2] (P. 37.) *The stones of the place should be fit for fuel.*—The limestone at Neby Mùsa is bituminous, and somewhat combustible.

VIII

[1] (P. 41.) " *The tower still bears his (David's) name.*"—This tower is situated just inside the city, near the Jaffa Gate. It is often called the Tower of Hippicus, though its base measurements agree more nearly with those of Herod's tower Phasælus.

[2] (P. 43.) *The Kharrûb.*—The Carob tree (*Ceratonia siliqua*), said by tradition to have furnished, in its pods, the locusts which the Baptist ate; and also the husks on which the swine, in the parable of the Prodigal Son, were fed.

[3] (P. 45.) *Stones left unfinished at the death of Solomon.*— These stones are generally called " Hajar el Hibleh " or stone of the pregnant woman, from the belief that the work of cutting and carrying them had been assigned to female jinns in that condition. One such stone is pointed out in the south wall of Jerusalem, and another huge block, on a

hill-top near Hirsha, is said to have been left there by a jinniyeh who dropped it when she heard the welcome news of Solomon's death. (See Clermont-Ganneau's *Archæological Researches*, Vol. I. 69,)

Like Abraham and El Khudr, David appears sometimes in order to protect the Jews. Some instances will be mentioned in Section II in connection with legends possibly founded on facts.

IX

[1] (P. 46.) *Dhu'lkarneim.*—See Sale's *Koran*, Chandos Classics Edition, chap. xviii. pp. 224–25 and footnotes.

[2] (P. 48.) *Elijah's cave on Carmel.*—For other particulars concerning this place and the " treatment " here practised, see Dr. Thomson's *The Land and the Book* (1886), Vol. I. pp. 329 ff.

X

[1] (Pp. 54 ff.) Compare 3 Macc. i. 28, 29; ii. 21–24, with Dean Stanley's *Jewish Church*, Vol. III. p. 248.

NOTES

SECTION II

I

¹ (P. 61.) *Bâb el Khalìl.*—The Western Gate of Jerusalem is called Bâb el Khalìl (the Gate of the Friend, *i.e.* Abraham) probably because it is that by which anyone who is going to Hebron (El Khalìl) would leave the city. But an ornamental Arabic inscription, just inside the sixteenth-century gateway, reminding the passer-by that " Ibrahim was the Friend of Allah," may have given the name. This gate was at one time called " Bâb mihrab Daûd " (Gate of the Oratory of David) because of its proximity to the traditional Tower of David mentioned in the first section of this book. The present Zion Gate, now called by the natives " Bâb en Nebi Daûd " (Gate of the Prophet David) used then to be known as " The Gate of Zion," or " of the Jews' Quarter."

² (P. 61.) *'Isa ibn Maryam and El Messìh ed-Dejjâl.*—The minds of Moslem theologians have been much exercised by the difficult task of reconciling these conflicting traditions with actual topography, especially as another apocalyptic statement represents the Dejjâl as coming from the East, and being met and slain, on his reaching the bank of the Jordan, by 'Isa, who will descend upon the minaret bearing his name at the Mosque of the Ommayades at Damascus and then with his believing followers will leave El-Kuds to withstand him. The Dejjâl will come either from the 'Irak or from Khorassan, accompanied by an army of 70,000 Jews, who, having acknowledged him as the Messiah son of David, hope to be restored to their kingdom under his guidance. From Jerusalem 'Isa will bring with him three stones which he will throw at the fleeing impostor; saying, with the first, " In the Name of the God of Abraham "; with the second,

" In the Name of the God of Isaac "; and with the third,
" In the name of the God of Jacob." His aim will be un-
erring and fatal. The Jews, discomfited, will seek to hide
themselves; but their places of concealment will be endued
with miraculous power, the very stones behind which they
crouch crying out, " There is a Jew behind me." As the
Jordan is east, and Lydda west of Jerusalem, the difficulty of
reconciling these statements is obvious.

[3] (P. 63). *Jeremiah's Grotto.*—Jeremiah's Grotto is so
called from the belief that the Book of Lamentations was
composed and written there; while the sheer artificial
precipice, at the foot of which it opens, is identified by modern
Jewish legend as the "Beth-ha-Sekelah," or place of execution
by stoning, mentioned in the Mishna. From this circumstance some have supposed that St. Stephen was stoned here,
and also that the top of the hillock, now occupied by a
Moslem cemetery, was Calvary. This is not the place to
discuss such speculations. The spot where the relics of the
proto-martyr, said to have been discovered about A.D. 415,
as the result of a vision vouchsafed to Lucianus, a priest of
Kaphar-Gamala—wherever that village may have been—
were buried with solemn rites, is shown in the recently and
totally rebuilt church just north of the hillock which stands
on the site of that erected by the Empress Eudocia and
consecrated in A.D. 460. It was a remarkable fact which
can be proved by reference to pilgrim writers, that at different
periods of the history of Jerusalem, various spots, north, south,
east and west of the city, have been pointed out in connection
with the death and burial of St. Stephen.

II

[1] (P. 64.) *Turbet Birket Mamilla.*—The great Mohammedan cemetery bearing this name is situated about half a
mile west of Jerusalem. Modern research has shown that in
Crusading times and long before, it was a Christian burial-
ground, the last resting-place of the canons of the Church
and Abbey of the Holy Sepulchre. It is remarkable for a
large pool or birket called by Christian tradition the upper
pool of Gihon, by Jewish, Millo. In the cemetery itself are

the tombs of several distinguished Moslems, and, as might be expected, some interesting legends are connected with it. The oldest of these is attached to a cave some distance west of the pool and called the " Charnel-house of the Lion." Its story is as follows :—

Many hundreds of years ago there lived in Persia a great king who was both an idolater and a magician. He dwelt in a lofty tower in the topmost story of which was a temple where he worshipped the heavenly bodies with unholy rites, such as the sacrifice of new-born babes. In this temple might be seen very curious machinery which caused images of the deities, that the heathen supposed to rule the different heavenly bodies, such as Jupiter, Mars, and Venus, to move as if they were endued with life. Now this monarch, whose name was Khorsu, was as ambitious as he was wicked. He sent a great army to overrun the Holy Land, massacre the monks at Mar-Saba, and then take Jerusalem. They slew every human being in the city, and having destroyed all the churches and carried off everything of value, including the true Cross, which had been enclosed in a strong chest and sealed up by the Patriarch of Jerusalem some time before the arrival of the invaders, they returned to their own country. The skulls of the recluses martyred at Mar-Saba are shown there to this day. The Persians were obliged to leave Jerusalem, where they had slain 60,000 persons, because of the stench arising from the vast number of unburied corpses. As there was no one to inter the fallen, God inspired a lion with pity for the remains of His servants slain by pagans ; and the wild beast not only drove off all others which would have devoured the dead, but actually conveyed their corpses, one by one, to this cavern, which was originally very deep, and had a hundred steps leading down into it, and laid them there reverently side by side. [According to Williams' *Holy City*, Vol. I. p. 303, this legend is first mentioned by Eugesippus about A.D. 1120, and is introduced in order to account for the name by which the cavern was then known, namely " Caverna " or " Spelunca Leonis," as William of Tyre writes when mentioning the adjacent pool. In a tract by an earlier writer, supposed by

Williams to have been Modestus, there is a statement to the
effect that the pious care of " a Nicodemus and a Magdalen "
provided for the decent sepulture of those slain by the
Persians. The name of the man is said to have been
Thomas; whilst a third version of the legend makes out that
the corpses were buried by an aged woman and her female
dog. Quite a different story is that the bodies buried in this
cave were those of the Holy Innocents.] Several years later
St. Mamilla erected a church on the spot, and there prayers
used to be said daily for the repose of the souls of the martyrs
buried in the cave. In connection with this story, it may
be worth while to notice that in several legends of Palestinian
saints, lions figure in a remarkable manner. Thus St.
Jerome (died A.D. 410) is, in mediæval art, very frequently
represented in company of a lion whose wounded paw the
saint had healed in the desert of Chalcis, and who, in
gratitude, became Jerome's faithful servant and protector.
(See Prothero's *The Psalms in Human Life*, p. 27.) In like
manner, visitors to the convent of Mar-Saba are shown the
cave where the founder of that monastery took up his abode
with a lion, the former tenant, and are gravely told that when
the saint expressed his opinion that the place was too small
to accommodate two lodgers, the king of beasts courteously
took the hint and found a dwelling elsewhere; while in the
Chapel of St. Mary the Egyptian, close to the Church of the
Holy Sepulchre, pilgrims admire a painting showing how a
certain hermit, when on his way to visit the saint, found her
dead, and a lion engaged in the pious task of burial.

[2] (P. 65.) *One kirât.*—" It is customary in the East to
measure everything by a standard of twenty-four kirâts.
The kirât literally means an inch, or the twenty-fourth part
of the dra'a or Arabic ell. The English expression ' eighteen
carats fine ' for gold is a survival of this usage. It signifies
that the metal contains eighteen parts of gold in twenty-four
of the alloy. Everything in the East is supposed to be made
up of twenty-four kirâts or carats. Thus a patient or his
friends will ask a physician how many kirâts of hope there
are in his case. A man will say there are twenty-three
kirâts of probability that such an occurrence will take

place. A company divides its shares into kirâts, etc. (See Dr. Post on " Land Tenure, Agriculture, etc.," in the Pal. Exp. Quarterly Statement for 1891, p. 100, footnote.)

III

[1] (P. 69.) *En Nebi Daûd.*—Although it is only since the twelfth century that Jewish and Christian traditions have located the tomb of David at the spot situated outside the Zion Gate and known as the Cœnaculum, or upper room where Christ instituted the Lord's Supper, it is only since A.D. 1560 that Mohammedans have recognised it as such (Robinson's *Biblical Researches,* Vol. I. p. 242, etc.). Though, indeed, in 1479, Tucher of Nüremberg found a mosque installed in the lower part of the building, which already contained what were shown as the tombs of David and Solomon and other Jewish kings, there is evidence that the Moslems did not believe in the tradition, and they probably had the mosque there, in the first place, to be on terms of equality with the Christians, and in the next, because of their belief in the Cœnaculum as the place where 'Isa ibn Maryam " miraculously caused a table to descend from heaven " (*Uns el Jelîl,* Vol. I. p. 145. Cairo edition). As a matter of fact, we know, from the special statement of Mejr-ed-dîn (A.D. 1495), that in his day Mohammedans believed that David and Solomon were buried near Gethsemane (*ibid.,* pp. 105 and 131). He indeed mentions the Cœnaculum, but only as the " Church of Zion " (*ibid.,* Vol. II. p. 402). The group of buildings connected therewith was originally erected as a convent for the Franciscans, and this Order had its chief seat here from A.D. 1313 to 1561. They had been expelled from it before the latter date, but had succeeded in regaining possession. The tradition concerning their final expulsion is as follows:—

In A.D. 1560 a wealthy and influential Jew from Constantinople came to Jerusalem, and begged to be allowed to pray at the tomb of David. The request being indignantly refused by the Latins, he vowed to be revenged, and accordingly, on his return to Constantinople, he told the

NOTES 253

Grand Wazìr that it was very wrong to permit the tomb
of one of the great prophets of Islàm to remain in the hands
of infidels. As a result of his representations, aided it is
said by bribes, the Moslems were persuaded that the tomb
of David was where both Jews and Christians agreed in
stating it to be, and accordingly the Franciscans were again
expelled, and had to find new quarters. Since that time the
place has been in Moslem hands.

The following is the well-known story first told by Rabbi
Benjamin of Tudela, who visited Jerusalem soon after
A.D. 1160: "On Mount Sion are the sepulchres of the house
of David, and those of the kings who reigned after him. In
consequence of the following circumstance, however, this
place is hardly to be recognised at present. Fifteen years
ago one of the walls of the place of worship on Mount Sion
fell down, which the Patriarch ordered the priest to repair.
He commanded him to take stones from the original wall of
Sion, and to employ them for that purpose, which command
was obeyed. Two labourers, who were engaged in digging
stones from the very foundation of the walls of Sion, happened
to meet with one which formed the mouth of the cavern.
They agreed to enter the cave and search for treasure; and
in pursuit of this object they penetrated to a large hall,
supported by pillars of marble, encrusted with gold and
silver, before which stood a table with a golden sceptre and
crown. This was the sepulchre of David, king of Israel, to
the left of which they saw that of Solomon, and of all the
kings of Judah who were buried there. They further saw
the locked chests, and desired to enter the hall to examine
them, but a blast of wind, like a storm, issued forth from the
mouth of the cavern, and prostrated them almost lifeless on
the ground. They lay in this state until evening, when they
heard a voice commanding them to rise up and go forth
from the place. They proceeded terror-stricken to the
Patriarch, and informed him of what had occurred. He
summoned Rabbi Abraham el Constantini, a pious ascetic,
one of the mourners of the downfall of Jerusalem, and caused
the two labourers to repeat the occurrence in his presence.
Rabbi Abraham hereupon informed the Patriarch that they

had discovered the sepulchre of the house of David and the kings of Judah. The Patriarch ordered the place to be walled up, so as to hide it effectually from everyone to the present day. The above-mentioned Rabbi Abraham told me all this." (See Williams' *Holy City*, Vol. II. pp. 509, 510.)

IV

[1] (P. 73.) *Birket Israìl.*—This great pool, which twenty years ago, before the discovery of the Double-pools at St. Anne's was made public, used to be pointed out as " the Pool of Bethesda," is now being rapidly filled up with rubbish.

[2] (P. 73.) *Bridge at Lydda.*—This bridge at Lydda was built by the same Emìr of Ramleh who treacherously sent assassins to kill the Crusading Heir-Apparent of England, who afterwards became Edward I.

V

[1] (P. 77.) *Detective stories.*—A good many tales are current respecting the means used by specially gifted persons for the detection of criminals. Some of them remind one of the Biblical story of Solomon and the two mothers (1 Kings iii. 16 to end) and also the Apocryphal account of Daniel's procedure in the " History of Susanna."

For two other and similar stories, versions of which are current in this country, see Dr. Thomson's *The Land and the Book*, edition of 1873, p. 153.

[2] (P. 78.) *Burial of Kolonimos.*—It is no uncommon thing for very pious Jews to give orders that after their death, and by way of expiating sins committed during their lifetime, their bodies should be ill-treated. Some even direct that the four modes of capital punishment ordered in the Law, viz. beheading, strangling, burning and stoning, should be executed on their corpses. Others arrange that they are, after death, to have the *malkoth*, or public scourging with forty stripes save one, inflicted upon them; whilst others, again, as in the case of a lately deceased Grand Rabbi of Jerusalem, give orders that their bodies shall be dragged

along the path to their graves. In the case just mentioned, the bier on which the corpse was lying was so dragged for a short distance.

[3] (P. 101.) *Grave of Kolonimos.*—It is said that the small cairn now shown as the tomb of Kolonimos was thus formed, and that the last stone was thrown upon it during the early part of the nineteenth century. It is in the bed of the Kedron, a little south-west of the so-called tomb of Zechariah.

The above story may contain an historical kernel. Kolonimos was a well-known person, and in his days very few people in Palestine could either read or write. Those who possessed these accomplishments exercised a tremendous influence over their contemporaries, knowledge in their case being indeed power, as is proved by the following fact preserved traditionally:—

During the Greek War of Independence (1821–28), a Tatar courier arrived one day from Constantinople bringing a written order from the Sublime Porte to the Governor of Jerusalem directing him to put to death at once the Greek Orthodox Patriarch and several of his chief ecclesiastics. It happened, however, fortunately for the condemned, that of all the Government officials, from the Pasha downwards, the only one who could read and write was an effendi well-disposed to the Christians. The letter from Stambûl was therefore placed in his hands to be deciphered. Having read it through, he informed his colleagues that it referred to a totally different matter. No one doubted his word, and the document was left in his possession to be answered. As soon as he could do so unobserved, he called on the Greek Patriarch and the other clergy mentioned on the order, and, having demanded a private interview, showed them the death-warrant, but promised to keep its real import secret. This promise he kept loyally, and the Orthodox Greek community, out of gratitude for this great service, accorded to his descendants the right, which they still enjoy, of being entertained as honoured guests not only at the Greek convent at Jerusalem, but also in all other Orthodox monasteries within the Patriarchate of Jerusalem.

Now if this was the condition of things a century ago, it

must have been worse in the time of Kolonimos. What really took place was probably something like this:—Whilst the rabbi was writing and muttering his hocus-pocus, he was furtively scanning the faces of the spectators in order to see whether there were any present who seemed particularly interested in the matter or in the result of his action.

Noticing fear or anxiety depicted on the features of one of them, he concluded that it was caused by an evil conscience, and, having made up his mind, he needed only to point to the shrinking culprit in order to elicit the truth. Such methods for surprising wrongdoers into confession of their guilt are in vogue at the present day.

VI

[1] (P. 82.)   *The people of Deyr es Sinneh.*—*Vide* Josephus, *Antiq.*, xv. 10, 5; *Wars*, ii. 8, 6; *Antiq.*, xiii. 5, 9; xvii. 13, 3; xviii. 1, 5, 6.

The suggestive name and the tales told of the eccentric people of Deyr es Sinneh are supposed to be reminiscences of the once famous sect of the Essenes, of whom mention is often made by Josephus, but of whom, as far as the writer is aware, no actual traces have as yet been discovered, except those of the cistern and baths above referred to.

[2] (P. 84.)   " *The times of the infidels.*"—This is the way in which the Moslem peasants usually refer to the period when Palestine was under Christian rule.

[3] (P. 84.)   *Tombs on the site of the present Greek convent of St. Onuphrius.*—Ecclesiastical tradition says that these tombs and the ruined mediæval building close by, which covers a deep rock-hewn pit, mark the site of Aceldama. During the Middle Ages the earth from the hill-terraces here used to be carried to Europe by the ship-load to various cemeteries, such as the Campo Santo at Pisa, because of the general belief that it possessed the peculiar property of accelerating decomposition. It also was endued with the strange gift of knowing the difference between one nationality and another. Thus we are informed that " By order of the Empress Helena, two hundred and seventy ship-loads of it were translated to Rome and deposited in the Campo Santo near the Vatican, where it

was wont to reject the bodies of the Romans and only consume those of strangers." (Monroe, as quoted by Barclay, *City of the Great King*, p. 208.)

⁴ (P. 85.) *Christians beyond Jordan in the time of the Crusades.*—Baldwin I tempted many of the Christians living beyond Jordan to come and settle at Jerusalem. They were granted special privileges and immunities, and in A.D. 1121, his successor passed a free-trade measure remitting all customary dues on articles of commerce. (William of Tyre, xii., xv.; Williams' *Holy City*, Vol. I, p. 404 and footnote.) It has for centuries been customary for criminals and outlaws to flee to the district east of the Jordan, and take refuge there under the protection of some Bedawi sheykh. The custom illustrates such episodes as the flight of Jephthah (Judges xi. 2), and David's sojourn in Philistia (1 Sam. xxi. 10; xxvii. 1, 2).

VII

¹ (P. 93.) *The judgments of Karakash.*—The expression " This is one of the judgments of Karakash," is usual among the natives of Palestine when a decision arrived at is hopelessly absurd, though based strictly upon the evidence in the case. It is said to have originated several hundred years ago during the administration of the Emir Beha-ed-din Karakash, or Karakush, who lived during the latter part of the twelfth Christian century, and was a faithful lieutenant of the great Saladin, who entrusted to him the construction of the new fortifications on the Jebel el Mokattam at Cairo. The rock-hewn trench protecting the citadel there is said to have been dug by his orders. He was also in chief command of the garrison at Acre when that town was taken by Cœur de Lion, about A.D. 1192. He was therefore an historical personage, and the judicial eccentricities for which he is remembered may have originated in lampoons circulated by his enemies. (Bohaeddin's *Life of Saladin*, P.E.P., Col. Conder's translation, p. 107, footnote, and also pp. 202, 209, 238, 269.)

² (P. 95.) " *Hang the first short man you can find.*"—In 1857, an American subject was murdered at Jaffa. The United

States Government sent a man-of-war, the crime was investigated, and the supposed criminal hanged at the yard-arm of the vessel. However, to this day the tradition is current at Jaffa that the victim was not the real murderer, but a poor negro bread-seller who was sacrificed in his stead.

IX

[1] (P. 99.) *Mohammad's "Night-journey" from Mecca to Jerusalem.*—" From Jerusalem he is said to have been carried through the seven heavens into the presence of God, and brought back again to Mecca the same night." " It is a matter of dispute amongst Mohammedan divines, whether their Prophet's night-journey was really performed by him corporeally, or whether it was only a dream or vision. Some think the whole was no more than a vision; and allege an express tradition of Moawiyeh, one of the Khalifehs, to that effect. Others suppose that he was carried bodily to Jerusalem, but no further, and that he ascended thence to heaven in spirit only. But the received opinion is, that it was no vision, but that he was actually transported in the body to his journey's end, and if any impossibility be objected, they think it is sufficient answer to say, that it might easily be effected by an omnipotent agent." Sale's footnote to verse 1 of Koran Sûra xvii, entitled " The Night-Journey " (Chandos Classics, pp. 206, 207).

X

[1] (P. 100.) *A Sultan dreamt that all his teeth fell out.*—To dream that one has lost a single tooth is a fearful omen. Grown-up people suffering with their teeth make vows, and children, losing their first set, take each of the old ones as it falls out, and throw it up to the sun, crying: " O sun! take this donkey's tooth and give me instead the tooth of a gazelle." The formula differs amongst the fellahìn of Silwan, whose children are taught to say: " O sun! take this donkey's tooth, and instead of it give me the tooth of one of thy children." Amongst native Arab Jews the tooth is thrown into a well with the formula given in the text. Others say:

" O sun! take this iron tooth and give me a tooth of pearl."

Up to the year 1868, when the new iron dome was placed over the Church of the Holy Sepulchre, a great number of human teeth were to be seen sticking, as witnesses to vows made by their owners, in the cracks and interstices of the clustered columns on the left-hand side of the great portal to the said church.

NOTES

SECTION III

I

[1] (P. 103.) *Folks gentle and simple.*—Considering the strange vicissitudes of Eastern history, it is not surprising that many people, now abjectly poor, should claim to be descendants of famous men. Orientals generally have great regard for pure blood and ancient lineage. Amongst the poor of Palestine there are many who, though obliged to do menial work to obtain a living, as household servants, labourers, etc., yet claim that they are " Awlad asl," *i.e.* " Children of stock " or of gentle descent, and that on this account, if they do their work faithfully, they should enjoy a degree of respect not shown to those low-born. It is related of one such that, being able-bodied and very strong, but having no other means of livelihood, he consented to accept employment from a poor peasant who had only one ox and could not plough for want of a second. The scion of nobility in his dire distress actually agreed to be yoked to the plough in the place of the missing animal; stipulating, however, that besides receiving food and wages, he was to be treated with the greatest respect, and always to be addressed as " O Emìr." In consequence of this arrangement the ploughman, while at work, was constantly calling out " Yamìnak, ya Emìr," or " Shemâlak, ya Emìr," *i.e.* " To the right, O Emìr," or " To the left, O Emìr."

There is at the present day a poor seamstress at Jerusalem whose family boast that they are descended from Chosroes, king of Persia. A fellâh for some time in the writer's service traced his lineage to the Fatimite Khalìfeh " Ed Dahìr," whilst a teacher in one of the Jerusalem Mission schools in 1874 asserted that he was descended from the ancient kings of Armenia. There are some of these high-born people who have been more fortunate than others. Thus, the family of the celebrated Khalid ibn Wlid, surnamed for his victories in the early days of Islam "The Sword of Allah," is still powerful at Jerusalem. The late Yussif Pasha El Khaldi, one of the representatives of Turkey at the Berlin Conference, and sometime Mayor of Jerusalem, belonged to this old family; so also one or two of the Imperial Ottoman Commissioners appointed to supervise the excavations of the Palestine Exploration Fund. There are, in the Lebanon, descendants of the great and chivalrous Saladin who were pensioners of the German Protestant Order of the "Johanniter" or Knights of St. John of Jerusalem up to the outbreak of the Great War. The value placed upon connection with a good family is popularly expressed in the saying, "Take good stock, even on the mat," *i.e.* marry a woman of good family, even though she possess nothing but a mat. On the other hand, persons assuming an arrogant demeanour solely on the strength of their supposed noble ancestry, and whilst lacking any personal merit themselves, are mercilessly ridiculed, as it is right that they should be. The principle "Noblesse oblige" is perfectly well appreciated, in theory at any rate.

II

1 (P. 108.) *"Affixed to the gates of the Ka'aba."*—It was customary among the ancient Arabs to reward poets of acknowledged eminence by allowing copies of their verses to be affixed to the gate of the Temple at Mecca. Seven such poems were thus distinguished, and are known in literature as the "Mo'allakat" (Suspended Poems).

2 (P. 108.) *"Mûkleh."*—An illustration of this form of head-dress will be found on page 49 of Lane's *Modern Egyptians*, Vol. I. It is not uncommon in Palestine, where there may, at the present day, be seen no fewer than sixty different forms of Oriental male headgear, by which Christians, Jews, Moslems, Bedû, different classes of derwìshes and peasants from various districts, etc., may be distinguished from each other.

3 (P. 110.) *Long hair of a priest of the Orthodox Church.*—

The ecclesiastics of the Orthodox Greek Community are remarkable for wearing their hair very long. Many Moslem derwìshes do the same, but amongst the Mohammedan peasantry it is customary to shave the head, leaving only a tuft called *shusheh* on the crown. The tale often told by Christian dragomans to tourists is, that this tuft is left in order that Mohammed or good angels may have something to lay hold of when carrying dead Mohammedans to heaven, in the same way that the Prophet Habakkuk was transported to Babylon. (See " Bel and the Dragon," verse 36.) However, the more reasonable explanation is that the custom originated in the fear that if a Moslem should fall into the hands of an infidel, and be slain, the latter might cut off the head of his victim, and, finding no hair by which to hold to, put his impure hand into his mouth, in order to carry it, for the beard might not be sufficiently long. (See Lane's *Modern Egyptians*, Vol. I. p. 40.)

III

[1] (P. 114.) *An afrìt.*—The *afrìt* is an especially malicious and mischief-loving demon whose abode is on house-tops and in corners behind doors, as well as in cracks in walls or under thresholds. It is considered very dangerous, for women especially, to sit on the thresholds of doors after sunset, as then the *afrìt* issue forth from their lurking-places and might do them serious injury.

[2] (P. 115.) *Karakoz and 'Iweyz.*—Karakoz and 'Iweyz, something like the English " Punch and Judy," are the names of the actors in Oriental puppet-shows, for a description of which see Lane's *Modern Egyptians*, Vol. II. p. 116.

[Karakoz is universal, but on the two occasions when I have seen Kheyyal-ez-Zull (shadow shapes) referred to, there was no 'Iweyz. On one occasion, in Egypt, Asfur was leading character.—M. P.]

IV

[1] (P. 124.) " *The Kadi Abdullah el Mustakìm lived at Baghdad.*—El-Mansûr, A.D. 941, having established his court

at El Hashemìeh, was compelled by an insurrection to erect a new capital, and in the 145th year of the Hejìra laid the foundation of Baghdad, which for nearly five centuries remained the seat of Imperial Oriental luxury. (See Crichton's *History of Arabia*, Vol. XXXIII, p. 16.)

V

1 (P. 130.) *Azrael and his son.*—As a version of the foregoing story, which entirely, and also in scraps, the writer has several times heard told by natives of Palestine, is said to be found in Grimm's collection of fairy tales, it is difficult to determine whether its origin is Oriental or the contrary. The name of the hero of the story, which is in circulation among the peasantry of the native Christian village of Ramallah, situated about ten miles to the north of Jerusalem, would seem to indicate that it has been introduced by some Spanish or Italian monk. It has been told to the writer by four different persons, all of whom were natives, and on as many different occasions.

2 (P. 135.) *Francesco's card-playing.*—Though at first sight it may seem an anachronism to mention cards as having been played in the days of the Herods, seeing that the first actual mention of them as having been used in Europe dates back to the year A.D. 1388, and that their first introduction into France was during the reign of Charles VII (1432–1461), yet some German savants are of the opinion that they were an invention of the Chinese, and reached Europe through an Arabian channel. (See Brockhaus, *Conversations-Lexikon* on " Spielkarten.")

VI

1 (P. 142.) *The plant feyjan.*—This Arabic name is evidently only another form of the Greek πήγανον = peganon. According to Bishop Jeremy Taylor it was used by pretended exorcists in his day. He says: " They are to try the devil by holy water, incense, sulphur and rue, which from thence, as we suppose, came to be called the ' herb of grace.' "

2 (P. 148.) *Baklâweh.*—A kind of mince-pie pastry covered

with syrup of sugar, and of which the natives are particularly fond. A story is told of an Arab who, when threatened with immediate death if he took any more of it, coolly commended his family to the protection of the would-be murderer, who stood over him with a drawn sword—and took another mouthful. (See *Tales told in Palestine.*)

[3] (P. 153.) "*The Sultan could not make up his mind to kill her, as was his duty since she had no brothers.*"—According to Oriental social ideas, the result, doubtless, of the fact that polygamy is allowed, it is the brother, and not the father, who is a girl's natural protector, her avenger if wronged, and her executioner in case she disgrace herself. This should be borne in mind when reading such Scripture narratives as Genesis xxxiv. or 2 Samuel xiii.

[4] (P. 157.) [*Wedding procession of the Jân.*—Ten years ago, I was told in Jerusalem the story of a servant of the Latin Patriarch who played upon the reed-pipes very beautifully. This man was sent one night on an urgent errand to the head of a religious house at Nazareth, and as he rode out from the city down into the gloomy valley, he amused himself and supported his courage with the music of his favourite instrument. Suddenly he was surrounded with torches lighting dusky faces, and found himself in the middle of a wedding procession, the members of which besought him to stop and play for them. He cited the urgency of his errand, but they told him not to worry about that; they could take him further in an hour than he could hope to ride in a night. By that and their peculiar faces he knew them for the Jân, so was afraid to deny them.

At an early hour of the next morning, when the Patriarch was saying his first mass, he turned and saw this man kneeling in the church behind him. The service over, he called him and asked why he had not gone to Nazareth as he had been told to do. The man replied: "I have been and come again," and in proof of the assertion, presented the answer to the message with which he had been sent. The Patriarch led him straight to the confessional, and having heard his story, as a penance forbade him ever again to play the pipes, of whose music the Jân are known to be fond.—M. P.]

VII

[1] (Pp. 160 ff.) *Uhdey-dûn.*—This, at first sight, appears a foolish story, but I seem to detect in it a legendary reminiscence of a savage and cannibal race or their subjugation by men more civilised. The name Uhdey-dûn, which is a diminutive of *Haddâd* (blacksmith), and the fact that his enemy had a copper cauldron, temptingly suggests the Age of Iron conquering that of Bronze.

VIII

[1] (P. 173.) *The magic mirror of ink and the sand table.*—For a description of the wonders performed by Oriental wizards with the Mirror of Ink, see Lane's *Modern Egyptians*, Vol. I. pp. 367 ff., or Thomson's *The Land and the Book*, in which Lane is quoted at p. 157 (edition of 1873). For the sand table see Lane as above, p. 362.

[2] (P. 173.) *Mahajaneh* (more properly *Mahjaneh*).—A stick with a peculiar crotch at one end, always cut from an almond tree and carried by derwìshes. Its handle is the same in shape as that of some symbolic staves often represented by the ancient Egyptians in the hands of their deities.

[3] (P. 175.) *The ".maûsam," or season of pilgrimage.*—This varies according to the dignity of the *makâm*. Many of the greater shrines of famous saints, such as Neby Mûsa and Neby Rubìn, have their own *maûsam*, which lasts a whole week.

[4] (P. 176.) *The machicolated window above the gate.*—In the earlier part of the last century such " machicolations " or protected windows over doorways were very common in Jerusalem, not only over the entrances of monasteries and public buildings, but even in private dwellings. They are rarely met with nowadays.

[5] (P. 178.) *Ignorance of Christian priests.*—The Christians of various sects in Palestine now generally appreciate the value of education, and vie with each other in providing schools, especially for the training of ecclesiastics. In and near Jerusalem there are several of these seminaries, and though there are still, in out-of-the-way places more par-

ticularly, ignorant ecclesiastics, yet the number of the latter is by no means so great as it was during the early part of the last century, when the rural clergy belonging to the Orthodox Greek Church was notorious for its dense ignorance, and no adequate provision was made for the instruction of the parochial ministers. Even in Jerusalem it was the custom for the Sunday preacher to have to go during the previous week to a learned archimandrite in order to be instructed in a sermon for the occasion. (See Williams' *Holy City*, Vol. II. p. 548.) It was also then the custom to provide a successor for a village priest who was becoming old or feeble, by selecting a likely lad from the hamlet, and sending him as a servant to the convent at Jerusalem. Here he had to attend the various services of the Church and commit to memory the liturgies for Sundays, feast-days, baptism, etc., so that when occasion required he could read them, if nothing else, from the prayer-books.

IX

[1] (P. 187.) *The hoopoe* (*Upupa epops*).—For particulars concerning the hoopoe, see Tristram's *Natural History of the Bible*, pp. 208 ff., and Hastings' *Bible Dictionary*, article "Lapwing"; also the Koran xxvii. 20, where, however, Sale wrongly renders the Arabic name "Hud-hud" by "lapwing." It is also mentioned by that name in the English Bible (Lev. xi. 19). For the story of the hoopoe in connection with Solomon and Belkis, see *Mejr-ed-din*, Vol. I. p. 115, Cairo edition.

X

Most of the Animal stories in this chapter appeared originally in the P. E. F. Quarterly Statements for July 1904 and April 1905. In the present reproduction I have altered some details and added others which I did not mention in my original paper. Other stories, for instance that about the old woman and those on plant-lore, are, as far as I know, new to the English-speaking public.

[1] (P. 194.) *The dog who earned his right to decent burial.*—Since I first contributed this story to the Quarterly State-

ment, as above noted, I have, to my surprise, come across a version of it in an old eighteenth-century Spanish edition of *Gil Blas.*

² (P. 195.) *Bìr el Kelb.*—It seems probable that the true origin of the legend about the " Bìr el Kelb " is the fact that the Tombs of the Kings, only a few yards distant, are generally called by the Jews " The Tomb of Kalba Shebua." This person is said by tradition to have been the father-in-law of Akiba. He is said to have distinguished himself by supplying food, at his own cost, to the poor of Jerusalem during the time of the great famine. (This tradition is probably based upon the historical fact connected with Helena of Adiabene and her almsgiving.) The grotto where Kalba Shebua distributed his bounty is pointed out in the vicinity of the traditional tomb of Simon the Just.

³ (P. 202.) " *When a male hyæna is seven years old it becomes either a female of the same species or else a bat.*"—See Dr. J. Levy's *Neu-Hebräische und Chaldäisches Wörterbuch,* twelfth part. " A male hyæna after seven years becomes a bat, a bat after seven years becomes a vampire, that animal after seven years becomes a nettle, a nettle after seven years becomes a thorn, a thorn after seven years becomes a demon." *Bava Kama,* fol. 16, col. i. Quoted by Hershon, *Talmudical Commentary on Genesis,* p. 136. [The hyæna from its habit of digging up and devouring dead bodies is often called *ghûleh* by the fellahìn, and confused with the genuine ghoul. Indeed there seems a general tendency among the ignorant to impute a demoniacal character to wild animals. A fellâh in Egypt described a travelling menagerie to me as " All kinds of *afarìt* in cages," and I spent a strange morning in the Zoological Gardens at Ghizeh with a hashash, who took the majority of the creatures there displayed for devils and mocked them, exulting in their captivity.—M. P.]

⁴ (P. 204.) *Story of the man who won the heart of the hyæna.*— I relate the story as told me by a lady who had heard it from a fellaheh. It seems to be Seneca's well-known tale of the runaway slave and his grateful king of beasts (first mentioned, so it is said, in his *De Beneficiis*). The lion has been extinct in Palestine for centuries, the leopard is rare, though

now and then met with, and so the hyæna, at present the largest of the Judean carnivora (the bear being found only in the Lebanon and the anti-Libanus), whose name " Ed-Daba " is somewhat like the name " Es-Seba," by which the lion is most frequently known, has taken his place in the story.

[5] (P. 208.) *The fox, the eagle, and the leopard.*—A version of this fox story is related by Ph. Baldensperger in the Quarterly Statement for July 1905, pp. 199, 201.

[6] (P. 211.) Since the story of the " Dib-dib " was first published in 1907, Miss Bartle Frere has pointed out to me that it is clearly an Indian tale, the original of which is " The Valiant Chatee-Maker " of her *Old Deccan Tales* (John Murray, Albemarle Street, London, 1898). It is also evident that the jan, ghuls, rassads, marids and shedim of Jewish, Christian and Moslem superstition are the Palestinian representatives of the Indian " sakshas " or beast-headed, human-bodied and bird-footed demons.

[7] (P. 211.) *The spinal cord of a man becomes a serpent.* See Hershon's commentary as above. See also Macaulay's account of Dodwell's writings A.D. 1689: *History of England*, chapter xiv.

[8] (P. 211.) *A serpent at the age of a thousand becomes a whale.*—Ph. Baldensperger in Quarterly Statement, 1905, p. 204.

[9] (P. 211.) *Time required by different creatures to reproduce their species.*—Twenty-one days are required for the full formation of a hen in the egg, and a similar period is required in the vegetable kingdom for that of almonds; fifty days for that of a dog and figs; fifty-two for that of a cat and mulberries; sixty for that of swine and apples; six months for that of foxes and all sorts of cereals; five months for that of small cattle and grapes; twelve months for that of large unclean animals (such as horses, etc.) and palm trees; nine months for that of large clean animals (as oxen) and olives; three years for that of the wolf, lion, bear, hyæna, elephant and chimpanzee and a fruit resembling figs; seventy years elapse before the viper can reproduce its own species, and a similar period is required for the carob tree. The wicked

serpent requires seven years, and nothing in the vegetable kingdom requires a similar period. . . . In so far, then, as there is nothing corresponding to it in the vegetable kingdom, the serpent is cursed above all cattle, and above every beast of the field. Bechoroth, fol. 8, col. i. Quoted by Hershon, p. 134.

[10] (P. 214.) A story somewhat similar to that of the woman turned into a tortoise is told, according to the Brothers Grimm, in the Tyrol concerning a certain " Frau Hutt." According to another tradition apes are the descendants of certain men of 'Akaba who were transformed into these creatures because, in David's time, they went fishing on the Sabbath day. Another variant to the story of the wicked woman is told at Petra in connection with two obelisks on the hill-top, which are said to have been "wives of Pharaoh" and guilty of the same desecration of bread.

<h3 style="text-align:center">XI</h3>

[1] (P. 217.) *The tortoise-herb.* Cf. "Einiges aus dem Pflanzenreich," by L. Baldensperger. In *Evangelische Blätter aus Bethlehem*, July 1906, pp. 21 *et seq.*

<h3 style="text-align:center">XIII</h3>

TRANSLATION OF A TYPICAL " KEMI " OR WRITTEN AMULET,
USED BY ORIENTAL JEWS IN PALESTINE

BINV.	AMI.	ASV.
Abbreviation for the Hebrew words " In the Name of God we shall do and prosper."	Abbreviation in Hebrew of " My help cometh from Jehovah."	Abbreviation of Hebrew of " The Maker of Heaven and Earth."

" And all people of the earth shall see that thou art called by the name of the Lord; and they shall be afraid of thee."

Deliver from fetters Bambina, daughter of Rena, to praise Thy Name, and may the merits of the Patriarchs shield her. A. N. S. V. (initials of the words 'Amen, Netzach, Tselah, Vaad).

In the Name of the Most High and the Cause of all Causes, the Exalted El Jah, the God of Israel, I am that I am, High and Exalted, the Dweller in Eternity; Whose name is Holy; And in the Name of the Almighty of Sabaoth, Lord of Lords, Living and Existent for everlasting Ages. Amen, Selah. And in the name of JVHT (tetragrammaton).

Prosper me in the writing of this parchment, that it be a preservative, deliverance, protection and a perfect cure to the wearer of this Charm from sundry and divers evil diseases existing in the world, from an evil eye and from an evil tongue. I adjure you, all ye kinds of evil eyes, a black eye, a hazel eye, blue eye, yellow eye, short eye, broad eye, straight eye, narrow eye, deep eye, protruding eye, eye of a male, eye of a female, the eye of a wife and the eye of a husband, eye of a woman and her daughter, eye of a woman and her kinsfolk, eye of an unmarried man, eye of an old man, eye of an old woman, eye of a virgin, eye of one not a virgin, eye of a widow, eye of a married wife, eye of a divorced wife, all kinds of evil eyes in the world which looked and spoke with an evil eye concerning or against the wearer of this charm, I command and adjure you by the Most Holy and Mighty and Exalted Eye, the Only Eye, the White Eye, the Mighty Eye, the Compassionate, the Ever-Watchful and Open Eye, the Eye that never slumbereth nor sleepeth, the Eye to Which all eyes are subject, the Wakeful Eye that preserveth Israel, as it is written, " The Eye of the Lord is upon them that fear Him, and upon them that trust in His Goodness."

By this Most High Eye I adjure you all evil eyes to depart and be eradicated and to flee away to a distance from the Wearer of this Amulet, and that you are to have no power whatever over her who wears this Charm. And by the power of this most Holy Seal, you shall have no authority to hurt either by day or by night, when asleep or when awake : nor over any of her two hundred and forty-eight limbs, nor over any of her three hundred and sixty-five veins, henceforth and for ever. A. N. S. V. (Abbreviation for 'Amen, Netzech, Tsilol, Ve'ad.)

NOTES 271

UZAH. ADIAH. LEHABIEL.
PL. JH. VH. JHVH. EHYEH. AH.
ASHER. HV. GH. VH.
Kinbijah. Baduomfiel. Beduftiel.

" Shaddyam " (probably meaning power of the sea).
And by the power of all the holy names and seals in this
Charm, I adjure all malignant powers, evil spirits, impure
powers and all kinds of plagues that molest human beings
to be scared away from, and fear the wearer of this Amulet,
and not to approach her, nor to come within the distance
of four cubits from her; nor to annoy her in any manner,
either by day or by night, when she is awake or when she is
dreaming. May she obtain a perfect cure from all malignant
diseases which are in the world, and from epilepsy, con-
vulsions, askara, paralysis, headache, a beclouded mind,
oppression and palpitation of the heart, and from all bondage
and witchcraft, fright and vexation, trembling, startling,
excitement, diseases of the womb, evil imaginations and
visions, male or female devils and demons, and all hurts;
and from Millelin, and Letlin, and all evil spirits and other
occult powers, and impure powers, a perfect cure, deliverance and shield from all evil diseases existing in the world
henceforth and for ever. And by the power of—
RVI. ASHA. VVTZ. TCHM. TRV. HSHT. ILICH.
And by the power and influence of VDA. HVI. SISH. IMI.
RTZM. TRM. HTB. VMCH. HHV. MRN. MAT. CIN.
CMM. LAB. KHSCH. IRL. TTSH. VDN. Kaa. LTI.
MLCH. all this shall be established and confirmed to the
wearer of this Charm. So be it, Amen.

Pishon, Gihon, Hiddekel, Euphrates.
Euphrates, Hiddekel, Gihon, Pishon, Euphrates.
Hiddekel, Gihon, Pishon, Euphrates.
Paghaf, Vidar, Shahekel, Vuleni.
Taluman, Rakuh, Padhach, Higeb.

Thou shalt not suffer a witch to live.
Thou shalt not suffer a witch to live.
Thou shalt not suffer a witch to live.

A perfect cure, deliverance and shield from all bondage and witchcraft from henceforth and for ever. Amen. Selah.

1. The apparently meaningless combinations in capital and other letters, shown in the above charm, are formed from the names of the angels, the four streams of Paradise, etc. The belief is, that the changes in the position of the letters make these various names more effective and therefore render the amulet more powerful.

2. In writing charms, etc., the father's name is never mentioned. The reason alleged is the example of the Psalmist, who prays, " O Lord, truly I am thy servant; thy servant and the son of thy handmaid."

3. It is not the object of this work to treat the question of Jewish and Eastern angelology and demonology, amulets, etc., exhaustively. Much interesting information on these and kindred subjects may be gathered from the following English works: Edersheim, *Life and Times of Jesus the Messiah*, Appendices XIII, XVI; Thompson, *Land and the Book*, 1873, pp. 150, 151, etc.; Lane's *Modern Egyptians*, Vol. I. pp. 300, 306, 317, 338, 361; Vol. II. pp. 177, 256, 371.

4. Besides written amulets like that of which a translation from the original Hebrew is given above, it is customary amongst Jews and other Orientals to wear different objects made of metal, glass, bone, etc., to keep away evil spirits and ward off the effects of the evil eye. Amongst these objects we may mention a wolf's bone, blue beads, and silver figures of a pair of frogs (the sex of each figure being clearly indicated), a sword, pistol, gun, battle-axe, pair of scissors, scimitar, a hand, tooth, etc., or to wear a sprig of rue or a copy of the Koran, etc.

5. The belief in the protective power of the name Jehovah or YHVH is shared by the Samaritans equally with the adherents of Orthodox Judaism. I have in my possession the photograph of a Samaritan charm written on parchment, said to be several centuries old, and to have been used by generation after generation of " The foolish people that

dwell in Sichem " (Ecclus. i. 26), in order to cure sick folk of
their ailments. It is written in seven columns divided from
each other by lines of Samaritan writing in larger characters
than those covering the greater part of the document. A
framework of two lines of such writing runs along the four
sides of the whole, and, on examination with a magnifier, is
easily decipherable as containing the account of the overthrow of Pharaoh and his hosts in the sea. The columns are
divided into sections by from two to five lines of similar
writing (the names of Jehovah, the words " and Moses
prayed," etc.), whilst between the divisions are paragraphs
of small and closely written lines. The sides of this precious
document, for which the trifling sum of five thousand francs
was coolly asked, is shown by the scale of centimetres photographed with it. It was in a terribly dirty and torn condition,
having been worn, rolled and folded up into a bundle about
two and a half inches cube, and apparently next the skin.
About the middle of the eighth column is a *zair'geh* table,
with letters arranged inside squares, like that shown by Lane,
Vol. I. p. 356.

TRANSLATION

PROTECTION (OR AMULET)
FOR AN INFANT AND A WOMAN IN CHILDBED

And in good luck.

Be reviled, O Satan!

Psalm cxxi., " A Psalm of degrees," from beginning to end.

Charm against Lilith vouched for as efficacious by several
famous Rabbis :—

" In the Name of YHVH, the God of Israel Whose Name
is great and to be feared.

" Elijah, may his memory be blessed, was walking out
one day when he came upon Lilith. He said to her,
' Unclean one! where art thou going? ' She said to him, ' I
am going to the house of So-and-So, who is in childbed; in
order to cause her death and to snatch and devour her child.'
He said unto her, ' Be thou smitten with the itch, and
imprisoned by the Name of the Most Holy One, and become

a silent stone.' She answered and said unto him, ' O my lord, let me off, and I swear, in the name of YHMH, to forsake this my way, and that whenever I shall see or hear any of my names I shall straightway flee. And now I will make known unto thee my names. And whenever my names shall be mentioned I shall have no power to do evil or to injure. I swear to thee to reveal my names, and if they be written and suspended in the dwellings of the child or the confined woman I shall at once flee.

" ' These are my names:—SATRINAH, LILITH, AVITU, AMIZ, RAPHI, AMIZU, KAKASH, ODEM, 'ik, PODS, 'ils, PETROTA, ABRO, KEMA, KALEE, BITUAH, THILTHO, PARTASHA.

" ' And whoever fixes up these my names I shall at once flee from the placard hung up in the house of the confined woman or the child. This is a charm, and the child as well as his mother shall never be hurt by me.' "

CABALISTIC DIRECTION.—Rabbi Eleazar of Garmiza (Worms in Germany), the author of the Josephta, may his memory be blessed, says:—" As a charm against pestilence and fire, from which may YHVH protect us, let this be hung against the window or against (opposite to) the door and at once they will flee." Thus also Rabbi Arieh the Saint has said in a MS. of his, " All this is very marvellous, as also Rabbi Eliezer Baal Shem Tore says."

In a good sign.

Shaddai.

Solemn Adjuration of the Evil Eye. (As this, though abbreviated, is almost identical with the amulet translated above, there is no need to reproduce it here.)

Picture of a hand, on the back of which is written " Shaddai " (Almighty) and " Adonai " (Lord), with permutations of letters forming names of angels, etc.

SQUARE DIAGRAM

and Eve.
and Sarah.
and Rebekah.
and Leah.

In the corners, pictures of Wailing Place, Machpelah, Rachel's Tomb and the Holy City Zion.

Adam.
Abraham.
Isaac.
Jacob.

Lilith and all appertaining to her, Avaunt!

Inside, a circle containing four magic words formed from these names.

Seni and Sensani and Simnaglûf, Be present!

Thou shalt not suffer a witch to live. To live thou shalt not suffer a witch. To live a witch thou shalt not suffer.

In the next inner circle other magic Cabalistic words.

Picture of the " Evil Eye " armed with claws and crab-like mandibles, etc., on which are other letters and magic words.

In the centre the words " El Shaddai," *i.e.* " God Almighty," followed by six lines of Cabalistic words, the last of which is " Keep," or " Preserve," *i.e.* " Protect."

A witch to live thou shalt not suffer. A witch thou shalt not suffer to live. Not a witch shalt thou suffer to live.

Note.—A remarkable thing in this charm is the omission of the names of the four angels, Gabriel, Michael, Raphael and Uriel.

GENERAL INDEX

Meaning of some Arabic Names used in the Index.

Ain, Fountain
Bab, Gate
Birket, Pool
Cadi or Kadi, Moslem Judge
Caliph or Khalif, Successor of Mohammad

Harat, Street or Quarter of Town
Kubbet, Dome
Neby or Nebi, Prophet
Sûk, Market
Tarik, Way or Road
Wady, Valley

277

A CATALOG OF SELECTED

DOVER BOOKS

IN ALL FIELDS OF INTEREST

A CATALOG OF SELECTED DOVER
BOOKS IN ALL FIELDS OF INTEREST

CONCERNING THE SPIRITUAL IN ART, Wassily Kandinsky. Pioneering work by father of abstract art. Thoughts on color theory, nature of art. Analysis of earlier masters. 12 illustrations. 80pp. of text. 5⅜ x 8½.   23411-8

ANIMALS: 1,419 Copyright-Free Illustrations of Mammals, Birds, Fish, Insects, etc., Jim Harter (ed.). Clear wood engravings present, in extremely lifelike poses, over 1,000 species of animals. One of the most extensive pictorial sourcebooks of its kind. Captions. Index. 284pp. 9 x 12.   23766-4

CELTIC ART: The Methods of Construction, George Bain. Simple geometric techniques for making Celtic interlacements, spirals, Kells-type initials, animals, humans, etc. Over 500 illustrations. 160pp. 9 x 12. (Available in U.S. only.)   22923-8

AN ATLAS OF ANATOMY FOR ARTISTS, Fritz Schider. Most thorough reference work on art anatomy in the world. Hundreds of illustrations, including selections from works by Vesalius, Leonardo, Goya, Ingres, Michelangelo, others. 593 illustrations. 192pp. 7⅛ x 10¼.   20241-0

CELTIC HAND STROKE-BY-STROKE (Irish Half-Uncial from "The Book of Kells"): An Arthur Baker Calligraphy Manual, Arthur Baker. Complete guide to creating each letter of the alphabet in distinctive Celtic manner. Covers hand position, strokes, pens, inks, paper, more. Illustrated. 48pp. 8¼ x 11.   24336-2

EASY ORIGAMI, John Montroll. Charming collection of 32 projects (hat, cup, pelican, piano, swan, many more) specially designed for the novice origami hobbyist. Clearly illustrated easy-to-follow instructions insure that even beginning papercrafters will achieve successful results. 48pp. 8¼ x 11.   27298-2

THE COMPLETE BOOK OF BIRDHOUSE CONSTRUCTION FOR WOODWORKERS, Scott D. Campbell. Detailed instructions, illustrations, tables. Also data on bird habitat and instinct patterns. Bibliography. 3 tables. 63 illustrations in 15 figures. 48pp. 5¼ x 8½.   24407-5

BLOOMINGDALE'S ILLUSTRATED 1886 CATALOG: Fashions, Dry Goods and Housewares, Bloomingdale Brothers. Famed merchants' extremely rare catalog depicting about 1,700 products: clothing, housewares, firearms, dry goods, jewelry, more. Invaluable for dating, identifying vintage items. Also, copyright-free graphics for artists, designers. Co-published with Henry Ford Museum & Greenfield Village. 160pp. 8¼ x 11.   25780-0

HISTORIC COSTUME IN PICTURES, Braun & Schneider. Over 1,450 costumed figures in clearly detailed engravings–from dawn of civilization to end of 19th century. Captions. Many folk costumes. 256pp. 8⅜ x 11¾.   23150-X

CATALOG OF DOVER BOOKS

STICKLEY CRAFTSMAN FURNITURE CATALOGS, Gustav Stickley and L. & J. G. Stickley. Beautiful, functional furniture in two authentic catalogs from 1910. 594 illustrations, including 277 photos, show settles, rockers, armchairs, reclining chairs, bookcases, desks, tables. 183pp. 6½ x 9¼. 23838-5

AMERICAN LOCOMOTIVES IN HISTORIC PHOTOGRAPHS: 1858 to 1949, Ron Ziel (ed.). A rare collection of 126 meticulously detailed official photographs, called "builder portraits," of American locomotives that majestically chronicle the rise of steam locomotive power in America. Introduction. Detailed captions. xi+ 129pp. 9 x 12. 27393-8

AMERICA'S LIGHTHOUSES: An Illustrated History, Francis Ross Holland, Jr. Delightfully written, profusely illustrated fact-filled survey of over 200 American lighthouses since 1716. History, anecdotes, technological advances, more. 240pp. 8 x 10¾. 25576-X

TOWARDS A NEW ARCHITECTURE, Le Corbusier. Pioneering manifesto by founder of "International School." Technical and aesthetic theories, views of industry, economics, relation of form to function, "mass-production split" and much more. Profusely illustrated. 320pp. 6⅛ x 9¼. (Available in U.S. only.) 25023-7

HOW THE OTHER HALF LIVES, Jacob Riis. Famous journalistic record, exposing poverty and degradation of New York slums around 1900, by major social reformer. 100 striking and influential photographs. 233pp. 10 x 7⅞. 22012-5

FRUIT KEY AND TWIG KEY TO TREES AND SHRUBS, William M. Harlow. One of the handiest and most widely used identification aids. Fruit key covers 120 deciduous and evergreen species; twig key 160 deciduous species. Easily used. Over 300 photographs. 126pp. 5⅜ x 8½. 20511-8

COMMON BIRD SONGS, Dr. Donald J. Borror. Songs of 60 most common U.S. birds: robins, sparrows, cardinals, bluejays, finches, more–arranged in order of increasing complexity. Up to 9 variations of songs of each species.
Cassette and manual 99911-4

ORCHIDS AS HOUSE PLANTS, Rebecca Tyson Northen. Grow cattleyas and many other kinds of orchids–in a window, in a case, or under artificial light. 63 illustrations. 148pp. 5⅜ x 8½. 23261-1

MONSTER MAZES, Dave Phillips. Masterful mazes at four levels of difficulty. Avoid deadly perils and evil creatures to find magical treasures. Solutions for all 32 exciting illustrated puzzles. 48pp. 8¼ x 11. 26005-4

MOZART'S DON GIOVANNI (DOVER OPERA LIBRETTO SERIES), Wolfgang Amadeus Mozart. Introduced and translated by Ellen H. Bleiler. Standard Italian libretto, with complete English translation. Convenient and thoroughly portable–an ideal companion for reading along with a recording or the performance itself. Introduction. List of characters. Plot summary. 121pp. 5¼ x 8½. 24944-1

TECHNICAL MANUAL AND DICTIONARY OF CLASSICAL BALLET, Gail Grant. Defines, explains, comments on steps, movements, poses and concepts. 15-page pictorial section. Basic book for student, viewer. 127pp. 5⅜ x 8½. 21843-0

THE CLARINET AND CLARINET PLAYING, David Pino. Lively, comprehensive work features suggestions about technique, musicianship, and musical interpretation, as well as guidelines for teaching, making your own reeds, and preparing for public performance. Includes an intriguing look at clarinet history. "A godsend," *The Clarinet,* Journal of the International Clarinet Society. Appendixes. 7 illus. 320pp. 5⅜ x 8½. 40270-3

HOLLYWOOD GLAMOR PORTRAITS, John Kobal (ed.). 145 photos from 1926-49. Harlow, Gable, Bogart, Bacall; 94 stars in all. Full background on photographers, technical aspects. 160pp. 8⅜ x 11¼. 23352-9

THE ANNOTATED CASEY AT THE BAT: A Collection of Ballads about the Mighty Casey/Third, Revised Edition, Martin Gardner (ed.). Amusing sequels and parodies of one of America's best-loved poems: Casey's Revenge, Why Casey Whiffed, Casey's Sister at the Bat, others. 256pp. 5⅜ x 8½. 28598-7

THE RAVEN AND OTHER FAVORITE POEMS, Edgar Allan Poe. Over 40 of the author's most memorable poems: "The Bells," "Ulalume," "Israfel," "To Helen," "The Conqueror Worm," "Eldorado," "Annabel Lee," many more. Alphabetic lists of titles and first lines. 64pp. 5$\frac{3}{16}$ x 8¼. 26685-0

PERSONAL MEMOIRS OF U. S. GRANT, Ulysses Simpson Grant. Intelligent, deeply moving firsthand account of Civil War campaigns, considered by many the finest military memoirs ever written. Includes letters, historic photographs, maps and more. 528pp. 6⅛ x 9¼. 28587-1

ANCIENT EGYPTIAN MATERIALS AND INDUSTRIES, A. Lucas and J. Harris. Fascinating, comprehensive, thoroughly documented text describes this ancient civilization's vast resources and the processes that incorporated them in daily life, including the use of animal products, building materials, cosmetics, perfumes and incense, fibers, glazed ware, glass and its manufacture, materials used in the mummification process, and much more. 544pp. 6⅛ x 9¼. (Available in U.S. only.) 40446-3

RUSSIAN STORIES/RUSSKIE RASSKAZY: A Dual-Language Book, edited by Gleb Struve. Twelve tales by such masters as Chekhov, Tolstoy, Dostoevsky, Pushkin, others. Excellent word-for-word English translations on facing pages, plus teaching and study aids, Russian/English vocabulary, biographical/critical introductions, more. 416pp. 5⅜ x 8½. 26244-8

PHILADELPHIA THEN AND NOW: 60 Sites Photographed in the Past and Present, Kenneth Finkel and Susan Oyama. Rare photographs of City Hall, Logan Square, Independence Hall, Betsy Ross House, other landmarks juxtaposed with contemporary views. Captures changing face of historic city. Introduction. Captions. 128pp. 8¼ x 11. 25790-8

AIA ARCHITECTURAL GUIDE TO NASSAU AND SUFFOLK COUNTIES, LONG ISLAND, The American Institute of Architects, Long Island Chapter, and the Society for the Preservation of Long Island Antiquities. Comprehensive, well-researched and generously illustrated volume brings to life over three centuries of Long Island's great architectural heritage. More than 240 photographs with authoritative, extensively detailed captions. 176pp. 8¼ x 11. 26946-9

NORTH AMERICAN INDIAN LIFE: Customs and Traditions of 23 Tribes, Elsie Clews Parsons (ed.). 27 fictionalized essays by noted anthropologists examine religion, customs, government, additional facets of life among the Winnebago, Crow, Zuni, Eskimo, other tribes. 480pp. 6⅛ x 9¼. 27377-6

CATALOG OF DOVER BOOKS

FRANK LLOYD WRIGHT'S DANA HOUSE, Donald Hoffmann. Pictorial essay of residential masterpiece with over 160 interior and exterior photos, plans, elevations, sketches and studies. 128pp. 9¼ x 10¾. 29120-0

THE MALE AND FEMALE FIGURE IN MOTION: 60 Classic Photographic Sequences, Eadweard Muybridge. 60 true-action photographs of men and women walking, running, climbing, bending, turning, etc., reproduced from rare 19th-century masterpiece. vi + 121pp. 9 x 12. 24745-7

1001 QUESTIONS ANSWERED ABOUT THE SEASHORE, N. J. Berrill and Jacquelyn Berrill. Queries answered about dolphins, sea snails, sponges, starfish, fishes, shore birds, many others. Covers appearance, breeding, growth, feeding, much more. 305pp. 5¼ x 8¼. 23366-9

ATTRACTING BIRDS TO YOUR YARD, William J. Weber. Easy-to-follow guide offers advice on how to attract the greatest diversity of birds: birdhouses, feeders, water and waterers, much more. 96pp. 5³⁄₁₆ x 8¼. 28927-3

MEDICINAL AND OTHER USES OF NORTH AMERICAN PLANTS: A Historical Survey with Special Reference to the Eastern Indian Tribes, Charlotte Erichsen-Brown. Chronological historical citations document 500 years of usage of plants, trees, shrubs native to eastern Canada, northeastern U.S. Also complete identifying information. 343 illustrations. 544pp. 6½ x 9¼. 25951-X

STORYBOOK MAZES, Dave Phillips. 23 stories and mazes on two-page spreads: Wizard of Oz, Treasure Island, Robin Hood, etc. Solutions. 64pp. 8¼ x 11. 23628-5

AMERICAN NEGRO SONGS: 230 Folk Songs and Spirituals, Religious and Secular, John W. Work. This authoritative study traces the African influences of songs sung and played by black Americans at work, in church, and as entertainment. The author discusses the lyric significance of such songs as "Swing Low, Sweet Chariot," "John Henry," and others and offers the words and music for 230 songs. Bibliography. Index of Song Titles. 272pp. 6½ x 9¼. 40271-1

MOVIE-STAR PORTRAITS OF THE FORTIES, John Kobal (ed.). 163 glamor, studio photos of 106 stars of the 1940s: Rita Hayworth, Ava Gardner, Marlon Brando, Clark Gable, many more. 176pp. 8⅜ x 11¼. 23546-7

BENCHLEY LOST AND FOUND, Robert Benchley. Finest humor from early 30s, about pet peeves, child psychologists, post office and others. Mostly unavailable elsewhere. 73 illustrations by Peter Arno and others. 183pp. 5⅜ x 8½. 22410-4

YEKL and THE IMPORTED BRIDEGROOM AND OTHER STORIES OF YIDDISH NEW YORK, Abraham Cahan. Film Hester Street based on *Yekl* (1896). Novel, other stories among first about Jewish immigrants on N.Y.'s East Side. 240pp. 5⅜ x 8½. 22427-9

SELECTED POEMS, Walt Whitman. Generous sampling from *Leaves of Grass*. Twenty-four poems include "I Hear America Singing," "Song of the Open Road," "I Sing the Body Electric," "When Lilacs Last in the Dooryard Bloom'd," "O Captain! My Captain!"–all reprinted from an authoritative edition. Lists of titles and first lines. 128pp. 5³⁄₁₆ x 8¼. 26878-0

THE BEST TALES OF HOFFMANN, E. T. A. Hoffmann. 10 of Hoffmann's most important stories: "Nutcracker and the King of Mice," "The Golden Flowerpot," etc. 458pp. 5⅜ x 8½. 21793-0

FROM FETISH TO GOD IN ANCIENT EGYPT, E. A. Wallis Budge. Rich detailed survey of Egyptian conception of "God" and gods, magic, cult of animals, Osiris, more. Also, superb English translations of hymns and legends. 240 illustrations. 545pp. 5⅜ x 8½. 25803-3

FRENCH STORIES/CONTES FRANÇAIS: A Dual-Language Book, Wallace Fowlie. Ten stories by French masters, Voltaire to Camus: "Micromegas" by Voltaire; "The Atheist's Mass" by Balzac; "Minuet" by de Maupassant; "The Guest" by Camus, six more. Excellent English translations on facing pages. Also French-English vocabulary list, exercises, more. 352pp. 5⅜ x 8½. 26443-2

CHICAGO AT THE TURN OF THE CENTURY IN PHOTOGRAPHS: 122 Historic Views from the Collections of the Chicago Historical Society, Larry A. Viskochil. Rare large-format prints offer detailed views of City Hall, State Street, the Loop, Hull House, Union Station, many other landmarks, circa 1904-1913. Introduction. Captions. Maps. 144pp. 9⅜ x 12¼. 24656-6

OLD BROOKLYN IN EARLY PHOTOGRAPHS, 1865-1929, William Lee Younger. Luna Park, Gravesend race track, construction of Grand Army Plaza, moving of Hotel Brighton, etc. 157 previously unpublished photographs. 165pp. 8⅞ x 11¾. 23587-4

THE MYTHS OF THE NORTH AMERICAN INDIANS, Lewis Spence. Rich anthology of the myths and legends of the Algonquins, Iroquois, Pawnees and Sioux, prefaced by an extensive historical and ethnological commentary. 36 illustrations. 480pp. 5⅜ x 8½. 25967-6

AN ENCYCLOPEDIA OF BATTLES: Accounts of Over 1,560 Battles from 1479 B.C. to the Present, David Eggenberger. Essential details of every major battle in recorded history from the first battle of Megiddo in 1479 B.C. to Grenada in 1984. List of Battle Maps. New Appendix covering the years 1967-1984. Index. 99 illustrations. 544pp. 6½ x 9¼. 24913-1

SAILING ALONE AROUND THE WORLD, Captain Joshua Slocum. First man to sail around the world, alone, in small boat. One of great feats of seamanship told in delightful manner. 67 illustrations. 294pp. 5⅜ x 8½. 20326-3

ANARCHISM AND OTHER ESSAYS, Emma Goldman. Powerful, penetrating, prophetic essays on direct action, role of minorities, prison reform, puritan hypocrisy, violence, etc. 271pp. 5⅜ x 8½. 22484-8

MYTHS OF THE HINDUS AND BUDDHISTS, Ananda K. Coomaraswamy and Sister Nivedita. Great stories of the epics; deeds of Krishna, Shiva, taken from puranas, Vedas, folk tales; etc. 32 illustrations. 400pp. 5⅜ x 8½. 21759-0

THE TRAUMA OF BIRTH, Otto Rank. Rank's controversial thesis that anxiety neurosis is caused by profound psychological trauma which occurs at birth. 256pp. 5⅜ x 8½. 27974-X

A THEOLOGICO-POLITICAL TREATISE, Benedict Spinoza. Also contains unfinished Political Treatise. Great classic on religious liberty, theory of government on common consent. R. Elwes translation. Total of 421pp. 5⅜ x 8½. 20249-6

CATALOG OF DOVER BOOKS

MY BONDAGE AND MY FREEDOM, Frederick Douglass. Born a slave, Douglass became outspoken force in antislavery movement. The best of Douglass' autobiographies. Graphic description of slave life. 464pp. 5⅜ x 8½.   22457-0

FOLLOWING THE EQUATOR: A Journey Around the World, Mark Twain. Fascinating humorous account of 1897 voyage to Hawaii, Australia, India, New Zealand, etc. Ironic, bemused reports on peoples, customs, climate, flora and fauna, politics, much more. 197 illustrations. 720pp. 5⅜ x 8½.   26113-1

THE PEOPLE CALLED SHAKERS, Edward D. Andrews. Definitive study of Shakers: origins, beliefs, practices, dances, social organization, furniture and crafts, etc. 33 illustrations. 351pp. 5⅜ x 8½.   21081-2

THE MYTHS OF GREECE AND ROME, H. A. Guerber. A classic of mythology, generously illustrated, long prized for its simple, graphic, accurate retelling of the principal myths of Greece and Rome, and for its commentary on their origins and significance. With 64 illustrations by Michelangelo, Raphael, Titian, Rubens, Canova, Bernini and others. 480pp. 5⅜ x 8½.   27584-1

PSYCHOLOGY OF MUSIC, Carl E. Seashore. Classic work discusses music as a medium from psychological viewpoint. Clear treatment of physical acoustics, auditory apparatus, sound perception, development of musical skills, nature of musical feeling, host of other topics. 88 figures. 408pp. 5⅜ x 8½.   21851-1

THE PHILOSOPHY OF HISTORY, Georg W. Hegel. Great classic of Western thought develops concept that history is not chance but rational process, the evolution of freedom. 457pp. 5⅜ x 8½.   20112-0

THE BOOK OF TEA, Kakuzo Okakura. Minor classic of the Orient: entertaining, charming explanation, interpretation of traditional Japanese culture in terms of tea ceremony. 94pp. 5⅜ x 8½.   20070-1

LIFE IN ANCIENT EGYPT, Adolf Erman. Fullest, most thorough, detailed older account with much not in more recent books, domestic life, religion, magic, medicine, commerce, much more. Many illustrations reproduce tomb paintings, carvings, hieroglyphs, etc. 597pp. 5⅜ x 8½.   22632-8

SUNDIALS, Their Theory and Construction, Albert Waugh. Far and away the best, most thorough coverage of ideas, mathematics concerned, types, construction, adjusting anywhere. Simple, nontechnical treatment allows even children to build several of these dials. Over 100 illustrations. 230pp. 5⅜ x 8½.   22947-5

THEORETICAL HYDRODYNAMICS, L. M. Milne-Thomson. Classic exposition of the mathematical theory of fluid motion, applicable to both hydrodynamics and aerodynamics. Over 600 exercises. 768pp. 6⅛ x 9¼.   68970-0

SONGS OF EXPERIENCE: Facsimile Reproduction with 26 Plates in Full Color, William Blake. 26 full-color plates from a rare 1826 edition. Includes "The Tyger," "London," "Holy Thursday," and other poems. Printed text of poems. 48pp. 5¼ x 7.   24636-1

OLD-TIME VIGNETTES IN FULL COLOR, Carol Belanger Grafton (ed.). Over 390 charming, often sentimental illustrations, selected from archives of Victorian graphics—pretty women posing, children playing, food, flowers, kittens and puppies, smiling cherubs, birds and butterflies, much more. All copyright-free. 48pp. 9¼ x 12¼.   27269-9

PERSPECTIVE FOR ARTISTS, Rex Vicat Cole. Depth, perspective of sky and sea, shadows, much more, not usually covered. 391 diagrams, 81 reproductions of drawings and paintings. 279pp. 5⅜ x 8½. 22487-2

DRAWING THE LIVING FIGURE, Joseph Sheppard. Innovative approach to artistic anatomy focuses on specifics of surface anatomy, rather than muscles and bones. Over 170 drawings of live models in front, back and side views, and in widely varying poses. Accompanying diagrams. 177 illustrations. Introduction. Index. 144pp. 8⅜ x11¼. 26723-7

GOTHIC AND OLD ENGLISH ALPHABETS: 100 Complete Fonts, Dan X. Solo. Add power, elegance to posters, signs, other graphics with 100 stunning copyright-free alphabets: Blackstone, Dolbey, Germania, 97 more–including many lower-case, numerals, punctuation marks. 104pp. 8⅛ x 11. 24695-7

HOW TO DO BEADWORK, Mary White. Fundamental book on craft from simple projects to five-bead chains and woven works. 106 illustrations. 142pp. 5⅜ x 8. 20697-1

THE BOOK OF WOOD CARVING, Charles Marshall Sayers. Finest book for beginners discusses fundamentals and offers 34 designs. "Absolutely first rate . . . well thought out and well executed."–E. J. Tangerman. 118pp. 7¾ x 10⅝. 23654-4

ILLUSTRATED CATALOG OF CIVIL WAR MILITARY GOODS: Union Army Weapons, Insignia, Uniform Accessories, and Other Equipment, Schuyler, Hartley, and Graham. Rare, profusely illustrated 1846 catalog includes Union Army uniform and dress regulations, arms and ammunition, coats, insignia, flags, swords, rifles, etc. 226 illustrations. 160pp. 9 x 12. 24939-5

WOMEN'S FASHIONS OF THE EARLY 1900s: An Unabridged Republication of "New York Fashions, 1909," National Cloak & Suit Co. Rare catalog of mail-order fashions documents women's and children's clothing styles shortly after the turn of the century. Captions offer full descriptions, prices. Invaluable resource for fashion, costume historians. Approximately 725 illustrations. 128pp. 8⅜ x 11¼. 27276-1

THE 1912 AND 1915 GUSTAV STICKLEY FURNITURE CATALOGS, Gustav Stickley. With over 200 detailed illustrations and descriptions, these two catalogs are essential reading and reference materials and identification guides for Stickley furniture. Captions cite materials, dimensions and prices. 112pp. 6½ x 9¼. 26676-1

EARLY AMERICAN LOCOMOTIVES, John H. White, Jr. Finest locomotive engravings from early 19th century: historical (1804–74), main-line (after 1870), special, foreign, etc. 147 plates. 142pp. 11⅜ x 8¼. 22772-3

THE TALL SHIPS OF TODAY IN PHOTOGRAPHS, Frank O. Braynard. Lavishly illustrated tribute to nearly 100 majestic contemporary sailing vessels: Amerigo Vespucci, Clearwater, Constitution, Eagle, Mayflower, Sea Cloud, Victory, many more. Authoritative captions provide statistics, background on each ship. 190 black-and-white photographs and illustrations. Introduction. 128pp. 8⅞ x 11¾. 27163-3

CATALOG OF DOVER BOOKS

LITTLE BOOK OF EARLY AMERICAN CRAFTS AND TRADES, Peter Stockham (ed.). 1807 children's book explains crafts and trades: baker, hatter, cooper, potter, and many others. 23 copperplate illustrations. 140pp. 4⅝ x 6.   23336-7

VICTORIAN FASHIONS AND COSTUMES FROM HARPER'S BAZAR, 1867–1898, Stella Blum (ed.). Day costumes, evening wear, sports clothes, shoes, hats, other accessories in over 1,000 detailed engravings. 320pp. 9⅜ x 12¼. 22990-4

GUSTAV STICKLEY, THE CRAFTSMAN, Mary Ann Smith. Superb study surveys broad scope of Stickley's achievement, especially in architecture. Design philosophy, rise and fall of the Craftsman empire, descriptions and floor plans for many Craftsman houses, more. 86 black-and-white halftones. 31 line illustrations. Introduction 208pp. 6½ x 9¼.   27210-9

THE LONG ISLAND RAIL ROAD IN EARLY PHOTOGRAPHS, Ron Ziel. Over 220 rare photos, informative text document origin (1844) and development of rail service on Long Island. Vintage views of early trains, locomotives, stations, passengers, crews, much more. Captions. 8⅞ x 11¾.   26301-0

VOYAGE OF THE LIBERDADE, Joshua Slocum. Great 19th-century mariner's thrilling, first-hand account of the wreck of his ship off South America, the 35-foot boat he built from the wreckage, and its remarkable voyage home. 128pp. 5⅜ x 8½.
40022-0

TEN BOOKS ON ARCHITECTURE, Vitruvius. The most important book ever written on architecture. Early Roman aesthetics, technology, classical orders, site selection, all other aspects. Morgan translation. 331pp. 5⅜ x 8½.   20645-9

THE HUMAN FIGURE IN MOTION, Eadweard Muybridge. More than 4,500 stopped-action photos, in action series, showing undraped men, women, children jumping, lying down, throwing, sitting, wrestling, carrying, etc. 390pp. 7⅞ x 10⅝.
20204-6 Clothbd.

TREES OF THE EASTERN AND CENTRAL UNITED STATES AND CANADA, William M. Harlow. Best one-volume guide to 140 trees. Full descriptions, woodlore, range, etc. Over 600 illustrations. Handy size. 288pp. 4½ x 6⅜.   20395-6

SONGS OF WESTERN BIRDS, Dr. Donald J. Borror. Complete song and call repertoire of 60 western species, including flycatchers, juncoes, cactus wrens, many more–includes fully illustrated booklet.   Cassette and manual 99913-0

GROWING AND USING HERBS AND SPICES, Milo Miloradovich. Versatile handbook provides all the information needed for cultivation and use of all the herbs and spices available in North America. 4 illustrations. Index. Glossary. 236pp. 5⅜ x 8½.
25058-X

BIG BOOK OF MAZES AND LABYRINTHS, Walter Shepherd. 50 mazes and labyrinths in all–classical, solid, ripple, and more–in one great volume. Perfect inexpensive puzzler for clever youngsters. Full solutions. 112pp. 8⅛ x 11.   22951-3

PIANO TUNING, J. Cree Fischer. Clearest, best book for beginner, amateur. Simple repairs, raising dropped notes, tuning by easy method of flattened fifths. No previous skills needed. 4 illustrations. 201pp. 5⅜ x 8½. 23267-0

HINTS TO SINGERS, Lillian Nordica. Selecting the right teacher, developing confidence, overcoming stage fright, and many other important skills receive thoughtful discussion in this indispensible guide, written by a world-famous diva of four decades' experience. 96pp. 5⅜ x 8½. 40094-8

THE COMPLETE NONSENSE OF EDWARD LEAR, Edward Lear. All nonsense limericks, zany alphabets, Owl and Pussycat, songs, nonsense botany, etc., illustrated by Lear. Total of 320pp. 5⅜ x 8½. (Available in U.S. only.) 20167-8

VICTORIAN PARLOUR POETRY: An Annotated Anthology, Michael R. Turner. 117 gems by Longfellow, Tennyson, Browning, many lesser-known poets. "The Village Blacksmith," "Curfew Must Not Ring Tonight," "Only a Baby Small," dozens more, often difficult to find elsewhere. Index of poets, titles, first lines. xxiii + 325pp. 5⅜ x 8¼. 27044-0

DUBLINERS, James Joyce. Fifteen stories offer vivid, tightly focused observations of the lives of Dublin's poorer classes. At least one, "The Dead," is considered a masterpiece. Reprinted complete and unabridged from standard edition. 160pp. 5³⁄₁₆ x 8¼. 26870-5

GREAT WEIRD TALES: 14 Stories by Lovecraft, Blackwood, Machen and Others, S. T. Joshi (ed.). 14 spellbinding tales, including "The Sin Eater," by Fiona McLeod, "The Eye Above the Mantel," by Frank Belknap Long, as well as renowned works by R. H. Barlow, Lord Dunsany, Arthur Machen, W. C. Morrow and eight other masters of the genre. 256pp. 5⅜ x 8½. (Available in U.S. only.) 40436-6

THE BOOK OF THE SACRED MAGIC OF ABRAMELIN THE MAGE, translated by S. MacGregor Mathers. Medieval manuscript of ceremonial magic. Basic document in Aleister Crowley, Golden Dawn groups. 268pp. 5⅜ x 8½. 23211-5

NEW RUSSIAN-ENGLISH AND ENGLISH-RUSSIAN DICTIONARY, M. A. O'Brien. This is a remarkably handy Russian dictionary, containing a surprising amount of information, including over 70,000 entries. 366pp. 4½ x 6⅛. 20208-9

HISTORIC HOMES OF THE AMERICAN PRESIDENTS, Second, Revised Edition, Irvin Haas. A traveler's guide to American Presidential homes, most open to the public, depicting and describing homes occupied by every American President from George Washington to George Bush. With visiting hours, admission charges, travel routes. 175 photographs. Index. 160pp. 8¼ x 11. 26751-2

NEW YORK IN THE FORTIES, Andreas Feininger. 162 brilliant photographs by the well-known photographer, formerly with *Life* magazine. Commuters, shoppers, Times Square at night, much else from city at its peak. Captions by John von Hartz. 181pp. 9¼ x 10¾. 23585-8

INDIAN SIGN LANGUAGE, William Tomkins. Over 525 signs developed by Sioux and other tribes. Written instructions and diagrams. Also 290 pictographs. 111pp. 6⅛ x 9¼. 22029-X

ANATOMY: A Complete Guide for Artists, Joseph Sheppard. A master of figure drawing shows artists how to render human anatomy convincingly. Over 460 illustrations. 224pp. 8⅜ x 11¼. 27279-6

MEDIEVAL CALLIGRAPHY: Its History and Technique, Marc Drogin. Spirited history, comprehensive instruction manual covers 13 styles (ca. 4th century through 15th). Excellent photographs; directions for duplicating medieval techniques with modern tools. 224pp. 8⅜ x 11¼. 26142-5

DRIED FLOWERS: How to Prepare Them, Sarah Whitlock and Martha Rankin. Complete instructions on how to use silica gel, meal and borax, perlite aggregate, sand and borax, glycerine and water to create attractive permanent flower arrangements. 12 illustrations. 32pp. 5⅜ x 8½. 21802-3

EASY-TO-MAKE BIRD FEEDERS FOR WOODWORKERS, Scott D. Campbell. Detailed, simple-to-use guide for designing, constructing, caring for and using feeders. Text, illustrations for 12 classic and contemporary designs. 96pp. 5⅜ x 8½. 25847-5

SCOTTISH WONDER TALES FROM MYTH AND LEGEND, Donald A. Mackenzie. 16 lively tales tell of giants rumbling down mountainsides, of a magic wand that turns stone pillars into warriors, of gods and goddesses, evil hags, powerful forces and more. 240pp. 5⅜ x 8½. 29677-6

THE HISTORY OF UNDERCLOTHES, C. Willett Cunnington and Phyllis Cunnington. Fascinating, well-documented survey covering six centuries of English undergarments, enhanced with over 100 illustrations: 12th-century laced-up bodice, footed long drawers (1795), 19th-century bustles, 19th-century corsets for men, Victorian "bust improvers," much more. 272pp. 5⅜ x 8¼. 27124-2

ARTS AND CRAFTS FURNITURE: The Complete Brooks Catalog of 1912, Brooks Manufacturing Co. Photos and detailed descriptions of more than 150 now very collectible furniture designs from the Arts and Crafts movement depict davenports, settees, buffets, desks, tables, chairs, bedsteads, dressers and more, all built of solid, quarter-sawed oak. Invaluable for students and enthusiasts of antiques, Americana and the decorative arts. 80pp. 6½ x 9¼. 27471-3

WILBUR AND ORVILLE: A Biography of the Wright Brothers, Fred Howard. Definitive, crisply written study tells the full story of the brothers' lives and work. A vividly written biography, unparalleled in scope and color, that also captures the spirit of an extraordinary era. 560pp. 6⅛ x 9¼. 40297-5

THE ARTS OF THE SAILOR: Knotting, Splicing and Ropework, Hervey Garrett Smith. Indispensable shipboard reference covers tools, basic knots and useful hitches; handsewing and canvas work, more. Over 100 illustrations. Delightful reading for sea lovers. 256pp. 5⅜ x 8½. 26440-8

FRANK LLOYD WRIGHT'S FALLINGWATER: The House and Its History, Second, Revised Edition, Donald Hoffmann. A total revision—both in text and illustrations—of the standard document on Fallingwater, the boldest, most personal architectural statement of Wright's mature years, updated with valuable new material from the recently opened Frank Lloyd Wright Archives. "Fascinating"—The New York Times. 116 illustrations. 128pp. 9¼ x 10¾. 27430-6

PHOTOGRAPHIC SKETCHBOOK OF THE CIVIL WAR, Alexander Gardner. 100 photos taken on field during the Civil War. Famous shots of Manassas Harper's Ferry, Lincoln, Richmond, slave pens, etc. 244pp. 10⅝ x 8¼. 22731-6

FIVE ACRES AND INDEPENDENCE, Maurice G. Kains. Great back-to-the-land classic explains basics of self-sufficient farming. The one book to get. 95 illustrations. 397pp. 5⅜ x 8½. 20974-1

SONGS OF EASTERN BIRDS, Dr. Donald J. Borror. Songs and calls of 60 species most common to eastern U.S.: warblers, woodpeckers, flycatchers, thrushes, larks, many more in high-quality recording. Cassette and manual 99912-2

A MODERN HERBAL, Margaret Grieve. Much the fullest, most exact, most useful compilation of herbal material. Gigantic alphabetical encyclopedia, from aconite to zedoary, gives botanical information, medical properties, folklore, economic uses, much else. Indispensable to serious reader. 161 illustrations. 888pp. 6½ x 9¼. 2-vol. set. (Available in U.S. only.) Vol. I: 22798-7
Vol. II: 22799-5

HIDDEN TREASURE MAZE BOOK, Dave Phillips. Solve 34 challenging mazes accompanied by heroic tales of adventure. Evil dragons, people-eating plants, blood-thirsty giants, many more dangerous adversaries lurk at every twist and turn. 34 mazes, stories, solutions. 48pp. 8¼ x 11. 24566-7

LETTERS OF W. A. MOZART, Wolfgang A. Mozart. Remarkable letters show bawdy wit, humor, imagination, musical insights, contemporary musical world; includes some letters from Leopold Mozart. 276pp. 5⅜ x 8½. 22859-2

BASIC PRINCIPLES OF CLASSICAL BALLET, Agrippina Vaganova. Great Russian theoretician, teacher explains methods for teaching classical ballet. 118 illustrations. 175pp. 5⅜ x 8½. 22036-2

THE JUMPING FROG, Mark Twain. Revenge edition. The original story of The Celebrated Jumping Frog of Calaveras County, a hapless French translation, and Twain's hilarious "retranslation" from the French. 12 illustrations. 66pp. 5⅜ x 8½. 22686-7

BEST REMEMBERED POEMS, Martin Gardner (ed.). The 126 poems in this superb collection of 19th- and 20th-century British and American verse range from Shelley's "To a Skylark" to the impassioned "Renascence" of Edna St. Vincent Millay and to Edward Lear's whimsical "The Owl and the Pussycat." 224pp. 5⅜ x 8½. 27165-X

COMPLETE SONNETS, William Shakespeare. Over 150 exquisite poems deal with love, friendship, the tyranny of time, beauty's evanescence, death and other themes in language of remarkable power, precision and beauty. Glossary of archaic terms. 80pp. 5$\frac{3}{16}$ x 8¼. 26686-9

THE BATTLES THAT CHANGED HISTORY, Fletcher Pratt. Eminent historian profiles 16 crucial conflicts, ancient to modern, that changed the course of civilization. 352pp. 5⅜ x 8½. 41129-X

THE WIT AND HUMOR OF OSCAR WILDE, Alvin Redman (ed.). More than 1,000 ripostes, paradoxes, wisecracks: Work is the curse of the drinking classes; I can resist everything except temptation; etc. 258pp. 5⅜ x 8½. 20602-5

SHAKESPEARE LEXICON AND QUOTATION DICTIONARY, Alexander Schmidt. Full definitions, locations, shades of meaning in every word in plays and poems. More than 50,000 exact quotations. 1,485pp. 6½ x 9¼. 2-vol. set.
Vol. 1: 22726-X
Vol. 2: 22727-8

SELECTED POEMS, Emily Dickinson. Over 100 best-known, best-loved poems by one of America's foremost poets, reprinted from authoritative early editions. No comparable edition at this price. Index of first lines. 64pp. 5³⁄₁₆ x 8¼. 26466-1

THE INSIDIOUS DR. FU-MANCHU, Sax Rohmer. The first of the popular mystery series introduces a pair of English detectives to their archnemesis, the diabolical Dr. Fu-Manchu. Flavorful atmosphere, fast-paced action, and colorful characters enliven this classic of the genre. 208pp. 5³⁄₁₆ x 8¼. 29898-1

THE MALLEUS MALEFICARUM OF KRAMER AND SPRENGER, translated by Montague Summers. Full text of most important witchhunter's "bible," used by both Catholics and Protestants. 278pp. 6⅝ x 10. 22802-9

SPANISH STORIES/CUENTOS ESPAÑOLES: A Dual-Language Book, Angel Flores (ed.). Unique format offers 13 great stories in Spanish by Cervantes, Borges, others. Faithful English translations on facing pages. 352pp. 5⅜ x 8½. 25399-6

GARDEN CITY, LONG ISLAND, IN EARLY PHOTOGRAPHS, 1869–1919, Mildred H. Smith. Handsome treasury of 118 vintage pictures, accompanied by carefully researched captions, document the Garden City Hotel fire (1899), the Vanderbilt Cup Race (1908), the first airmail flight departing from the Nassau Boulevard Aerodrome (1911), and much more. 96pp. 8⅞ x 11¾. 40669-5

OLD QUEENS, N.Y., IN EARLY PHOTOGRAPHS, Vincent F. Seyfried and William Asadorian. Over 160 rare photographs of Maspeth, Jamaica, Jackson Heights, and other areas. Vintage views of DeWitt Clinton mansion, 1939 World's Fair and more. Captions. 192pp. 8⅞ x 11. 26358-4

CAPTURED BY THE INDIANS: 15 Firsthand Accounts, 1750-1870, Frederick Drimmer. Astounding true historical accounts of grisly torture, bloody conflicts, relentless pursuits, miraculous escapes and more, by people who lived to tell the tale. 384pp. 5⅜ x 8½. 24901-8

THE WORLD'S GREAT SPEECHES (Fourth Enlarged Edition), Lewis Copeland, Lawrence W. Lamm, and Stephen J. McKenna. Nearly 300 speeches provide public speakers with a wealth of updated quotes and inspiration–from Pericles' funeral oration and William Jennings Bryan's "Cross of Gold Speech" to Malcolm X's powerful words on the Black Revolution and Earl of Spenser's tribute to his sister, Diana, Princess of Wales. 944pp. 5⅜ x 8⅜. 40903-1

THE BOOK OF THE SWORD, Sir Richard F. Burton. Great Victorian scholar/adventurer's eloquent, erudite history of the "queen of weapons"–from prehistory to early Roman Empire. Evolution and development of early swords, variations (sabre, broadsword, cutlass, scimitar, etc.), much more. 336pp. 6⅛ x 9¼.
25434-8

CATALOG OF DOVER BOOKS

AUTOBIOGRAPHY: The Story of My Experiments with Truth, Mohandas K. Gandhi. Boyhood, legal studies, purification, the growth of the Satyagraha (nonviolent protest) movement. Critical, inspiring work of the man responsible for the freedom of India. 480pp. 5⅜ x 8½. (Available in U.S. only.) 24593-4

CELTIC MYTHS AND LEGENDS, T. W. Rolleston. Masterful retelling of Irish and Welsh stories and tales. Cuchulain, King Arthur, Deirdre, the Grail, many more. First paperback edition. 58 full-page illustrations. 512pp. 5⅜ x 8½. 26507-2

THE PRINCIPLES OF PSYCHOLOGY, William James. Famous long course complete, unabridged. Stream of thought, time perception, memory, experimental methods; great work decades ahead of its time. 94 figures. 1,391pp. 5⅜ x 8½. 2-vol. set.
Vol. I: 20381-6   Vol. II: 20382-4

THE WORLD AS WILL AND REPRESENTATION, Arthur Schopenhauer. Definitive English translation of Schopenhauer's life work, correcting more than 1,000 errors, omissions in earlier translations. Translated by E. F. J. Payne. Total of 1,269pp. 5⅜ x 8½. 2-vol. set.   Vol. 1: 21761-2   Vol. 2: 21762-0

MAGIC AND MYSTERY IN TIBET, Madame Alexandra David-Neel. Experiences among lamas, magicians, sages, sorcerers, Bonpa wizards. A true psychic discovery. 32 illustrations. 321pp. 5⅜ x 8½. (Available in U.S. only.) 22682-4

THE EGYPTIAN BOOK OF THE DEAD, E. A. Wallis Budge. Complete reproduction of Ani's papyrus, finest ever found. Full hieroglyphic text, interlinear transliteration, word-for-word translation, smooth translation. 533pp. 6½ x 9¼. 21866-X

MATHEMATICS FOR THE NONMATHEMATICIAN, Morris Kline. Detailed, college-level treatment of mathematics in cultural and historical context, with numerous exercises. Recommended Reading Lists. Tables. Numerous figures. 641pp. 5⅜ x 8½. 24823-2

PROBABILISTIC METHODS IN THE THEORY OF STRUCTURES, Isaac Elishakoff. Well-written introduction covers the elements of the theory of probability from two or more random variables, the reliability of such multivariable structures, the theory of random function, Monte Carlo methods of treating problems incapable of exact solution, and more. Examples. 502pp. 5⅜ x 8½. 40691-1

THE RIME OF THE ANCIENT MARINER, Gustave Doré, S. T. Coleridge. Doré's finest work; 34 plates capture moods, subtleties of poem. Flawless full-size reproductions printed on facing pages with authoritative text of poem. "Beautiful. Simply beautiful."–*Publisher's Weekly.* 77pp. 9¼ x 12. 22305-1

NORTH AMERICAN INDIAN DESIGNS FOR ARTISTS AND CRAFTSPEOPLE, Eva Wilson. Over 360 authentic copyright-free designs adapted from Navajo blankets, Hopi pottery, Sioux buffalo hides, more. Geometrics, symbolic figures, plant and animal motifs, etc. 128pp. 8⅜ x 11. (Not for sale in the United Kingdom.) 25341-4

SCULPTURE: Principles and Practice, Louis Slobodkin. Step-by-step approach to clay, plaster, metals, stone; classical and modern. 253 drawings, photos. 255pp. 8⅛ x 11. 22960-2

THE INFLUENCE OF SEA POWER UPON HISTORY, 1660–1783, A. T. Mahan. Influential classic of naval history and tactics still used as text in war colleges. First paperback edition. 4 maps. 24 battle plans. 640pp. 5⅜ x 8½. 25509-3

CATALOG OF DOVER BOOKS

THE STORY OF THE TITANIC AS TOLD BY ITS SURVIVORS, Jack Winocour (ed.). What it was really like. Panic, despair, shocking inefficiency, and a little heroism. More thrilling than any fictional account. 26 illustrations. 320pp. 5⅜ x 8½.
20610-6

FAIRY AND FOLK TALES OF THE IRISH PEASANTRY, William Butler Yeats (ed.). Treasury of 64 tales from the twilight world of Celtic myth and legend: "The Soul Cages," "The Kildare Pooka," "King O'Toole and his Goose," many more. Introduction and Notes by W. B. Yeats. 352pp. 5⅜ x 8½.
26941-8

BUDDHIST MAHAYANA TEXTS, E. B. Cowell and others (eds.). Superb, accurate translations of basic documents in Mahayana Buddhism, highly important in history of religions. The Buddha-karita of Asvaghosha, Larger Sukhavativyuha, more. 448pp. 5⅜ x 8½.
25552-2

ONE TWO THREE . . . INFINITY: Facts and Speculations of Science, George Gamow. Great physicist's fascinating, readable overview of contemporary science: number theory, relativity, fourth dimension, entropy, genes, atomic structure, much more. 128 illustrations. Index. 352pp. 5⅜ x 8½.
25664-2

EXPERIMENTATION AND MEASUREMENT, W. J. Youden. Introductory manual explains laws of measurement in simple terms and offers tips for achieving accuracy and minimizing errors. Mathematics of measurement, use of instruments, experimenting with machines. 1994 edition. Foreword. Preface. Introduction. Epilogue. Selected Readings. Glossary. Index. Tables and figures. 128pp. 5⅜ x 8½.   40451-X

DALÍ ON MODERN ART: The Cuckolds of Antiquated Modern Art, Salvador Dalí. Influential painter skewers modern art and its practitioners. Outrageous evaluations of Picasso, Cézanne, Turner, more. 15 renderings of paintings discussed. 44 calligraphic decorations by Dalí. 96pp. 5⅜ x 8½. (Available in U.S. only.)   29220-7

ANTIQUE PLAYING CARDS: A Pictorial History, Henry René D'Allemagne. Over 900 elaborate, decorative images from rare playing cards (14th–20th centuries): Bacchus, death, dancing dogs, hunting scenes, royal coats of arms, players cheating, much more. 96pp. 9¼ x 12¼.   29265-7

MAKING FURNITURE MASTERPIECES: 30 Projects with Measured Drawings, Franklin H. Gottshall. Step-by-step instructions, illustrations for constructing handsome, useful pieces, among them a Sheraton desk, Chippendale chair, Spanish desk, Queen Anne table and a William and Mary dressing mirror. 224pp. 8⅛ x 11¼.
29338-6

THE FOSSIL BOOK: A Record of Prehistoric Life, Patricia V. Rich et al. Profusely illustrated definitive guide covers everything from single-celled organisms and dinosaurs to birds and mammals and the interplay between climate and man. Over 1,500 illustrations. 760pp. 7½ x 10⅛.   29371-8